The Hero's Journey

The Hero's Journey

A voyage of self-discovery

**Stephen Gilligan
and Robert Dilts**

Crown House Publishing Limited
www.crownhouse.co.uk
www.crownhousepublishing.com

First published by
Crown House Publishing Ltd
Crown Buildings, Bancyfelin, Carmarthen, Wales, SA33 5ND, UK
www.crownhouse.co.uk
and
Crown House Publishing Company LLC
6 Trowbridge Drive, Suite 5, Bethel, CT 06801-2858, USA
www.crownhousepublishing.com

Originally published in hardback 2009 (ISBN 978-184590286-5). Reprinted 2010,
2011. Transferred to digital printing 2016.

British Library Cataloguing-in-Publication Data
A catalogue entry for this book is available from the British Library.

Print ISBN 978-184590286-5 (Hardback)
Print ISBN 978-178583162-1 (Paperback)
Mobi ISBN 978-184590402-9
ePub ISBN 978-184590403-6
ePDF ISBN 978-184590404-3
LCCN 2009936660

Contents

Day 1

Introduction and Overview

We (authors Stephen Gilligan and Robert Dilts) have been on a journey together for more than 30 years that started back in the early 1970s when we were students at the University of California at Santa Cruz. It was there that we met and worked extensively with Richard Bandler and John Grinder, the founders of NeuroLinguistic Programming (NLP). We also had the tremendous opportunity to study with Gregory Bateson, who many consider one of the greatest minds of the last century, and Milton Erickson, who is arguably the most brilliant psychiatrist, hypnotherapist, and healer who has ever lived.

After we graduated, each of us went our own way, only to reconnect in the mid-1990s. We were both married and with growing children by then, and had both established our own separate and successful professional paths – Stephen in Ericksonian Hypnosis and Psychotherapy and Robert in NeuroLinguistic Programming. We discovered, however, that our different journeys had brought us to many similar experiences and conclusions.

The idea of each life being a potential "hero's journey" is one of our most passionate shared interests.

The essence of the hero's journey is: How do you live a meaningful life? What is the deepest life you are called to? How can you respond to that call?

If you don't find that calling, you're likely to live in a lot of misery – to be unhappy, feel lost or confused, or perhaps end up with some significant problems. Perhaps a health issue, a career confusion, or a dysfunctional relationship.

To live a hero's journey will provide the most amazing rewards, but to turn away from it may cause tremendous suffering. So what we hope to do in this book is to help you sense and discover what your journey is, and how you might live it fully and deeply. Our interest is to explore how you can connect and align with the deepest part of your spirit, so that everything that you feel and think and do in the world is aligned with the human spirit.

A hero's journey is about a type of awakening and a type of opening – an opening to what life is bringing you and calling from you. And this calling is not always easy. Otherwise you wouldn't need to be a hero to do it.

There's a great benefit of the hero's journey, which is a sense of a meaning, a sense of being alive in the world. But with that benefit comes also the challenge, the cost. Wherever there is light, there will always be shadows – and in fact you could say the brighter the light, the darker the shadows. And living a full life is about holding and addressing both, the shadows as well as the light.

Another way of talking about this is that we're going to be focusing equally on what we call the *gift* and the *wound*. We say that deep within each of us is a gift that we're here to give into the world. But equally deep within each of us is a woundedness. And a woundedness, of course, does not just start with our own personal life – we carry the wounds of our family; we carry the wounds of our culture; we carry the woundedness of our planet. So the hero's journey is about sensing how to be able to deeply connect in a positive way to both of these energies.

Thus, a hero's journey is simultaneously about living your gifts and healing your wounds. Your power and your fullness are in both of these energies. And those two things will be there as major influences on your intimate relationships, your professional life, your health, and your development as a person – this simultaneous process of healing and sharing your gifts will always be there.

The Beginning of the Journey

The majority of this book has been drawn from a transcript of a semi-
nar that we did on the topic of the hero's journey in Barcelona, Spain.
We believe that the hero's journey is a dynamic, alive, and constantly
evolving process. Thus, we feel it is appropriate for a book on the hero's
journey to preserve the spontaneity, humor, and feel of a live seminar. We
have indicated our names in relationship to our personal contributions in
order to maintain the unique flavor of our different perspectives. Enjoy
the journey!

Steve Gilligan: Good morning, everybody, and welcome! We've
got a lot to cover in this program.

Robert Dilts: *(In an excited voice)* Are you ready for a journey?

SG: *(Voice like a preacher)* Brothers and sisters, are you ready?

RD: Say amen!

("Amens" and laughter from the audience.)

SG: Mmmm . . . that's what we like to hear! So now that you're a
bit out of your rational selves, we want to take advantage of it and
deepen it by honoring our daily tradition of reading a poem. Partly
this is to honor our Irish roots.

RD: We're both half Irish. My half is the bad half. *(Laughter.)*

SG: And even more importantly than our Irish roots, in this search
we really want to emphasize language as metaphoric and poetic
at its base. We see literal language as a secondary language, and
we see metaphor and symbolic language as the primary language.

RD: There's an interesting book by a linguist named George Lakoff
that is called *Metaphors We Live By*. Lakoff points out that we usually think of metaphor as being a secondary language process to
the fundamental, literal language. But he argues, as do we, that
it's actually the other way around – our fundamental language is
metaphorical. A child lives in a world of stories and metaphors

long before he or she learns literality. So the language of our heart and the language of our soul is metaphorical, not literal.

SG: From a practical level, this means that we're especially interested in how language enters the body; how it touches the body and awakens experiential–symbolic experience in the body. So when we talk about the hero's journey, we're going to be exploring that not in terms of some intellectual concept, but as a distinction that, as you breathe it deeply through your body, begins to awaken all of this experience within your body.

RD: They say in Papua New Guinea culture that "knowledge is only a rumor until it's in the muscle." So your hero's journey and your calling are just rumors, just ideas, until they get in your muscle. Your goals, your resources, your potentials – they're rumors until they're brought into the muscle, the breath, the body. Then and only then do they become living ideas that can transform your lives. So we would like for you to leave here more alive. Anybody want to be more alive?

SG: *(Enthusiastically and playfully)* Say amen!

(Laughter and "amens" from the audience.)

SG: The poem that I want to share with you is by a British poet named Derek Walcott. You'll hear in this poem Walcott talking about the two selves that are part of the legacy of each of us as human beings. He (along with many others) suggests that we have two different selves – you might call one the experiencing or *performance* self, and the other the *witnessing* self. Another set of terms we'll use is the *somatic* self and the *cognitive* self. A big part of what we're going to be exploring is the connection between these two minds. Is their relationship hostile? Is it dissociated? Is it one of dominance and submission? Or are these two minds within you living in harmony? Because when they're living in harmony, then your hero's journey can really open up into the world. So here's what Derek Walcott has to say about this relationship:

Love After Love

The day will come
when, with elation
you will greet yourself arriving
at your own door, in your own mirror
and each will smile at the other's welcome,

and say sit here. Eat.
You will love again the stranger who was yourself.
Give wine. Give bread. Give back your heart
to itself, to the stranger who has loved you

all your life, whom you ignored
for another, who knows you by heart.
Take down the love letters from the bookshelf,

the photographs, the desperate notes,
peel your own image from the mirror.
Sit. Feast on your life.

SG: So we hope that by the end of our journey together here you can peel your image from the mirror and feast on your own life . . . that the two selves within you can unite into a deeper Generative Self that lives the hero's journey.

RD: In that same spirit, I have a couple of short readings. The first is a poem about growing older, hearing one's calling in the body, and of sensing the deeper power of spirit that emerges in aging. It's an excerpt from "Sailing to Byzantium" by the great Irish poet William Butler Yeats. It evokes for Stephen and me something of what we learned from Milton Erickson, who was a sponsor and teacher to both of us. When we knew him he was old and crippled, struggling with terrible pain, and yet he seemed to find a connection with a source deeper than his infirmities. For me this poem is about how in many ways the hero's journey never ends. Yeats writes:

An aged man is but a paltry thing,
A tattered coat upon a stick, unless
Soul clap its hands and sing, and louder sing
For every tatter in its mortal dress.

RD: So, during our journey together here, may soul come and visit you and clap its hands and sing, and let every mortal tatter of your being come alive with celebration and contribution.

The other quotation I have is from Martha Graham, who is considered to be one of the foremost pioneers of modern dance. She taught, choreographed, and danced well into her nineties, perhaps because of her approach to life which she describes in the following way:

> *There is a vitality, a life force, a quickening that is translated through you into action, and because there is only one of you in all time, this expression is unique. If you block it, it will never exist through any other medium and be lost. The world will not have it. It is not yours to determine how good it is; nor how it compares with other expressions. It is your business to keep the channel open.*

RD: This is the essence of the hero's journey: keeping your channel open. A key part of this journey is to identify and release what closes your channel down and causes you to lose your vitality and your life force. So we will be seeking to discover and transform the shadowy forces that block you from expressing your unique energy in the world. One of the main goals of this program is to help you develop tools through which you can keep your channel open – whether it's with your children, your intimate partner, at work, or just going about your daily life – even sitting in a seminar. It's your business on your hero's journey to keep your channel open – and let life flow through you.

First Premise: Spirit is Waking Up

SG: The first core premise that we want to offer for navigating the hero's journey is:

> *Spirit is awakening into the world.*

Everything else we can orient to – thoughts, behavior, experience, relationship dynamics – are all seen as expressions of *spirit waking up.* And it's using all these forms – behaviors, thoughts, time, space, identity, and so forth – as the means to do it. By sensing and aligning to spirit at each moment, the hero's journey activates.

RD: There's that old question: Are we animals pretending to be gods, or are we gods pretending to be animals?

SG: What are the choices again? *(Laughter.)*

RD: So we are spirit waking up, both divine and human.

SG: This idea of the primacy of spirit was presented in the book *Of Water and the Spirit*, an autobiography by Malidoma Somé, a beautiful man who was born and raised in West Africa before coming to the West to teach. He talks about how in his cultural tradition it is assumed that when a baby is born, that baby has just come from another world, the world of spirit. And that furthermore, the spirit has chosen this time, this family, and this culture to be born into because he or she has a gift to give to the world.

We have also suggested that in addition to a gift to give, spirit also has a wound to heal. But in both cases, you can sense underlying any experiential moment, this living, pulsating consciousness that is looking to awaken. And by aligning with that, good things will happen.

The name Malidoma, interestingly, means "one who brings ritual to the enemy." In his culture, the baby is taken by the elders shortly after birth, and for several days the circle of elders ask the spirit in a ritual language: "Why have you come? What is the gift you have come to bring?" In Malidoma's case, it was sensed that he had come to bring a healing gift of ritual to the West, which, in the view of Malidoma's people, had seriously lost its deeper connection to spirit and was wreaking havoc as a result. Malidoma's grandfather, a chief elder, prophesied that Malidoma would venture to the West to bring this gift. To shorten a very beautiful story of Malidoma's hero's journey, this is indeed what happened. There are many ways to sense the primacy of spirit. One common way is to hold a newborn or connect with a young child and feel his or her primacy of spirit.

RD: When you hold a newborn baby, it is easy to experience the sense of awe of being in the presence of spirit. You really feel what

Martha Graham was saying about this unique energy that is coming into the world. And to stay attuned to that unique living presence is what guides the hero's journey.

Second Premise: Spirit is Awakening through a Human Nervous System

SG: To this first core premise, we can add a second:

Spirit is awakening through a human nervous system.

At one level, of course, this seems like a trivial idea, because it's so obvious. But it's important to appreciate that the human nervous system is the most advanced, generative musical instrument or computational device that has ever existed. Nothing even comes close to it, in terms of its capacity, its complexity, its power. The Buddhists like to say that when you get a human nervous system, you've really hit the jackpot! You've won the grand lottery. You might imagine a bunch of spirits lined up, waiting to come into this world, each one waiting to be issued a nervous system for the journey. You watch the spirit in line ahead of you be given a snake nervous system, the next one gets a giraffe, and then when you step up to the desk, they say, "OK, you get a human nervous system." Perhaps you remember that amazing time . . . you were so extraordinarily excited, so lucky, so happy, because you knew that having a human nervous system gave you the most amazing potential for transformation and self-realization of consciousness. This human nervous system gives you all the possibilities to live the hero's journey.

But of course, it comes with no operating instructions. And you forget its brilliance once you enter human society, with the televisions turned on, the gossip going on, and the commercials humming. One of the downsides of having such a sensitive biocomputer is that if it's not tuned properly, some nasty experiences can be created through it.

Third Premise: Each Life is a Hero's Journey

SG: We mention this at the outset of this work on the hero's journey, so we can appreciate that to go on the journey, we first need to sense the spirit underlying it all, then tune the nervous system that's unfolding the journey. This leads us to the third basic premise:

> *Spirit is unfolding through time / space on a hero's journey.*

So in addition to spirit and nervous system, we emphasize this third component of the journey unfolding across an arc of time. We see a person's life as this beautiful path that includes past, present, and future – many experiential moments joined together to unfold a beautiful story, sing an amazing song, dance a unique movement. At one level of this journey you are alone. At another, you are being helped by many positive beings, some of whom you are not even aware are there.

RD: In the model of the hero's journey, we call such beings *guardians*. In Stephen's Generative Self work, which we will intertwine with the hero's journey, they are called *sponsors*. These positive figures remind you and support your deepest call in many ways.

For example, on the Pacific island of Togo, when a baby is born, the women of the village perform a ritual with the new mother. They take her and the baby into the forest and gather around the newly arrived spirit. They sit with this baby, sensing the unique spirit of this new life, and then at a certain moment, one of them begins to make a musical sound. Another woman adds to it, then another, and in this way the community unfolds the creation of a song for that baby. The song is completely unique and just for that baby.

Throughout his or her life, at birthdays and other ritual times, the women gather and sing the song. And if the child does something bad or becomes sick, instead of punishing or medicating the child, the women gather around and sing the song to remind the child of who he is or she is. So the song becomes a way to support the development of the hero's journey for that being throughout a lifetime. And when the person dies, the community sings the song one last time and then it's never sung again.

This is a beautiful example of how we all need guardians to reminds us of our true nature, to support us in opening our channel again and again and again.

SG: The need for such guardians is especially important when we consider all the counter-forces that try to hypnotically persuade us that we have no living spirit to unfold on this journey through life. Consider, for example, the dominant force of contemporary society, namely the trance of consumerism. This hypnotic spell says: "You have no spirit inside of you. You have no hero's journey. Your main purpose is to buy refrigerators. Your main purpose in this world is to eat cheeseburgers."

RD: McDonalds and Starbucks.

SG: Robert and I are proud to be Americans – for bringing all these wonderful gifts to the world. *(Laughter.)*

RD: And as you separate from your spirit, the channel begins to close. As the channel closes, you begin to become lost in your wounds – and there's an attempt to compensate for the pain by consuming more. "If I just have another color TV, a new car, new shoes, then I'll be OK. Then I'll be acceptable as a person. Then I'll feel more alive."

SG: Frequently, the symptoms that occur in a person's life are like the singing of the Togo women. Their purpose is to call you back to your spirit. In other words, you can understand a person's experience in each moment as, the spirit is trying to wake up into the world. And you can understand the particularly intense experiences that people have, both positive and negative, as what is referred to in the hero's journey as *the call*.

RD: A call to action. A call to adventure. A call to be. A call to return to your spirit.

SG: And some people may never hear the call. Others hear it, but refuse it. As a psychologist who does lots of psychotherapy, one of the major diagnoses that I give to clients is: "It appears to me that you are constitutionally incapable of being a couch potato." A couch potato is someone who sits on the couch watching TV, drinking beer, and eating potato chips for so long that he or she starts to actually look like a potato. *(Laughter.)* And at the end of this person's life, the gravestone reads: "He watched a lot of TV, ate a lot of potato chips, and complained all of his life. Next!" *(Laughter.)*

So we are asking you to deeply consider: At the end of it all, what would you like your gravestone to read?

Some people are contented to just live like couch potatoes, settling into what Thoreau called "lives of quiet desperation." Some can do that; just run out the clock and live in a fog all their lives. But others, what I call the lucky ones, cannot; and their soul creates terrible disturbances and suffering to say, "Wake up! Wake up! Your life is about something more than this low level trance!"

One of the things we will be touching upon in this work is how to recognize your problems as "calls to return" and "calls to awaken" on your hero's journey, so you can have a positive and helpful relationship to these inevitable problems, utilizing them for your own growth and awakening.

RD: I work a lot in companies and organizations as a coach and a consultant. To me, it is very obvious when an organization has lost its soul – or when people sell their souls or their integrity. The major job of a coach is to help people reawaken their connection to their souls.

At the level of identity, we can say that we have two dynamics – there's a soul and there's an ego. The ego is the part of us that is built from the wounds. It is related to what is called in psychology "the idealized self" – who I think I have to be in order to be loved, in order to be acceptable, in order to be OK. This ego becomes a type of trap for the soul – and you see this in companies. And then sometimes a magic happens, and that soul is there again, singing its unique song and unfolding its unique journey.

To give you an interesting organizational example: I have a colleague who was involved in a study conducted by a large telecommunications company as a result of a huge failure they had experienced. They had been in a very competitive situation and needed to develop a product quickly to keep their share of this particular market area. The project was so important that they put 1,000 people to work on it. As it turned out, one of their competitors was able to beat them to market with a product that was of better quality, more economical, and quicker to produce. The reason for the study was that this competitor accomplished this with a team of only 20 people. The big question was: How is it possible for 20 people to so soundly outperform 1,000? In the language of the hero's journey, we would say that 20 people with their channels open – 20 souls committed to a calling – will always outperform 1,000 egos who are just doing their job and nothing more.

So how does "soul clap its hands and sing" in an organization? What brings and sustains that sense of aliveness, creativity, and vision in the life of a person, a relationship, or a group? This is one of the core questions we want to explore in this work. We hope that the material and the processes that we explore will be relevant to all of you in an important way.

The Hero's Journey Framework

RD: To begin to develop a general framework for this journey, we start with the work of Joseph Campbell. Campbell was the American mythologist who for many years studied all the different stories, legends, and myths, involving both women and men, from different cultures throughout history. Campbell noticed that across all of these stories and examples there was a certain "deep structure" that he called the "hero's journey." His first book was entitled *Hero with a Thousand Faces*, to emphasize that there are many different ways that this hero's journey can be expressed, but they all share a common framework. The following steps represent a simple version of that roadmap offered by Campbell, and is the one we will use to help us navigate the course of our own hero's journeys during this program.

Steps in the Hero's Journey

1. Hearing the call
2. Committing to the call (overcoming the refusal)
3. Crossing the threshold (the initiation)
4. Finding guardians
5. Facing and transforming demons
6. Developing an inner self and new resources
7. The transformation
8. Returning home with the gift.

1. The Calling

RD: The journey begins with a calling. We come into the world, and the world presents circumstances to us that call for or draw out our unique life force or vitality, as Martha Graham would say. Author Eckhart Tolle, who wrote *The Power of Now*, says that the primary function of the soul is to awaken. We don't come into this world to sleep. We come to awaken, and awaken again, and to grow and evolve. So the calling is always a call to grow, to contribute, to bring more of that vitality or life energy into the world or back into the world.

SG: Often the call to action comes from a challenge, a crisis, a vision, or somebody in need. Something has been lost and needs to be regained; some power in the world has decayed and needs to be renewed; some core part of life has been wounded and needs to be healed; some great challenge has arisen and needs to be met. But equally the call may come from inspiration and joy: you hear a piece of great music and you awaken to a dimension of beauty that you passionately want to unfold more of in the world; you feel an amazing love for parenting, and it calls you to raise that archetypal power into the world; you fall in love with your work, and it's all you can think of. As we will see, the call to the hero's journey can come from both great suffering and great joy, sometimes both at the same time.

RD: We should emphasize that the calling of the hero is very different from a personal goal that comes from the ego. The ego would like another television set and some more beer, or at least to be rich and famous. The soul doesn't want or need that; it wants to awaken, heal, connect, create; it awakens to the call of deep challenges, not for ego glorification but to serve and honor life. When a fireman or a policeman runs into a burning building to save someone, this is not a desired goal. It's a challenge and it's a risk, and there's no guarantee of success. Otherwise you wouldn't need to be a hero. So the calling demands courage. It demands that you become more than you have been.

SG: Another thing we'll be exploring is that you may hear the call in very different ways at different points of your life. In one of our exercises, we will ask you to trace the history of your calling. For example, a simple version of that inquiry is the following: "Take a few moments and sense back through your life, letting yourself become aware of different experiences that really touched you, that awakened a deep sense of aliveness and beauty inside of you." A similar question is: "What do you do in your life that really brings you beyond your normal self?" Your responses to these questions will bring out some of the ways you have felt the call.

As we will continue to emphasize, your soul swells and your spirit brightens when you hear the call. By noticing when this happens, you can begin to sense, track, and support your hero's journey. This is what Campbell meant when he said, "Follow your bliss!" Many have misunderstood this as an encouragement to hedonism, rather than sensing that the places when your spirit burns the brightest – when you feel "bliss" – are signs of what you are most here to do in this world.

RD: As Stephen was saying earlier, sometimes the call comes from symptoms or suffering. When my mother was in her early fifties, she had a reoccurrence of breast cancer that had metastasized throughout her body – not only to her other breast, but also to her ovaries, bladder, and the bone marrow of every bone in her body. The doctors gave her at best a few months to live. As you can imagine, it was the worst thing that had ever happened to her. At first she felt very much a victim and not at all a hero.

I helped her to begin to explore questions such as: What is the calling in the cancer? What is the cancer calling me to become? My mother opened to this journey of inquiry deeply, and it completely changed her life. To the great surprise of her doctors, she had a remarkable recovery and lived another 18 years almost completely symptom free. She would later look back at that time and say: "That was the best thing that ever happened to me! I was lucky. I got to live two lives: the one before I got cancer the second time and the one after that. And the second life was so much better than the first."

The question we will be exploring in this program is: What is life calling from you? This calling is probably not particularly easy – it's probably not calling you to take a walk in the park. The calling is most likely difficult; a beautiful but challenging path. This path is typically disruptive of the status quo. When I work with people in companies, I point out that a calling is not simply an improvement of the present. A calling and a vision bring the future into the present and can completely disrupt the present, making it impossible to do things the way you used to.

A key part of the hero's journey is the acceptance of the calling and the commitment to the journey.

2. *The Refusal of the Call*

RD: Precisely because the call can seem so challenging, it is often accompanied by what Campbell calls "the refusal." The hero wants to avoid all the hassle it will bring. "No thanks. Let someone else do it. It's too hard for me. I don't have time for this. I'm not ready." These are the sorts of responses that are typically used to refuse the call.

SG: And while some of the negative responses to the call may come from within, some come from outside – from family, friends, critics (what Campbell calls "ogres"), or society. You may be told, "That is unrealistic." Or perhaps, as many girls and women are hypnotically told, "That would be selfish." Sometimes this leads you to turn away from your calling, although fortunately not always.

I had a friend named Allan. Allan was one of the great figures in American postmodern art. He had wanted to be an artist as long as he could remember. But his father was a major lawyer in New York and wanted his son to follow in his footsteps. He would repeatedly insist, "You're not going to be an artist. You're going to be my junior partner." He would bring the young Allan to his law offices and show him the office he had already reserved for him. Incredibly, his name was already on the door.

Allan's unconscious mind was very creative and insistent. He developed severe asthma that forced him to move to the better climate of Tucson, Arizona, far from the hypnotic reaches of his father. Allan developed his art while he grew up in Arizona. This is a beautiful illustration of how his unconscious mind ensured that he could respond to his call. Many people have such stories of how in different ways, small and big, they evaded oppression in order to keep following their spirit.

RD: In my mother's case, when she began to look within and make these changes in herself, her surgeon looked her straight in the eye and told her in no uncertain terms that this kind of exploration was "a bunch of poppycock" and would "drive her crazy." And the doctor for whom she worked as a nurse said to her, "If you really care about your family, you won't leave them unprepared" – which is an interesting "hypnotic suggestion." The suggestion comes in the form of a presupposition: "You're going to die, and to try to live is selfish. You should prepare yourself and all your loved ones for your death and stop making a fuss." She decided to stop working for him soon after this.

Interestingly, this doctor got a serious illness about six years later. It wasn't nearly as advanced as my mother's, but his response was to take his own life. And it was never clear if she was a willing participant, but his wife died with him. Because, of course, he couldn't "leave her unprepared."

So there are messages that can come from inside or outside to block the path of your calling. A key part of our work will be to recognize and move beyond these messages.

3. Crossing the Threshold

RD: Once you respond to the call and really make the commitment to your path and your hero's journey, it results in what Campbell calls the "crossing of the threshold." You are now on the journey, you're in the experience. "Let the games begin." The word "threshold" has several meanings. One is the implication that beyond the threshold is a new frontier, a new territory, the unknown, the uncertain, the unpredictable, the shadowy promised land.

Another meaning of threshold is that you have reached the outer limits of your comfort zone. Before the threshold, you're in known territory; you're in your comfort zone, you know the lay of the land. Once you cross the threshold, you're beyond your comfort zone. So it becomes difficult, challenging, risky, frequently painful, and perhaps even fatal. To enter this challenging new territory is a crucial challenge of the hero's journey.

The third implication of a threshold is that it is a point of no return. You can't go back. It's like if you have a baby – you can't easily say: "Oops, I made a mistake. This is too challenging. I don't want it anymore. Take it back please." Once across the threshold, there is only one way to go, and that is forward.

So your threshold is the point at which you're going to go into a new and challenging territory that you've never been in before, and there's no turning back.

SG: And it is precisely at that place that your ordinary mind will fail you. Your ordinary conscious mind only knows how to create different versions of what has already happened (a bit like "rearranging the deck chairs on the Titanic" in order to try to save the ship). It cannot generate new realities. So as you realize that your conscious mind can't be the lead system in the journey, it is common to experience disconcerting responses – paralysis, confusion, trembling, uncertainty, passing out, and so on. These are the "subtle cues" that you are being called beyond where you've ever been before.

This idea that your ordinary conscious mind cannot lead your hero's journey will be a central one in this work. Therefore, one of our major practical explorations will be how to reorganize your consciousness at those points to what we will be calling a Generative Self – one capable of supplying you with the wisdom and courage to navigate the hero's journey.

4. Finding Guardians

RD: As you begin to travel along your hero's journey, Campbell points out that you must find guardians. Who are the ones that are going to sing my song and remind me of who I am? Who are the ones that have the knowledge or the tools that I need and know nothing about? Who can remind me that the journey is possible, and offer support when I most need it? Who are my teachers, my mentors, my sponsors, my awakeners?

This is a significant part of your learning on the journey – a constant search. Of course, it's *your* journey and not one that anyone can do for you. You are the one you will most need to listen to, to learn from, and consult with. But at the same time, it's also not a journey that you can make alone. It's not an ego trip. It's something that will challenge you beyond the capabilities that you currently possess.

In this regard, we find it helpful to distinguish between a *hero* and a *champion*. A hero is generally a normal human being who is called to an extraordinary circumstance by life. A champion is somebody who is fighting for an ideal that they think is the right way, the right map of the world. This ideal is right and anybody who opposes it is the enemy. So the champion imposes his or her own map of the world upon others.

SG: So the champion will says things like, "You're either with us or against us," and other memorable lines that you will hear from many priests and politicians. (*Laughter.*)

RD: "We fight for truth, justice and the American way . . . all over the world." (*Laughter.*) "And we're going to free your country by occupying it."

SG: A small point about guardians. They can be actual people – friends, mentors, family members. They may also be historical figures or mythological entities. For example, when I consider my path as a healer and therapist, I sometimes meditate on all those who have gone before me, the great lineages of beings who have given their love and devoted their lives to forging traditions and ways of healing. In the meditation, I sense their support flowing through time, from different cultures and different places, coming to me as support for my humble journey. So another one of the great questions we'll be exploring is: How do I sense and stay connected with those guardians that can guide and support me on my journey?

5. *Facing Your Demons and Shadows*

SG: A key difference between the hero and the champion is in the relationship to what Campbell called the "demons." Demons are the entities that try to block your journey, at times even threatening your very existence and the existence of those with whom you are connected. One of the main challenges in the hero's journey is how you deal with "negative otherness," both within you and around you. The champion looks to dominate and destroy everything that's different from his or her ego ideal. The hero operates at a higher level, one of relational transformation with the demons. The hero is called to do something that not only transforms his or her self, but also transforms the larger relational field in which he or she lives. This is change at a deeper level and, again, one that requires a different sort of consciousness, which is one of the main topics for our journey together.

RD: In many ways the climax of the hero's journey is the confrontation with what we will call "the demon"; the seemingly malevolent presence that threatens you and is determined to keep you from achieving your calling. Campbell points out that while initially the demon is perceived as outside of you and against you, the hero's journey brings you to recognize that the problem is not what is outside of you, it is what is within you. And that the demon is ultimately just an energy that is neither good nor bad. It is just an energy; a phenomenon.

What makes something a demon is the fact that I'm afraid of it or intimidated by it. If I wasn't afraid, it wouldn't be a demon. What turns something or someone into a demon is my response to it – my anger, my frustration, my grief, my guilt, my shame about it, and so on. That's what makes the problem seem so difficult. The demon holds a mirror to us. It reveals our inner *shadow* – the responses, feelings, or parts of ourselves that we don't know how to be with. I sometimes refer to them as our "internal terrorists."

SG: In practical terms, the demon might be an addiction, a depression, an ex-wife . . . *(Laughter.)*

RD: In a company it can be a financial crisis, the recession, a new competitor, and so on.

SG: Your demon could be Saddam Hussein, Osama Bin Laden, or George Bush. *(Laughter.)*

RD: The demon could be a health issue, or it could be your boss, your mother, your mother-in-law, or your child. The point is that what we (and Joseph Campbell) are ultimately suggesting is: *What makes something a demon is your relationship with it.*

6. Developing an Inner Self

RD: So a hero's journey is always a journey of transformation, especially a transformation of oneself. When I work in companies and organizations, I talk about the difference between the outer game of a business and what author Timothy Gallwey calls "the inner game." Success in any activity – whether it's a sport, your work, your intimate relationship, an artistic pursuit – requires a certain degree of mastery of the outer game (e.g. the specific players, the setting, the rules, the physical skills needed, the behavior patterning). Many people can learn the outer game fairly well, but the highest level of performance can only be reached by also mastering the inner game. This is a function of one's ability to deal with stress, failure, pressure, criticism, slumps, drops in confidence, and so on.

One of the things that a hero must learn is how to play this inner game. It involves much more than our cognitive mind. It is a function of emotional intelligence, somatic intelligence, and spiritual wisdom, which involves the connection to a larger field of consciousness – the deep sensing of an intelligence beyond the ego and intellect. On a hero's journey, you have to grow. You cannot be a hero and refuse to learn and grow.

SG: The cultivation of the inner game can be described in many ways. We will call it here the development of an inner self, an intuitive intelligence that connects the conscious mind with a larger consciousness that allows greater confidence, deeper understanding, more subtle awareness, and increased capacity at many levels.

7. The Transformation

RD: As you develop new resources within yourself and find your guardians you become ready to face your demons (and ultimately your own inner shadows) and engage in the great transformational challenge of the journey. Campbell refers to these challenges as your "trials."

SG: This is the time of great struggle, dedication, and battle that leads to the creation of new learnings and resources. It is here that you create within yourself and in the world that which has never existed before. This is what we mean by *generative*: going beyond what has ever been to create something completely new. This process, of course, can take a long period of time. It could be 20 years of a marriage, a lifetime of work, or years of exploration and innovation. There will be many setbacks and failures; times when all seems lost and the future bleak. These are predictable elements of the hero's journey. The hero is someone who can respond to these challenges and create new resources in order to successfully meet them. The transformation stage is when you have succeeded in your journey.

8. The Return Home

RD: The final stage of the hero's journey is the return home. This return has several important purposes with respect to the journey. One of them is to share what you've learned on your journey with others. A hero's journey is not just an individual ego trip; it is a transformational process done for both the person and for the larger community. So when a hero returns, he or she must find a way to share his or her realizations with others. Heroes frequently become teachers. In addition to giving, the hero must receive the recognition of others to complete the journey. Now you are transformed, you are different than you used to be. There needs to be an honoring of the journey.

SG: For example, a good friend of mine is a well known psychologist who has done some very interesting work. He shared with me that as a child, he would love to watch old movies on the lives of great scientists – people like Marie Curie, Louis Pasteur, and Sigmund Freud. Each of these movies follows a general "hero's journey" pattern: the early calling, the commitment, the great battles, the hard-earned discoveries, and so forth. The typical end of such movies has the scientist standing in front of a large audience – the same people that scorned and attacked him or her earlier in the journey – and being given some great reward or acknowledgment for their life's work. My friend would always find himself welling up at such movies, feeling within him a calling to contribute something very meaningful in the world. He told me this recently, after being given a lifetime achievement award in front of thousands of people, and sensing that movie ending happening in his own real world, just as he hypnotically attuned to it on the movie screen many years earlier. Those movies reflected his calling, and the award was a recognition that he had succeeded in the great challenge of his journey.

However, as Campbell points out, there can also be a lot of resistance at this stage. Sometimes the hero doesn't want to come back. He or she is tired, perhaps wary that others won't understand, or perhaps exalted in the new found state of higher consciousness. So just as there might be a refusal to answer the call, there might be a refusal to return. Sometimes, as Campbell explains, another person or being has to come and get the hero, to call them back home.

Another problem is that the community may not welcome the leader. Moses may come off the mountain to discover his people engaged in partying; warriors may return home from battle and not be welcomed, or their horrors not witnessed and honored; people may not want to listen to a story from a person whose journey reflects the needs for others in the community to do their own healing. So once the great struggle has been achieved within a higher state of consciousness, its integration into the ordinary consciousness of everyday living is a further great challenge.

Still, there are plenty of examples of heroes who have accomplished this final stage. We mentioned that Milton Erickson was a major mentor for both of us. He is a really good example of a complete hero's journey. One of many interesting details of his life was that he was paralyzed from severe polio at the age of 17, which incidentally is around the (initiation into adulthood) age that a classic "wounded healer" is struck down with a severe illness or wound. So instead of being able to move through the traditional path of the mainstream society, such a person is separated from regular life and must begin his own healing journey. In Erickson's case, the doctors told him he would never move again. Rather than merely submit to this negative suggestion, Erickson began a long series of mind–body explorations to see just what was possible in terms of healing his condition. Amazingly, he succeeded in regaining his ability to walk, and developed new understandings and resources about mind–body healing in the process. He then used these radical new learnings in his long career as a psychiatrist, helping others to learn about their own unique capacity for healing and transformation.

When we knew him, he was an aged man. He was in a lot of pain and quite weak, and couldn't reliably handle a heavy patient load, so he was mostly seeing students. When I met him, I was a poor college student. I lived on ten dollars a week for food, which even back then wasn't much. But I knew I had to study with this guy because he awakened something very deep in me. I asked him: "Dr. Erickson, can I come back regularly and be your student?"

"Yes," he replied.

"How much money do I need to pay you?" I asked. "I'm pretty sure I can get some college loans, so if you tell me how much, I'll make arrangements."

He said: "Oh, that's all right. You don't have to pay me anything." Which is what he said to all of us young students. He was retired, his house was paid off, his kids were out of the house, he had no major financial responsibilities. He was just giving back – donating his hard-earned hero's gifts to the community. I went to see him for almost six years, and I never paid him any money. He would let us stay in his guest room or his office building. What he did say was, "The way that you can repay me is by passing on to others anything that you find here that is helpful to you. That's how you can repay me!" There are many times I wish I had just paid off the old man with money to satisfy my debt *(laughter)* . . . but not really.

I think you can sense that this is a beautiful story of a hero's journey. And when I encountered him, he was in the final phase of returning to the community and passing on to others.

RD: By the way, not only did the doctors tell Erickson that he would never move again, when Erickson had just contracted the polio and was laying in bed he overheard them telling his mother that he wouldn't live till the morning. He thought that was a terrible thing for anybody to say to a mother, so he felt he just had to make sure their judgment was not correct. He went on a journey in his body to try to find what he could move. The only things he could willfully move were his eyes. And so for several hours when his mother would come by, he would try to move his eyes to get her attention. Once he had managed this, for several more hours he struggled to work out a signal system and finally succeeded in communicating to her to turn his bed toward the window, so he could be sure to watch the sun come up the next day. So, "soul claps its hands" again! Something deep within consciousness is awakened, and the journey continues.

SG: These are the basic steps of the hero's journey. This is the framework we will use through the rest of the program to allow you to discover and deepen your own hero's journey. We'll be exploring this mostly experientially. We'll be doing demonstrations, especially asking you to work with each other to develop your own learnings and understandings. So you will be asked to work with yourself as well as be a good coach for others.

RD: A part of learning to be a good hero is also to be a good guardian. For those of you who are coaches and therapists, it will be important to do this from the awareness that it is your client's journey, not yours. I see a lot of people, especially in the NLP world, who say, "Oh, my client is facing a demon! *I'm* the hero. I'm going to kill my client's demon with my great technique! Swish it. Reframe it. Anchor it." When you try to "rescue" or "cure" your client, you are sending the message, "Yes, you're a victim. Stay a victim. *I'm* the hero." Or on another level: "I'm a champion. I need a victim in order to have my ego feel good. I'm doing this for me, not you." So keep this in mind: you are the guardian when you are the coach. You have your own hero's journey, but so does your partner or client. Your job is not to be the hero on their journey, but rather a good guardian and resource.

So this is our map. The next step is to get it "in the muscle."

The Generative Self

RD: We have gone over the basic road map of the hero's journey, and we have suggested that there are certain principles and tools that can help in traveling that path. When you reach a threshold, for instance, when you reach a place where you have to step into unknown territory, you can no longer rely simply on the functioning and resources of your ordinary mind, the conscious cognitive mind. The good news is, you don't have to. You have more than one mind. And the hero's journey is an opportunity to get to learn more deeply about your other minds.

SG: So this is the second of the two major frameworks that we're going to be exploring. The first framework relates to the steps of the hero's journey. The second has to do with developing the tools and the consciousness necessary to make that journey. A key part of this second framework is called Generative Self. It is primarily based on the work I've developed over the past 30 years, starting out as a student of Erickson and then incorporating other work such as martial arts.

Figure 1.1 shows the core premises of the Generative Self. We touched upon the first three earlier, namely: (1) Spirit is waking up (2) through a human nervous system (3) on a hero's journey. We now will move to (4), that the Generative Self has three minds that can be distinguished – somatic, cognitive, and field – and (5) each of these minds can operate at three different levels of consciousness: primitive (or regressive), basic, and generative. To travel your own hero's journey, you will need to attune these three minds to their highest level, generative, so that transformation, creativity, and healing are possible. Our focus will be on raising your body, mind, and field consciousness to their highest generative levels, so that you can succeed on your hero's journey.

1. **"SPIRIT IS WAKING UP. . .**
- Spirit has *gift* to give AND *wound* to heal
- Spirit is deepest identity
- Spirit activates whenever ordinary identity is destabilized (e.g. ecstasy or agony)

2. **into HUMAN CONSCIOUSNESS**
- The human nervous system is the most advanced instrument of consciousness ever developed
- If you don't learn to play the instrument, you're in trouble
- Your experience is a function of your state
- Attuned human conscious PLUS spirit EQUALS Generative Self

3. **on HERO'S JOURNEY**
- Each person's life is an arc unfolding over time into the world
- The journey has many death and rebirth cycles
- At heart of hero's journey is spirit waking up
- Suffering is a signal of misalignment with the call/journey

4. **utilizing THREE MINDS**
- Somatic, cognitive, and field
- Integration of three minds awakens the Generative Self

5. **operating at THREE LEVELS OF CONSCIOUSNESS"**
- *Primitive* (unconscious wholeness, field without self-awareness)
- *Ego* (conscious separateness, awareness without field)
- *Generative* (conscious differentiated wholeness, parts and whole simultaneously)

Source: Stephen Gilligan, *The five premises of the Generative Self* (2004)

Figure 1.1: Five core ideas of the Generative Self approach.

The Three Minds: Somatic, Cognitive, and Field

SG: The first is the mind within your body. We call this the *somatic mind*. This is the mammal mind; the primary mind for young children. There is a whole pattern of intelligence and wisdom within the body to which you may or may not be attuned.

RD: We're suggesting that the body is not just a machine that is controlled by the brain in your head, but that there is also a brain in your body. In fact, there are multiple brains in your body.

SG: Who was it that said: "God gave man two brains, but only enough oxygen to supply one at a time"? George Bush? *(Laughter.)*

RD: I think that was John Lennon. *(Laughter.)*

One of the brains in the body is called the enteric brain or enteric nervous system in the belly (*enteric* literally means "inside the stomach"). Modern neuroscientists calculate that the system of nerves surrounding the large intestine and the other digestive organs in the belly has a sophistication and complexity roughly equivalent to the brain of a cat. So you have a cat's brain in your belly. *(Laughter.)* When everything is going its way, it purrs. But if it feels threatened . . . pssssst! *(More laughter.)*

There is also a growing body of research illustrating that your heart is not just a mechanical pump. It is a brain of its own (see Gershon, 2002). I have a colleague who has been a specialist in general surgery (and of the digestive apparatus) for more than 25 years. He is a Fellow in Surgery at Harvard University Medical School and is a member of the American Association for the Advancement of Science. At a recent conference, he was talking about the case of a heart transplant patient. After the recipient's recovery, he started exhibiting unusual behaviors. He began craving foods he had never liked before. He found himself obsessed with music that he had never liked previously. He found himself attracted to places that he had no conscious memory of.[1]

---

[1] For a beautiful account of personality changes in heart transplant patients, see Paul Pearsall's book, *The Heart's Code* (1998).

It was all a big mystery until they investigated the life patterns of the heart donor. They discovered that these foods had been the favorite foods of the donor, that the donor had been a musician who performed the music the recipient had become obsessed with, and that the places the recipient found himself going to were places where significant events had happened in the life of the donor. Due to strict confidentiality rules, neither the patient nor the doctors had had previous access to information about the donor nor his personal history. Somehow the preferences had been transferred through the donor's heart.

SG: It's interesting when we talk about some of these core experiences of the hero's journey – namely the gifts and the wound – that one of the chief characteristics of these is that you experience them deeply in your body. So when you're in a place of suffering, it's not just an intellectual experience; something deep in your body begins to activate. Similarly, when you feel the deepest part of your gift, there's something deep in your body that swells and "sings the body electric." So the somatic mind is the first mind – it is the base for all else. And the quality of your consciousness depends in no small apart on the quality of that somatic mind.

The second mind is the *cognitive mind* – the mind in the head, so to speak . . .

RD: The logical, analytical mind . . .

SG: . . . the mind that makes maps, representations, sequences, symbols, plans, meanings, and all those wonderful human activities.

The third mind is the *mind of the field*. Not only is there consciousness within you, there's consciousness all around you. We all live in multiple, coexisting dynamic fields: history, family, culture, environment. You may work in the field of NLP, or live in an oppressive field of fear. How you relationally engage with these fields, and hopefully what is beyond these fields, is one of the great challenges of a human life.

RD: In Third Generation NLP, the notion of field is most characterized by the fourth perceptual or "we" position. First, second, and third perceptual positions (self, other, and observer) relate to the significant individual perspectives in a system of human interaction, which could be called the "space" of the interaction. The relational field is created by the patterns of relationship and interaction which occur in that space. Fourth position simultaneously includes and transcends the other three perspectives.

As an illustration of this notion of field, if you combine two hydrogen atoms and an oxygen atom you get something rather astonishing. You get water, which is neither hydrogen nor oxygen. It includes them but transcends them. If you took the hydrogen away, there would be no water. If you took the oxygen away there would be no water. But water is something more than either hydrogen or oxygen. It is a third entity created from, or immanent in, their relationship.

The notion of field mind is reflected in Gregory Bateson's claim:

> *The individual mind is immanent but not only in the body. It is immanent in pathways and messages outside the body; and there is a larger Mind of which the individual mind is only a sub-system. This larger Mind is comparable to God and is perhaps what people mean by "God," but it is still immanent in the total interconnected social system and planetary ecology.*
>
> *(Steps to an Ecology of Mind,* 1972)

Bateson's "larger mind" is an example of what we are referring to as "field mind."

SG: So a major point here is that in order to perform the hero's journey, you need to be aligned and connected with each of these three minds. Those of you who were brought up Catholic will be delighted to discover that perhaps you have your first practical application of the sign of the cross . . . because the three minds are . . . (touches forehead, then heart, then opens arms outwards). (Laughter.)

RD: The father is the cognitive mind (touches forehead).

SG: Jesus . . .

RD: . . . the son, is the somatic mind (touches heart).

SG: And the Holy Spirit . . . (opens arms outwards)

RD: . . . is the field mind.

SG: So we've been searching for some practical application of our childhood Catholicism; and we will present this as the mystery of the trinity. *(Laughter.)*

Three Levels of Consciousness: Primitive, Ego, and Generative

RD: Now, to get to the generative aspect of each of these minds, there are certain principles that allow us to tap the generative resources of each one.

SG: Each mind can operate at different levels. It may sound a little complicated at first, but I think it will soon become clear. The ordinary level, what we will call the *ego level*, is the "ordinary" inside-the-box mind. So when you're operating from the basic state of consciousness with regard to your somatic mind, just walking through your day doing your daily business, the body is generally regarded as an "it." Or you may regard it as a dumb animal that needs to be pushed through the day. You load it up with caffeine in the morning and rush off to work, pushing your body through a hectic day. Then at night, you come home, put food and maybe alcohol in the body, and "relax." You pass out, go to sleep, get up the next morning, and do it again.

At the ego level of somatic mind, you're not experiencing the magic in your body. You're not experiencing the creative mysteries of the body. You don't sense its connection to ancestral wisdom, to intuitive knowing, to courage and tenderness. So if you are facing a challenge in your hero's journey, you're going to have to shift the consciousness in your body to a higher state.

RD: What we are calling the *generative state.*

SG: Individuals who are excellent performers – artists, athletes, business leaders, healers – know how to shift into a higher state of consciousness in their body. They know that to do something generative, they need to first move their somatic mind to the highest level of consciousness. Such peak performers engage in intense practice to reach and sustain these states of generative somatic mind. And how you can do that is one of our major teaching focuses in this work, so you can be successful in meeting the great challenges and callings of your life.

RD: These levels are analogous to the gears in your car. You've got to shift to another gear in order to be able to address the situations and challenges you meet along the road.

SG: Ironically, the typical thing that happens for most people is that when they encounter a challenge, they shift gear to a lower level, not the higher level needed to meet the challenge. This is what makes a challenge into an impasse; in the face of the challenge, a person's consciousness degrades to a primitive state where no new responses or learnings are possible.

For example, when the 9/11 tragedy hit the United States, the ordinary box of identity of the American psyche was cracked. I remember watching it on TV and there was a voice inside of me that said: "Now all of the old distinctions are gone. All of the old ways are gone." And I thought, perhaps in retrospect a little too optimistically: "This is a great opportunity for us all, to come together and move to a higher level." And we had a lot of "guardians," lots of support to do that – this opportunity to grow our consciousness. It's very sad for me to see what happened instead – that in my humble view the United States deeply lost its way in response to the challenge.

RD: So there can be a type of degenerative process as well. This might be thought of as a regression to a more *primitive state* of consciousness.

SG: Where there's no longer an intelligent way of responding, you go to a more basic, primordial, pre-ego state. More emotional energy, less linearity, more intense imagery. We return to the primordial soup of consciousness. We are suggesting this happens any time you lose your identity. This can be the consequence of a trauma or loss or failure. You have a failure in business, and the normal order falls apart. You have a crisis in a personal relationship, and your normal order falls apart.

But it can also be a voluntary, positive process. You fall in love, and you reconnect with the ocean of being. You jump out of an airplane (hopefully with a parachute!), you go for a night of ecstatic dancing, you giggle the night away with your friends. All these activities deliberately move you out of the box of your ego consciousness and back into the fluid swell of the original mind.

And we're emphasizing that this is actually not a bad thing – because it's bringing you deeply into primitive consciousness. You *need* to lose your mind on a periodic basis, to get back to the primitive level, to regenerate and recreate your presence in the world. Shifting from the ego to the primitive, whether it happens under positive or negative conditions, brings you down into the roots of consciousness from which new life can be generated. Primitive consciousness is needed to recreate your identity and to generate something beyond where you've been before.

Once you drop into the primitive level, the great question is whether you will get stuck there, or whether you can stay connected with the resources of the primitive consciousness, while also adding the important resources of the generative level. In other words, what can you do to let go of the limitations of the ego level, drop into the creative waters of the primitive, and then move forward to the transformational level of the generative mind?

The Principles for Creating a Generative Self

SG: One way we will do this is by focusing on the generative principles for each mind. To move to a generative somatic level, the general principle is, *Align and center*. To move to a generative cognitive level, the principle is, *Accept and transform*. To move to a generative field level, the principle is, *Open beyond (e.g. the problem), then open beyond that*.

RD: In other words, getting outside of the old box into a whole new world of possibilities.

SG: By the end of this program, we hope you will have a reasonably good understanding of these principles, and some knowledge of how to put them into practice. To begin, we will be focusing on the generative somatic, and how mind–body centering can get you there. Centering is a practice by which you unify and align your somatic state. It is a process where you take your mindful awareness, drop it into your body, then open through your body into the world. In doing so, you bring all of your embodiment into a unified field from which emerges many generative properties.

RD: When we lose our center or become uncentered, there's a type of chaos, or confusion, or insecurity that makes you much more susceptible to external influences. When you are centered, the channel is open and strong, and you feel peaceful and confident, connected to many resources.

SG: When you center, your worrying mind settles down. Your awareness is able to open. So you have calmness and clarity; the capacity to be at rest even while you think and respond to difficult challenges.

RD: Another common quality of centering is *presence*. There's a full presence of all of your consciousness – as opposed to what the Buddhists call the agitation and clouded awareness of the "monkey mind," which is jumping around, from tree to tree, from branch to branch, from worry to worry.

SG: On your hero's journey there will be many times where you lose your ordinary capacity to understand things and to act confidently. Your ego-intellect does not have the capacity to generate new consciousness, so it will crumble in the face of challenges that require you to be generative. You will lose your mind on a regular basis – isn't that wonderful to look forward to? *(Laughter.)*

Seriously, though, centering is what will allow you to let go of the need for your ego-intellect to control and explain everything. Centering allows you to experience stability, attunement, intelligent sensing, and intuitive responsiveness, so you can perform at a high level under trying circumstances.

RD: And once you get centered, your next challenge will be to transform your cognitive mind. To move it from having to dominate or control things to being able to blend and flow with relationships, like an aikido master, so that transformation and new possibilities emerge. The operating principle for the generative cognitive level is called *sponsorship,* which is the term Stephen coined in his Self Relations work to describe "the process of awakening awareness of the goodness and gifts within each person, within the world, and the connections between them." It is like the example of the community of women in Togo singing to the baby. Sponsorship is what awakens or reawakens you to who you really are.

SG: Following our exploration of centering we'll focus on the skills of sponsorship.

RD: We'll see how, through sponsorship, the generative cognitive mind becomes a sort of a creative field, not any position in that field. That's why we call it a "mind of minds." It operates like a field or container, something that creatively holds all of its contents with a vitality, energy, and a creative curiosity that allows new relational connections to begin to emerge within that field.

SG: Milton Erickson is one of our major models for sponsorship, of how to accept what's there in a way that allows new experiences to emerge. During the first half of his psychiatric career, Erickson worked in a hospital with "crazy" people. One guy on the ward claimed he was Jesus Christ. Now this isn't generally a problem – there's always one Jesus Christ on every locked ward. The only problem is when two or more patients claim they're Jesus. *(Laughter.)* Anyway, all the therapy with "Jesus" had basically consisted of trying to convince him that he wasn't Jesus. Of course, "Jesus" would just respond by blessing the psychiatrists, saying, "Go in peace, my son."

Erickson took an immediate liking to "Jesus," and thought about how to creatively accept and sponsor his awakening. He walked up to "Jesus," introduced himself, and said, "I understand you're Jesus."

The guy said: "That's right, I'm Jesus."

Erickson replied: "And you're a carpenter, right?"

Jesus replied: "Of course, everybody knows I'm a carpenter."

"And you really like to help others?" Erickson continued.

"That's why I'm here," Jesus confirmed.

"Well," Erickson said. "There is a building project on the hospital wing next door, and they're short a few carpenters. And I wonder if you wouldn't mind going over there every day and helping in the building project."

Jesus graciously agreed, and over the next few weeks he left the hospital ward every day and put in a good day's work as a carpenter. He gradually became connected to the others on the crew, and began to operate less as a psychiatric patient and more as a working citizen in the world. This was the basis for the therapy that Erickson did with him, and it is a typically beautiful example of how he utilized the generative cognitive mind to blend with what was there, in a way that opened beyond it.

RD: So the principle of sponsorship is about receiving and accepting what's there, but holding it within a bigger framework. Sponsorship is about holding what's there in a way that allows other possibilities to emerge.

SG: And it carries this very key idea that within every experience and every person are the seeds of goodness and gifts. So it is a process of "change through no-change"; that is, letting go of trying to change something and instead receiving it with a skillful curiosity, holding it in a way that allows it to unfold further, into new patterns.

RD: What we're going to find is that it's often very easy to sponsor the gift – to give it space, to allow it to grow. The greater challenge is often to sponsor the wound, the "demon," or the shadow. We don't want to sponsor it – we want to get rid of it, we want to cure it, we want to control it, we want to fight it. But true healing and transformation come from being able to sponsor the wound, sponsor the demon, sponsor the shadow. That's a type of skillfulness that we'll be exploring a lot in the second part of this program.

SG: The third part of this work involves how to open generative fields of consciousness. This is especially about releasing the hypnotic grip of focal attention to a problem or person, and opening to a larger field of consciousness around that pattern or person, so that you have expanded awareness and resources available. We will see how we can do this at several different levels of field consciousness, to attune to larger fields of intelligence, so that you're not walking in the world as an isolated, disembodied, ego-intellect, but rather as an embodied and centered human presence that's deeply connected to generative fields of awareness.

In working with each of these three minds – somatic, cognitive, and field – the basic idea is that you are as good as your state of consciousness. If you are in a low level somatic state, you're not going to be able to successfully meet the challenges of your journey. If your cognitive patterning is rigid and controlling, you're going to fail at any transformational tasks. If you're not connected to larger fields of resources, you're not going to get very far.

Developing a Generative Somatic Consciousness

SG: So we're saying your state will determine what you experience, the meaning you place on it, the capacity you have to respond to it, and your general quality of life. That's a lot! The good news is that it is *you* who has primary control of your state, should you wish to claim it. And what we're doing here is exploring how you can upgrade your state to a high level so that you can indeed experience success on your life journey.

RD: In NLP we like to say: it all starts with the state. And Steve's Generative Self model is about attuning to different aspects of that state, and learning how to bring each one to its highest levels.

Exercise: Connecting with Your Center

SG: The first stage is: How can you develop and utilize a generative somatic state? To explore that, we'd like to introduce a few experiential exercises around centering.

RD: This is an exercise for centering yourself. And there's a reason that we're doing it as the first exercise. We're suggesting that it is the first and primary skill that you need for your hero's journey. And we're going to return to this over and over throughout the program – the practice and discipline of dropping into your center.

SG: Then we're going to have you do a second exercise with a partner in which you use your connection to the center to begin to explore your calling.

RD: So we're saying: from the center comes the calling. We've probably all had the experience that when something challenging or extraordinary happens, it activates your center. You know something is up because you start to feel that energy, that activity in your center. If you're not aligned with your center, the energy moving in your center can be frightening and overwhelming. You can get lost in that energy, it can take over in a negative way. But if you're grounded in your center, the energy coming through can be sponsored in a positive and creative way.

(Note: We begin now to do a group experiential process of centering. During this and other group experiences, our communications generally shift to a softer, slower, more hypnotic style, thereby encouraging and supporting participants in shifting from their ego-intellect to their experiential consciousness. We use ellipses at those points to indicate where a pause of several seconds or more is made between words (for the purposes of allowing experiential deepening) and italics (where certain words or phrases are tonally marked out for experiential emphasis).)

SG: To begin the exercise, sit in a comfortable position. Begin to settle in and settle down . . .

RD: . . . and place both feet on the floor, so you can feel them grounded in the earth.

SG: Another word for centering is *balancing*. In centering, we're attuning to that balance point in every dimension of our consciousness. So you're not too far out (opens arm outwards), you're not too far in (hunches inward), but you find the balance point where you can be both in and out at the same time. While centering involves relaxation, it's not just relaxation – like watching TV or drinking beers in a bar – it's relaxation plus attention, as artists and athletes learn to do. Being relaxed *and* aware, both at the same time.

RD: You're going to become centered and aware, not disconnected. A good starting place is to sense your awareness dropping down. Coming down into and through the body. Begin to feel the soles of your feet. There is a whole universe of sensation in the soles of your feet that is always there, but not always in your awareness.

SG: So just take a few moments to begin that process. You can do it with your eyes open or closed. Experiment. This is your own process of learning for yourself from inside.

RD: And remember, the key thing we're saying is that as you go inside, it's not like you're going to sleep. In fact it's the opposite – you're awakening more and more; connecting and awakening.

SG: Settling in . . . and settling down.

RD: The next step is *breathe*.

SG: As you move into centering . . . you're shifting from thinking to breathing.

RD: Your breath is always in the present. When you connect to your breath, you will be in the present.

SG: And as you settle into your breathing, you might also begin to sense the alignment in your spine. Sense your spine as soft . . . and luminous.

RD: In a centered state you're not hunched forward. You can imagine a gentle thread of light at the crown of your head just gently pulling you up, lifting the crown of your head up to the sky.

SG: We human beings have taken a long time getting vertical. Let's take advantage of that.

RD: Another way to help your spine become longer is to gently lift and open your chest.

SG: You might just take a few moments to breathe up and down . . . inside . . . of your spine . . . So your consciousness begins to shift from muscle tension to that simple energetic, subtle feeling in your spine.

RD: And remember, as you follow our words: don't got away, don't space out. Stay here.

SG: At the same time, our words can really be in the background . . . What emerges in the foreground . . . is just that pleasant sense of breathing . . . *up and down through the spine.*

RD: As if your breath can bring energy all the way up from the earth through the soles of your feet and up through your spine to your neck.

SG: As you breathe up . . . and down . . . through the inside of your spine . . . you might just bring a very simple sort of self-blessing . . . a simple suggestion for yourself . . . maybe it's a word like *self-care* . . . or . . . *self-love* . . . *self-acceptance* . . . Something that you can use to begin to bring a blessing or self-affirmation for yourself through your spinal awareness.

RD: Maybe it's a simple blessing like: *opening* . . . or . . . *awake.*

SG: And as you let yourself attune to your breathing . . . to your spinal awareness . . . to the energy moving up and down, inside the tube of the spine . . . and begin to drop that simple self-suggestion through the spine . . . then you can add several more suggestions to deepen the state . . . The first is, *Nothing to do in the body except relaxation . . . Nothing to do in the body except relaxation . . . Nothing to do in the body except relaxation . . . Letting go of all tension as you open deeper into that centered awareness.*

RD: And as you do, you might continue to sense that string . . . *lifting* through your crown chakra . . . gently *lifting* your spine and head up . . . deeply feeling your channel *opening . . . opening . . .*

SG: And to help you further, you can add one more simple suggestion into the mix: *Nothing for the mind to cling to . . . Nothing for the mind to cling to . . . Nothing for the mind to cling to . . . that's good . . . that's good . . . Breathing . . . that's good . . . that's good . . . Spinal attunement . . . that's good . . . that's good . . . Nothing to do in the body except relaxation . . . that's good . . . that's good . . . Nothing for the mind to cling to . . . that's very good . . . that's very good . . .*

RD: Breathing . . .

SG: Letting go of all thoughts, letting go of all beliefs . . .

RD: . . . and breathing . . .

SG: . . . into the mind of no-mind . . . the mind of no content . . . nothing to do . . . except relaxation . . . nothing to cling to . . .

RD: . . . and breathing.

SG: And from that place of centered aligned . . . no-mind . . . it's a wonderful thing to discover that you can receive experiences from beyond your conscious mind . . .

RD: . . . an opening to a larger mind . . .

SG: . . . and one of the experiences that you can receive from the superconscious mind . . . is an experience of deep well-being and centeredness that you've had in the past.

RD: Remembering those positive transcendent experiences of your channel being *open* . . . your center being connected *to something deeper.*

SG: Let the superconscious mind bring back on the gentle rivers . . . of breath . . . times in your life . . . where you felt deeply . . . deeply whole . . . and at peace.

RD: When you were able to *feel that vitality* . . . and *feel that life force* . . . fully *flowing* through you . . . a state of *effortless excellence.*

SG: And as you *receive those experiences* . . . *breathe* them into the present moment . . . concentrate all of your awareness . . . to *breathing them* into the present moment, into your body.

RD: And as you do . . . *notice* . . . where is your attention focused in these experiences . . . *in your body?* Where is your center *in your body* . . . when you're in *these experiences of well-being?*

SG: If you were to walk in the world with this sense of well-being . . . *where is your center?*

RD: And as you sense . . . where is your center in your body . . . you can take your hands . . . and begin to place them on your body where you . . . *feel your center most focused and present.*

SG: If you were going to speak from this state of well-being . . . *where is the center* for your speech?

RD: Make sure that center is somewhere below the neck . . . and above the legs . . . in the body. Find this center in the body.

SG: Notice how you can . . . *touch your center* . . . in the same way that you would *touch somebody that you deeply love* . . . so the quality of the touch . . . is able to *awaken the center* . . . and *awaken yourself* as well . . . Find that way of connecting to your center . . . that allows your consciousness . . . your spirit . . . your deepest awareness . . . to *become one with it.*

RD: You can also find times of challenge in your life . . . where you were able to *stay centered* . . . to *stay deeply connected* with yourself . . . knowing that no matter what was going on outside, in you, or around you . . . that you'd always *stay connected with your center.*

SG: And as you just feel . . . and explore . . . that quality of simple . . . *deep connection* with your center . . . it's a great thing to appreci-ate . . . *that's your base.* You can leave it, but it can never leave you . . . It's always there, a song for the asking . . . And that when you *feel from that base* . . . when you *speak from that base* . . . when you *think from that base* . . . *good things are going to happen in your life.* So you may just want to have a sense . . . before we begin to bring clo-sure to this first experiment . . . is there any simple vow, any simple commitment that you want to make?

RD: And what will be your anchor for this state . . . your symbol . . . that allows you to come back to this place . . . more and more easily . . . as a base line in your life?

SG: Knowing that whenever you want, you can touch that place . . . sense that anchor . . . to allow yourself to know: *I return now to my center. I come back home to myself . . . I connect back to my source . . .* And as the great Irish poet Yeats said, "When I am at home with myself, everything I do ends as a love poem" . . . *Long live the hero's journey . . . Long live the hero's journey . . . Long live the hero's journey!*

RD: *(Voice gently becomes less hypnotic, beginning to non-verbally reorient attention back into the room)* Now take a moment and breathe deeply into your center. Allow your breath to bring energy to the center

... to animate the center, to bring it more and more alive ... and as you do so, let yourself come back into this world out here. Yet even as your attention begins to reorient externally, also keep your awareness attuned to your center.

Too often we easily just give away our center as soon as we open our eyes or shift our awareness. So keep your first attention on that center as you look around the room, and as you begin to move your body. So you're not leaving your center or letting it go – you're looking out from and engaging the world from your center. Welcome back!

We hope you had a good first experience. Take a moment and reflect on what happened for you. Was it easy or hard to let go? What was your blessing or self-suggestion? How did that work for you? What was it like finding and connecting to your center? If you had a symbol, what was it?

SG: There are so many things we could say about the importance of centering. We talked about it as a base, as a channel for the spirit to awaken into the world. We talked about it as an integration point, where all the different parts of mind–body consciousness can become unified. In the martial arts, this is called "one point." When a martial artist is facing multiple violent attacks, he or she is trained to stay attuned to center, so the mind stays calm and aware, and the body is organized for optimal responsiveness.

In this regard, we're talking about centering as an attentional process: Where and how do you give your attention? We're especially talking about what might be called "first attention." Where is your first focus, your base focus of attention? You have this precious gift of attention, and you can focus it anywhere, on anything.

I can place it outside of me, on another person, such as Robert here, but then he will become my higher power. I will look to Robert for everything, and disconnect from my own presence. I could place it on my internal dialogue, and then my attention will be caught within all of my words. I could place it on some image or memory: "This is what happened before; that's going to happen all the time."

All of these are different possibilities, and they represent ways that people satisfy this important need of stabilizing their consciousness, by fixating in on some (hopefully) unchanging content. But each has significant costs – they lock you into a content-static connection, away from your center and locked in an unchanging representation. Psychologically, this is called *fundamentalism*, the rigid adherence to a static text, and we see it as the great opponent of generative consciousness.

Of course, the "positive intention" of such fundamentalisms is to stabilize consciousness. However, we are suggesting that centering is a higher level response to this need. Since the center is content-free, you can stabilize your consciousness around it, yet still be completely open to the ever-changing patterns and energies of the moment. This "stability plus openness" is a characteristic of generative consciousness, and a necessary skill for the hero's journey.

RD: Transformational teacher Richard Moss maintains that "the greatest gift you can give to yourself or another person is the quality of your attention." Those of you who are coaches know that. We're suggesting that to do that with others, you first need to give that quality of attention to yourself. Richard Moss also points out that "the distance between yourself and another person is the same as the distance between yourself and yourself." So, again, we're saying: the starting place is within, and centering is the mind–body process for doing that. Who was it who said: "The answer is within"?

SG: George Bush? *(Laughter.)* Somebody. George Bush, Madonna, or Robert Dilts, I can't remember. *(Laughter.)* I confuse them after a while. *(Both laugh.)* By the way, we emphasize laughter as a crucial skill for the hero's journey – life is much too serious to not have a sense of humor!

Another quality of centering is that it connects you with the deeper mind. You can call it by many names – creative unconscious, super-conscious, archetypal intelligence, field. And through your center comes your calling, comes that spirit looking to awaken into the world.

RD: Think of your center as your access to a deeper mind. According to NLP, eye movements are accessing cues to cognitive information; they're the pathways that your cognitive mind uses in order to think. In the same way, your center is the accessing cue to that which is deeper than the cognitive mind.

SG: And when you are on your hero's journey, that is a crucial access that you need. You need to connect with yourself beneath your thinking mind.

RD: So we're suggesting the first thing that you should always say to yourself when you get into any kind of a difficult situation is: relax, drop down, center, open into the world through your center. This hooks up your cognitive mind with your somatic mind, thereby allowing a greater degree of wisdom.

Exercise: Speaking and Listening from Your Center

SG: What comes from that mind–body unity, that somatic/cognitive integration, is a deeper type of intelligence. To see how this might relate to sensing and speaking your calling for your hero's journey, we want to do a second exercise now. Robert and I will demonstrate it with each other.

(Steve and Robert sit in chairs facing each other.)

RD: We're going to be asking you to first connect with your own center, then connect with your partner. This will allow you to explore the principle that the distance between myself and myself determines the distance between myself and another. In order for me to really connect with Steve, I have to first be connected with myself.

SG: So the first step in this process, and in every exercise we will do as part of this work, is to take the time to connect with your center. Rather than performing for our partner – trying to fix them, impress them, seduce them, take care of them – we're going to take a few moments of silence to settle in and settle down, and find the center within. Then we're going to very gently let our eyes open, so that we can connect with our partner, even as we remain connected with our center. To do that, it's important to let your eyes open primarily to the peripheral field. You don't want to get into a staring contest with your partner, or lock your attention onto any part of them; you want to see beyond them, then open very wide to the peripheral. In the martial art of aikido, we call this "soft eyes," which is how the aikidoist visually orients so he or she can be aware of a large field, not locking onto anything, being able to respond creatively to everything. So it's not a groggy or undifferentiated awareness; quite the contrary. You're letting yourself develop a centered field awareness, which we will see is a crucial skill for the Generative Self.

RD: As you look at your partner, see if you can soften and widen your visual field so you can also see the corners of the walls behind him or her. Just experiment with that, finding that tuning point where you can be aware of focal content while also opening to a larger field of awareness. Just notice as you attune: Can you soften your eyes to see more?

SG: Practice this process when connecting with your partner: centering, opening to your partner, opening your visual field beyond your partner. You're looking to develop a beautiful field consciousness – wide and deep awareness, with sensitivity to subtle patterns within that field.

RD: Remember, the greatest gift I can give to my partner is the quality of my attention. So give your attention to your partner as if it's a precious gift. *(Steve and Robert take a few moments to attune to each other.)*

SG: As we connect, we first find our center and then find an open connection with our partner. When you've completed these first two steps, you'll signal it by simply nodding your head, so your partner knows you're ready to move to the next step.

Then one of you is going to be Person A, the other will be Person B. In this demonstration, Robert will be person B and I will be person A.

Giving your first attention to staying non-verbally connected to yourself and to your partner, Person A is going to make a simple statement: "My deepest calling is about _____." For the content, it could be a word or phrase, or a body movement, or a symbolic image that comes to you. Whatever shows up when you make the statement, express that.

So, for example . . . *(attunes with Robert)* . . . Robert, my deepest calling is about . . . and then I'm waiting for the response to come from my center. Not from here *(points to head)*, but from here *(points to center in belly)*. *Robert, my deepest calling is about . . . healing violence.*

RD: As Person B, I'm giving my full attention to Steve. I'm allowing his sharing to touch me deeply. I want to be touched and awakened by his calling, so I can drink it in and mirror it back. Once I somatically resonate with his statement, I as the receiver respond with: *Stephen, I really get; I really sense that your deepest calling is to heal violence.*

SG: *(Pauses to breathe in.)* And Person A just receives that as a sort of a blessing. Breathe it in, let it take you deeper.

That's one side. Then person B makes his or her statement.

RD: I make my statement allowing it to come from my center. I might say *(Robert pauses, breathes and attunes to Steve) Steve, my deepest calling is . . . to continue to open myself fearlessly to the mystery that I live.*

SG: *(Pauses to absorb and sense the statement.)* I really drink that in . . . feel the beauty of it . . . and then simply feed back: *Robert, I really sense your calling in opening to that mystery. And I send you much support.*

RD: *(Pauses and breathes.)* And I receive that.

That's one round. And then we repeat the process for four or five rounds. We find it takes a few times to let yourself settle in and really start speaking and listening from your center.

In terms of the calling, you don't have to use words. You could simply make a gesture with your body. As Isadora Duncan, the famous dancer, said: "If I could say it, I wouldn't have to dance it."

SG: So you might find that what comes out of a center is a movement. *(Steve and Robert slowly make different gestures – arms opening, hands touching heart, finger pointing to the future – to show examples.)*

RD: It could also be an image, a symbol that maybe your cognitive mind doesn't understand what it means, but it's just a symbol that comes to you. My calling is . . . a thunderbolt from the sky, or a group of people singing, or the color purple. All these could be symbols or metaphors that come when you open the space to speak your calling from your center.

SG: We're just looking to breathe a connection that holds all that. Remember: *go slow.* This is not the Oprah Winfrey talk show; you're not trying to impress your partner with your personality. You're looking to sense a deeper connection with your center and your calling. Let it come from a deeper place.

Now we are going to demonstrate the whole process again to give you the whole sense of it. So we'll take a few moments to settle in and settle down.

RD: Begin this process by feeling your breath in your spine, becoming present in your body, connecting to yourself in your center. *(Moments of silence as both Steve and Robert close their eyes and center.)*

SG: And when you feel that connection with your own center, you can gently let your attention open to the field that includes your partner. *(Steve and Robert connect with each other silently for a few moments, then each nods head to indicate readiness.)*

Robert, my deepest calling is about . . . healing woundedness.

RD: *Stephen, I see . . . and I honor . . . that your deepest calling is about healing woundedness.*

Stephen, my deepest calling is about . . . (Robert opens arms slowly into the field.)

SG: *Yes, Robert, I* really *sense that your deepest calling is about (repeats Robert's movement) . . . and I send you much support for that calling.*

Robert, my deepest calling is about . . . (Touches hands to heart, then opens them into the world.)

RD: *Stephen, I really, really feel . . . I can sense . . . that your deepest calling is about . . . (makes Stephen's gesture) . . . and I support that with everything in my being.*

Stephen, my deepest calling is about . . . seeing everything as light . . . even the darkness as light.

SG: *I really see, Robert, this very deep calling . . . to see everything, including the darkness . . . as . . . part of the light . . . and I send you much support. Much support.*

(Stephen and Robert, now deeply attuned, take a few moments to silently share the space, before turning to the group.)

RD: *(With mischievous smile)* And so, Stephen and Robert turned to the multitude and said: "Go forth, and share your deepest calling!" *(Laughter.)*

We hope you can sense from our demonstration that the key here – when you're a coach, a therapist, a consultant, a friend – is the quality of listening that you give to allow somebody to touch those deep places in themselves. And I want to suggest that you can give that quality of attention anytime, with anybody, anywhere. For example, sitting on an airplane, or waiting in line at the bank, or being at a stuffy dinner party. I have – and it's quite miraculous what happens if you just give that attention to somebody, listen from that centered place. People discover themselves sharing very deep and personal things with you without even knowing why. That is one very important learning from this exercise.

The other part is really connecting to your calling by giving the same quality of attention to listening to your inner self. What is your calling? How can you sense it, speak it, live it, realize it?

SG: We suggest that you practice this exercise with someone that you're deeply unconsciously attracted to. *(Laughter.)*

RD: And if you can't find someone you're deeply unconsciously attracted to, find someone you're unconsciously repelled by. *(Laughter.)*

SG: And in order to keep the mystery of life alive, don't tell them on what basis you've selected them! *(Laughter.)* OK, go where no man nor woman has gone before. And may the Force be with you!

Bringing the Three Minds Together in Support of the Calling

SG: We want to continue to build on what we've explored in the previous section, and in particular we would like to start out by addressing the notion of the hero's journey in terms of connection with the three minds: somatic, cognitive, and field.

RD: In our previous two exercises, you were connecting into your center and exploring your calling. And we assume that you have taken the time to practice this and have found some statements that touched you. Once you sense the calling, a next step is making the commitment by accepting and moving forward with that calling.

SG: Campbell talks about this in terms of crossing a first threshold. You get beyond all the ego fears and self-criticism that are keeping you from your calling, and step into the world and begin the journey. You're no longer trapped in the soap operas, the endless language games, and the ego insecurities. You're actually walking in the larger world of consciousness.

We are suggesting the Generative Self as an approach that can help you to do that. One of the main questions we're exploring here is how to realize your power and potency. How can you organize yourself so that your commitments and ideas and actions really can make a difference in the world? This is what we mean by being potent.

When you do coaching or therapy, your clients are generally starting out with a state of impotency. And both men and women suffer equally from this type of impotency. *(Laughter.)* Seriously, one of the great sufferings that people experience results from the sense that, "What I say and what I do don't make a difference. What I say and what I do isn't creating the results that I want in my life." So the task of the hero's journey, as well as coaching or therapy, is to shift from a state of impotency – what I do doesn't make a difference

– to a state of potency – what I do and say and think *does* make a difference.

RD: "Yes, you can!" as President Obama would say. *(Laughter.)*

SG: The Generative Self work suggests that you can do this by integrating the three minds – somatic, cognitive, and field – to forge a higher state of consciousness. What we want to explore here are three simple ways to do that: (1) *sense your calling and set it as a clear and resonant intention* in the cognitive mind, (2) *align the calling with the center* in the somatic mind, and (3) *bring your calling into the world* by opening your center into the field.

RD: The following exercise in Aligning the Three Minds, which Stephen developed, is a powerful way to bring our life force and unique vitality out into the world.

Exercise: Aligning the Three Minds to Realize Your Calling

1. Write down your calling(s). Be succinct and positive – no more than five words in addition to: "My deepest calling is to _____."

2. Speak your calling three or four times, noting your feelings each time.

3. Somatically attune, with your hand on your center, and then speak your goal again, making sure your voice is resonant with center. Slow down significantly, just to sense the connection between your voice and center. Notice any differences.

4. Somatically attune with a hand on your center, and point with the other hand into the "future." Make sure you feel your energy *both* connecting to center *and* extending through and beyond your finger. While you extend into the future and hold center with equal resonance, speak your calling again. Notice any differences.

5. Once you find the resonant alignment of the three minds, maintain it while you meditate on the commitment to realize the call.

SG: In the first step of the exercise, you're identifying and speaking the calling. Begin by getting a piece of paper and taking a few moments to sit with the open statement, "My deepest calling is about X" or "My deepest calling is to X." For example, "My deepest calling is to be a loving presence in the world," or "My deepest calling is to bring more integrity into politics," or "My deepest calling is about social justice." Take your time to center and listen in to your deeper voice. Remember, your calling doesn't come from your ego-intellect, it comes from your deeper center. Write down whatever comes, using five words or less for each response. Then sit with it for a few moments, let it go, and come back to the statement again, seeing if a different response comes. Take a couple of minutes and see if you can come up with four or five statements of, "My deepest calling is about _____."

RD: Before continuing, do this now. Write down several statements, reflecting your calling.

(Pause.)

SG: We are now going to demonstrate the rest of exercise, and then invite you to practice it with a partner. This process of aligning the three minds to realize an intention is an example of what Robert was calling "translating yourself from a rumor into a reality."

Demonstration with Marcos

SG: Welcome, Marcos. What I would like to do in this very short time is to really support you to explore how you can speak your calling into reality. For our first step, can you please select one of the callings you just wrote down, and go ahead and speak it aloud.

Marcos: Yes. *My deepest calling is to relieve suffering.*

SG: *Your deepest calling is to relieve suffering.* That's good. *(Takes deep breath, then speaks to the group.)* If you are the coach, any time and every time that you hear somebody speak anything like their calling, any time you sense somebody speaking with their spirit, you want to breathe it deeply into your body. You want to absorb it at the deepest level of your being, really breathe it, let it touch you and awaken you at a deep level. Because you're here to absorb their spirit, bring it deep inside your center, feel its power and beauty, and let it guide you in your connection with the person.

(To Marcos) Great, Marcos. So what I'm going to ask you to do for the exercise is to take that simple but important statement, *"My deepest calling is to relieve suffering,"* and speak it aloud a number of times, under three different conditions.

The first couple of times, I'm going to ask you to speak it without any reference to centering or to field extension. Just speak it in a regular sort of way. And each time you do, just notice where it takes you when you speak it like that.

(To audience) And the receiving field – all of you out there, and also Robert and me – we'll move into a receptive listening place, also noticing how we're touched – or not – each time the calling is spoken. Because if we're going to realize our calling, we have to be able to touch other people with it. We need support from others. And if I speak my calling in a weak, uncentered way, you don't get touched, you don't get it that I'm up to something big. So we'll tune ourselves into a receptive mode so we can give feedback to the "hero" about whether and how they are touching us with their spirit.

(To Marcos) OK. So after we do the first round, we'll start the second round. In the second round I'm going to first coach you, hopefully very straightforwardly, to find your center, so that before you speak again, you will feel deeply connected to your center. And for this second part of the exercise, I'm going to ask you to speak very, very slowly – actually, about four or five times more slowly than usual – because what we're interested in during this round is how you can sense the vibration of your speaking voice against the vibration of your center. *This is one of the major parts of generative consciousness: to learn to think, speak, and act with deep connection to your center.* So for this training exercise, I'll be asking you to speak incredibly slowly, becoming more interested in the non-verbal vibration of your voice aligning with the center. And we'll see what difference that makes – in terms of where it brings you, and what effect it has on the receiving field.

And then third, I'm going to ask you to focus on bringing the calling resonating in your center out into the field; to lift the energy and the intention from inside of you into the world. For this part, I'll be asking you to speak like an opera singer *(makes slow, dramatic waving of hand and arm from center out into the room)* . . . or like a bull-fighter . . . OLÉ! *(makes dramatic movement like bullfighter waving bull through cape)*.

So in each of these forms, we want to see how we can extend our center all the way into the field, then release our energy in a beautiful, artistic way. In this exercise you'll see the different places where you hold your energy back, where your energy stops unfolding into the world, which is where your intention can no longer become realized. And as you open that energy fully from your center into the world, we'll see what sort of effect that has, for you and for the field. OK?

Marcos: OK.

SG: And most of all, really make this a self-learning experience for yourself. You're not here to perform for others. Use it to explore the connection to yourself.

OK, so let's begin. Tune back to the statement, "My deepest calling is to relieve suffering in others." Take a moment, and then when you're ready, I'm just going to have you speak the statement aloud. Then pause, sense where it takes you, and then try again.

Marcos: The first time I do it without centering?

SG: Yes. That's right. No centering the first time.

Marcos: My deepest calling is to relieve suffering. My deepest calling is to relieve suffering. My deepest calling is to relieve suffering. My deepest calling is . . . to relieve suffering. My deepest calling is to relieve suffering. My deepest calling is to relieve suffering.

SG: Great, so let's stop there, and you take a moment just to sense inside . . . what happened in that process. Did you feel more connected, less connected, self-conscious?

Marcos: I don't feel much connection.

SG: Yes, you don't feel much connection when you speak it that way. I'm sure that makes sense. And if it's OK, I'd like to share my experience listening as a coach. I can see the calling is very important for you. I can see there's a lot of deep emotion connected to it. And what I experience as a witness is when the feeling starts to open, it quickly gets pulled back. (*Makes a few repetitive movements to show opening, then closing down.*) And that evokes in me wanting to help you. But then, again, I'm a psychotherapist – so everything evokes in me wanting to help people! (*Laughter.*)

So let's see what happens when you speak it from a mind–body state of centering. To let go of the first condition, perhaps you'd like to step back, shake out the first state, then step forward when you're ready to center.

(*Marcos does that.*)

SG: Take a deep breath. (*Marcus breathes.*) I'd like to invite you, with your eyes closed, to just *take a few deep breaths . . . that's good . . . and let yourself sense in a simple way . . . that's good . . . that's it time to return . . . back into your center . . . that's good . . . Let go of everything else . . . that's good . . . relax through the spine . . . tune to your center . . . that's good . . . and if there are any specific experiences, any particular ways, that you use . . . to find that place of well-being, that place of connection, that place of centering . . . then go ahead and use those pathways . . . Use my support in whatever ways are helpful . . . to attune to your center . . . and when you sense it . . . let yourself take one of your hands and touch it there . . . so that you can begin to let your attention direct . . . to a place beneath your thinking . . . to a place beneath any worries or concerns . . . come back to your base.* (*Marcos places hand on heart.*) . . . *That's good, that's great . . . and just take a few moments to breathe into that connection, sense the connection between your mind and your center, your self and your center . . .*

Good. Now in a moment I'm going to ask you to speak the calling again. You can keep your eyes closed, keep your hand tuned to your center, keep your first attention connected to the energy of the center. And as you keep that connection, I'm going to ask you to speak the calling. Again, I'll ask you to speak it abnormally slow, this time really just exploring how to let your voice connect and express the vibrational energy of your center. At any time if you feel your voice disconnect from your center, slow down even more, breathe back into your center, establish a deeper connection before speaking again. It might sound something like this. *(Steve begins to speak in a slow, drawn out voice.)* Myyyyyyyyyy ... deeeeeeeeeepst ... callllllllllllling. Like that, just play with the non-verbal vibration, hooking it to the center. So whenever you're ready, go ahead and experiment with that.

Marcos: Mmmy ... deeepest ... caalling ... is ... to relieve ... suffferinngg.

SG: Good. That's good. And notice any differences in terms of where that takes you. And now try it again, this time feeling for vibration in the body. And play around with extending the vibration out into the world, letting it touch the back of the room perhaps. In my listening, the vibration is sort of pointing downwards into the ground, not outward into the living world. So try again.

Marcos: *(Speaks with much resonance.)* Mmmyyy ... deeeepest ... caaallling ... is ... to reelieevve ... suffferinngg.

SG: That's it! That's it! Good! *(Marcus stays connected to center, breathing, looking deeply connected.) And just breathe with that awareness ... and notice any differences when you connect to your intention in that way.* Notice what happens when you let go of the upper world of verbal language and social masks, and instead connect with your somatic energy, your body base. That's good, Marcos ... And then, when you're ready, take a nice breath and come on back out here.

(Marcos takes a deep breath and reorients into the room. He looks much more relaxed and centered.)

So what happened that time?

Marcos: Uhhhhhh. *(Smiles, hardly able to talk.)*

SG: *(Smiles in return)* Anything else? *(Laughter.)*

Marcos: It was a *very* deep experience.

SG: Yes. I can see: it was a very deep experience.

Marcos: The vibration connected to something very deep inside of me. I felt emotion also.

SG: Yes. I feel it in me, too. This time, I felt like you were actually creating a space – a big energy space began to open around you and extend from you.

Marcos: Yes, I felt that too . . .

SG: It was great to feel. And rather than being interested in helping you, this time I was interested in getting therapy from you!

(Marcos and group laughs.)

Whatever you were touching, I was touched by it, drawn to it. I felt like I wanted to be connected to that energy.

(To audience) So in this step, we're letting go of having to make clear sense in the head and concentrating on dropping down into the somatic energy, the somatic vibration, and stay with that as our base. This is our formula for the Generative Self: *When your cognitive ego-intellect self aligns with your embodied somatically centered self and attunes through vibration and resonance, good things happen.*

(To Marcos) OK, ready for the third step?

Marcos: Yes.

SG: This is where you get to be the famous opera star. Of course, this is a metaphor for talking about the process of feeling deeply into the resonance of your center, then lifting that energy out into the world, letting your intention be sung into the living world. So this time I'm going to ask you to speak like this . . . *(Steve shifts posture to be like a singer, and stretches his arm out in the group.) What I really want is to . . . relieve suffering . . . (Makes grand gesture, projecting the words and energy into the world.)* I'm going to ask you to play with this a bit – let it be playful yet serious, really finding an exaggerated movement, just like you're throwing a ball. *(Again, makes exaggerated slow movement, like throwing a ball.)* Once you extend it, just release it. Extend your intention into the world like you're throwing a ball *(makes gesture)* . . . or your're singing an opera *(makes gesture)* . . . or you're releasing flowers into a big crowd *(makes gesture)*. Touch it in you . . . *(reaches in to center)* . . . Release it into the world . . . *(repeats gestures several times)* . . . then let it go. Once you release it, let go, you're done with it, come back to center . . . then try again. OK?

Marcos: Yes.

SG: OK, so let yourself stand with your right foot forward. Take a few moments to center and sense the intention of your calling in your center. Once you connect with that, let your hand reach in, touch the calling, and open it into the world *(makes sweeping gesture)* as you speak the calling.

Marcos: *(Takes a few moments to silently center and connect with intention, then opens his eyes, and extends his arm forward as he speaks the calling.)* What I really want most in the world is to relieve suffering! *(Comes back to resting position and silently pauses.)*

SG: That's good. Let's just pause for a moment. I want to add just a little bit of coaching. Remember the part about releasing the intention with a graceful movement? *(Steve makes movement.)* So once you let go, make sure to really release your muscles, just like throwing a ball. *(Demonstrates.)* Releasing after extending will allow you to return to center. If we extend into the world and stay tense, there's no breath in the process; the link between inner and outer is broken, the energy loop of "dropping into center, opening into field, coming back to center" is broken. Feel it, open and extend it, release it, come back to center, and find it again. OK, try again.

Marcos: *(Silently centers and breathes, then makes gesture.)* What I want most in the world is . . . to relieve suffering.

SG: *Breathe . . . Deep breath . . . Follow the energy from your center into the world . . . Let your eyes extend beyond yourself, beyond any person, open into the infinite . . . Then release as you stay centered.* Try again, really work on it, releasing after the extension, and then keep your mind here.

Marcos: What I want most in the world is . . . to relieve suffering. *(Breathes.)*

SG: That's good. That's good . . . But notice how you begin to space out, your eyes look away, you're breaking the extension of your intention. Try again, keep the extension, just like Tiger Woods after he hits a golf ball. Keep relaxed but intentional focus after you release it. Follow through . . . Try again.

Marcos: *What I want most in the world is . . . to relieve suffering.*

SG: Say it with your whole heart and your whole mind and your whole being.

Marcos: *What I want most in the world is . . . to relieve suffering. (His energy rises.) . . . What I want most is to relieve suffering! (Energy increases.) . . . To relieve suffering . . . What I want most in the world is . . . to relieve suffering. (Audience members spontaneously begin to clap. Marcos smiles and beams.)*

SG: Wow . . . That's really amazing! Beautiful. *(Audience still calling out support and giving applause.)* That's what we're talking about! I really get that, Marcos . . . And as you can see *(makes gesture to audience)*, so does the field! Congratulations! *(Steve and Marcos exchange hugs.)* Any comments you would like to make on this third step?

Marcos: There was a total difference between saying it at the beginning and at the end feeling it – because internally, emotionally, the vibration was there . . . everything. And to feel to release it with a connection to myself . . . it's something I didn't know I could quite feel and experience at such a level. *(Smiles and beams.)*

SG: Yes . . . And now you know . . . and we certainly all know as well. You really can realize that intention deeply in the world, each day in every way. May your calling indeed be realized! Thank you very much, Marcos. *(They hug again, and Marcos leaves stage to audience applause.)*

RD: By the way, this is very much the kind of process that I use when I am coaching managers and company executives to express their visions. This is a key skill of leadership. What draws people to join you? If you ever watch videos of great leaders like Martin Luther King, you don't see them saying something like *(Robert speaks in a soft monotone while looking down at floor)*, "I have a dream." *(Audience laughs.)*

SG: And after he says it . . . "I have a dream". . . he doesn't pull away and say *(Steve shrugs shoulders, looks uninterested)*, "Oh well . . . whatever." *(Laughter.)*

RD: So this notion of being able to extend your centered intention out into the field – it's a really powerful idea for those of you who are teachers, coaches, or leaders in some other way. Not just for a hero's journey, but for any kind of communication capability. This is what might be called "giving power to the world." We all know how when some people talk, you just hear "blah blah blah blah". . . and you just get bored. But when others might say the same words, it grabs your heart, it wakes you up, it lifts your level of consciousness. What's that difference that makes the difference? That's what this exercise is about – bringing your words and your calling alive by speaking your intention in a centered and extended way.

SG: Take some time and find a few people to practice this with now.

The Challenge of Sustaining Your Connection to Your Center

SG: We want to make a simple point about this last exercise that will lead us into the next one. When you're coaching people, you're paying special attention to getting them connected to their centers, and then sustaining that connection. So you need to be able to observe your partner's non-verbal state, to see where tension is held. So if I'm the client and Robert is my coach, he's noticing my non-verbal state as he asks me to step into a generative state. If, as he does that, he sees me develop tension, he can immediately just coach me into a more relaxed state. *(Steve playfully becomes very tense, and Robert steps in to make gentle adjustments, non-verbally guiding Steve back to a relaxed, aligned posture.)*

RD: Yes, that's it . . . that's good. *(More laughter as Steve looks almost drunk with relaxation.)*

SG: Good. That feels great. So I have hired him as my coach. He's really expensive so I'm only hiring him for five minutes. *(Laughter.)* But seriously, it's like we're imagining if you took a pebble and dropped it through a body *(makes gesture of letting a pebble drop from the crown of the head into the body)*, would it be able to flow through – because that means the mind–body connection is open and generative – or would it get stopped and blocked at some point *(makes clenching sound)* – because that's where the generative life force becomes blocked and non-generative.

RD: That's where the channel isn't completely open. This is an exercise to learn how to more fully "open your channel."

SG: So the first challenge as a coach is to see if the client can really somatically connect to his or her center. The second challenge is to make sure the client doesn't lose his or her connection to center when directing attention into the outside world. For many of us, we can find our center if we withdraw from the performance world, but we lose it as soon as we have to engage with another human being. In coaching people with the exercise, we see a lot of this . . . *(Demonstrates extending into world and losing balance.)*

RD: If you do this, you're losing your vertical axis; the heaven–earth connection that grounds you and opens you to a higher level while you engage in the world.

SG: The type of posture you want to take is like the "warrior" pose in yoga, or literally like holding a bow and arrow. There's a relaxed tension that grounds you and keeps your center even as you release toward the target. So your attention is grounding down into the earth.

RD: Really feel your feet.

SG: Because there's going to be a lot of storms in the field. If you're going to live your hero's journey, there are a lot of nasty people that don't want you to succeed. If your first attention gets lost in that negative field, you're dead meat.

RD: But notice, for example, if Stephen is the negative storm coming at me *(Steve approaches Robert with menace)*, and rather than give my first attention him, I keep it in my center *(Robert becomes aligned and centered as Stephen pushes him, staying relaxed and open, looking beyond Stephen)*, then it's OK. I am not losing my way. By keeping my center and my vertical alignment, I don't give myself away to the problem.

SG: What was interesting in that brief encounter we just had was what I felt when "attacking" Robert. I felt this centered field open all around him, sort of like a force field. Something in me said, "Don't even think about attacking this guy." Not because he was vicious – that's another part of Robert that we'll find out about later *(laughter)* – but because I felt his energy field extending in a vibrant and supple way. As we say in aikido, he gave me no opening.

Exercise: Active Centering

RD: So we want to do another exercise around this skill of keeping your center, and that we call "active centering." On the hero's journey, your call is often met with strong resistance, both from within yourself and from others around you. So the great challenge is to find a way to make and maintain the commitment to your calling, even when the storms of negativity are pummeling you. This is a powerful characteristic of both the hero and the leader: when the going gets tough, you need to stay centered. So this exercise is about getting that calling even more deeply in the muscle and grounding in it.

People who practice martial arts (aikido, karate, judo, kung fu, etc.), for instance, often talk about the importance of being centered and calm, even when they are in the middle of intense competition. In fact, as Stephen alluded to earlier, "if you give away your center to your opponent, you have already lost the competition." When you lose your center and get upset, you begin to lose other resources and often start working against yourself.

There are two ways to stay centered: grounding and flowing. When grounding, we root our center to one spot, making ourselves solid and able to "stand our ground" despite any force acting against us. When flowing, we meet and move with whatever force comes our way. Staying centered, we step out of the line of the force and move in a circle around it so that we end up slightly behind and beside it. Both of these can be appropriate and useful strategies depending upon the situation we are in.

The following is an overview of the exercise.

1. Using memory or imagination, relive a situation in which it is difficult for you to stay centered and resourceful.

2. Step out of the experience and enter an inner state in which you feel aligned, relaxed, and centered.

3. When you are ready, ask your partner to gently begin to physically push and pull you in different directions, from different angles (from the shoulders, waist, front, back, side to side, etc.), while you practice staying centered, rooted, balanced, and aligned, both physically and mentally. Do this by meeting and energetically mirroring the pressure coming from your partner and directing it down through your center, through your feet, and into the ground. Remain relaxed with your knees flexible and breathe in the belly. As you become more comfortable and confident with your ability to remain in the state, you can make it more challenging by asking your partner to push or pull a little harder. When practicing flowing, have your partner pull and push you so you are no longer standing in the same place but moving through space. Turn in a circle around your partner so that you end up slightly behind and beside your partner. Remain rooted by staying grounded and connected to your center as you move.

4. When you feel ready, hold the centered state, step back into the challenging situation and notice how your experience is different. You should feel much more able to deal with the situation in a resourceful manner.

RD: So what we've been doing so far is having you connect with your calling, then connect with your center to live your calling into the world. We want to deepen this exploration by having you work with situations where it's not so easy for you to stay connected with your calling or your center. Let's just assume that there will be energies coming from the outside world that are going to disturb you, like Stephen was saying, these intense storms of negativity. When you start to bring your spirit into the world, you can easily become a target.

SG: This is, of course, a major reason why people don't live their hero's journey. Surely most people would agree with the statement, "I really want to be able to live fully in the world." The problem is there's a big "but" that creates a fear and holding back: "*But* I'd probably get hurt . . . *But* people wouldn't like me . . . *But* it would be too hard."

RD: These resistances and disturbances are frequently the result of programming that starts at a very young age. You express your life energy, and someone says: "Shh!! Shh!! Shh!! Children should be seen and not heard." So we get these messages from the very beginning: "Don't show your unique vitality." The question is, how can we hold that centered sense of our calling even in such turbulence? This turbulence could come from your family, your colleagues at work, your boss, your doctors . . .

SG: . . . or your own mind. You start thinking "Oh, my God! What if . . . ? What if . . . ? What if . . . ?" So, when people first start exploring centering, we hear excited comments like: "This is great! I'm going to stay centered for the rest of my life! – I'm never going to ever, ever, *ever* lose my center again!" And we're saying: "You're going to lose it a hundred times each day at least." But we're trying to explore how to keep getting it back. Let it go, bring it back. Let it go, reconnect with it.

RD: Now let's say I want to hold my center and Steve comes along aggressively (*Steve puts his hand on Robert's shoulder, begins to push him*). If I become rigid (*Robert stiffens up and almost falls over*) I am actually giving my center away. *You cannot be rigid or tense and centered at the same time!* It is not a strength based on muscular might, but rather on the aligned and centered life force that is within all living things.

So the goal is to be supple yet grounded, like a tree. And that's what this exercise is about. Also, centering is not something you do with your cognitive mind. If when centering I go up into my head, I've left my body and I have no rootedness or grounding. This could become a panic attack. If you've ever observed the physiology of a panic attack, the body gets locked and rigid, and the mental attention becomes lost in the tight box of the head. Centering is an antidote to such negative states. Again, the principle here is: Drop (your attention) down. Relax. Drop down.

Demonstration with Carmen

RD: So we'd like to demonstrate this and have you practice it. I'm curious if there's anybody here who is struggling with this challenge of staying connected with your calling, and is interested in getting some coaching with it? *(Robert selects Carmen from the audience to come on stage for the exercise.)*

OK, let's start this way. Please tell me a little bit about where you are getting pulled away from your calling. Where does that happen? What exactly does happen, both in the inner and outer worlds?

Carmen: There are places in my life that when I'm trying to do something, some negative thoughts just come along and then I feel these sensations or feelings of just being frozen.

RD: In which situations in your life do these things most emerge for you?

Carmen: In my company.

RD: In your company. Are there moments in your company where that seems to be more of a struggle, like during a meeting, or a presentation, or where?

Carmen: In specific meetings.

RD: So there are certain meetings. Are there certain people, or types of people?

(Carmen nods.)

(To audience) So to start the exercise, identify some concrete situations where a person loses their center and gets caught up in negative fields. I was coaching somebody the other day who, every time he would go in to make a presentation to the board of directors of his company, he said that the feeling in the room felt so thick and heavy with tension that he got smaller and smaller. So that was a particular situation where he lost that connection to his calling and to his center.

(To Carmen.) So I understand, Carmen, that for you, in your world, there are moments in your company, in certain meetings, with certain people, where it's a challenge. *(Carmen nods.)*

OK, so let's explore how you might shift that state. In the first step, I'm going to ask you to very briefly dip into that challenging situation. We call this "tasting the poison." So when you're ready, take a step forward and step into that situation, letting yourself experientially sense what it's like. *(Carmen steps forward.)*

And just let yourself see what you see, hear what you hear, and feel what you feel in that state . . . and when you're ready, let me know what you become aware of.

Carmen: *(Tenses up.)* . . . I'm back in a situation at work.

RD: Yes. And as you're back in that situation, do you feel tension in your body?

Carmen: Yes, very much.

RD: This is like what Stephen was talking about. As the coach, you're dropping an imaginary pebble through the mind–body of the client, sensing where the energy blocks are in the client. Where are the places that the channel is closed down? And then you can check with the client . . . *Carmen, where do you feel this constriction or contraction?*

(Carmen points to chest and shoulders.)

Thanks. And if you were to put words to this disruption . . . where you feel this turbulence . . . what would be the negative message that it carries?

Carmen: They don't listen.

RD: And why don't they listen? What are they saying about you? What is their message to you?

Carmen: I want to bring innovation and change.

65

RD: You want to bring innovation and change. That is your calling. And what is their response. Is it like, "We don't like that here" or "You're not good enough"?

Carmen: "We don't understand."

RD: Yes. They say," We don't understand. You don't make sense." And as you hear that, is there a feeling that goes with that?

Carmen: *(Carmen tenses up more, looking very uncomfortable and nods her head.)* Yes.

RD: *(To audience)* So you can see pretty clearly, as Carmen steps into her work situation, she loses her center. It's like her channel gets smaller and smaller. Her spirit is no longer opening into the field, it is contracted. The challenge is how to shift this.

(To Carmen) So Carmen, I'd like you now to take a step back, and step out of that situation. *(Carmen steps back, takes a breath.)* Good. And now let's attune to your calling. Remember the previous exercise where you were centering and then speaking your calling. Take a few moments to sense that, then go ahead and speak your calling aloud.

Carmen: *My calling is to walk the path of communication.*

RD: OK, good. And notice if you feel centered when you say that, especially when I gently push you. *(Robert very gently pushes Carmen's shoulder.)*

Carmen: No.

RD: It didn't look or feel like it from here, either.

SG: And that's the norm, by the way. When a person touches their problem state, the center is lost. *This is what makes a challenging situation into an impossible problem.*

RD: OK, Carmen, so let's take a little time to make sure you can find your center. You remember we said centering is about dropping down, lowering your center of gravity, bringing it closer to the ground. And one way to do that is that instead of locking your knees, let your knees bend. That's good, just bend your knees, breathe, and let yourself drop down into your center.

Good. Is that better? *(Carmen nods.)* Good, what I'd like to do next is ask you to explore a little bit about how to meet and interact with energies that are coming from outside of you. I'm going to do this by gently pushing you from different directions, and ask you to see how you can absorb the push into your center, stay centered, even while staying flexible.

The first thing I'd like to explore is how you meet my energy when I push you a little. *(Robert begins to gently push, sensing how Carmen responds.)* Mmmm, when I do this *(pushing gently)*, I don't feel much connection. It feels like you just surrender your center to me. I don't feel your presence – it's like you kind of go away. *(Carmen nods.)* That's the one way to respond to pressures from the outside – just give up and let them take you over.

The other option is muscular resistance. When I push, you can brace yourself, maybe push back. Let's try that. *(Robert pushes, Carmen stiffens. Robert then releases the pressure quickly and Carmen stumbles off balance.)* And you can see there, too, that when you resist, you also give your center to me. *(Carmen laughs and nods.)*

You can lose your center to an outside force either through passive submission or stubborn resistance. But as traditions like aikido teach us, there is a third "middle way" where you can use a supple center to give and receive energy and stay connected to both yourself and beyond you. I'm going to ask you to explore that by energetically mirroring me. So, for example, when I touch your shoulder *(Robert touches shoulder)*, receive it, then extend it back to me, like a wave. Stay relaxed, draw it into your center, extend it back, like a dance of giving and receiving.

In NLP we talk about mirroring, but we usually don't talk about energetic mirroring. It is a relational process that goes both ways. You can see that Carmen is not pushing against me, she's meeting me so I can feel her, and she can feel me.

(To Carmen) Now the next thing that I'd like to have you do is meet my energy and take it down through your feet. And what you're going to find is instead of my energy pushing you away or you

losing energy because you're resisting it, my energy will actually add to yours and make you stronger. *Use the energy coming from the push to feed your center and make yourself more grounded.*

Good, and actually bend your knees and let the energy move down through your legs into the ground. Meet, receive, and channel the energy down through your center . . . *There you go . . . that's good . . . (Robert and Carmen smile as their movements and energies blend into a type of stationary dance.)* And does it feel like you are using much effort here?

Carmen: No.

RD: So there's strength without effort, a power without muscular force. *That's what centering gives you! (Robert and Carmen continue the exercise until at one moment Carmen appears to lose her balance slightly.)* OK, right there, did you feel that? *(Carmen nods.)* You started to go up from your center into your head. *(Carmen smiles and nods.)* This is why we need somatic coaching – we've got to get this skill into our somatic patterning. It's not just an intellectual idea, it's a somatic skill. So, let's try again *(Robert pushes)* . . . that's it . . . that's it.

SG: *Relax through your eyes, Carmen . . . Relax through your eyes . . . That's good.*

RD: *(Carmen appears to lose her balance slightly.)* Right there, you lost your center again, could you feel that? *(Carmen nods.)* OK, so let's go more slowly now so you can really feel your center and the energy relating from it *(keeps pushing)*. That's good! . . . Can you feel how you're beginning to move around your center?

Carmen: *(Smiles.)* Yes!

RD: OK, let's pause for a moment . . . You can begin to sense that within you there is a center that is constant. From that center you can feel both great strength and amazing flexibility. You can sit down into it. We sometimes call that "the kangaroo tail" or the "dinosaur tail." It's an energetic tail you feel behind you, and you sit on it. *(Demonstrates.)*

SG: Let's hear from Carmen in terms of what that was like for you?

Carmen: When I let myself respond from my center as I was being pushed, it felt like my body was handling itself, it had its own natural way. I wasn't having to do it. It felt like a dance.

SG: That's what we call the "generative somatic mind" beginning to open up. And you may have noticed that her eyes started behaving in a very different way. They were soft focus, and wide open, looking beyond Robert to some open field. *(Carmen nods.)* To do centering, you move from focal vision to attuning to a peripheral field, opening a big space so that energy can just enter and move through and then beyond your body.

RD: Now that we've got the first part of the somatic entering in place, I want to add one more piece, which has to do with the "negative hypnosis" words that are part of that problem state. And so as we begin the dance again . . . *(Robert and Carmen move through the active centering process of Robert gently trying to move Carmen "off center" with his words and hands, while Carmen explores how she can keep her center during unsettling experiences)* . . . just notice how you can stay centered as I add the words: *You don't make sense . . . I don't understand you . . . You don't make any sense . . . I don't understand you. What are you talking about? . . . I don't understand . . . I can't listen to you. (Carmen is moving gracefully, like bamboo in the wind, appearing centered and relaxed.)*

Good, Carmen . . . that's great. (Robert and Carmen smile.)

(To audience) So you get the idea: I'm now adding the energy of the words – because that energy can throw you off, too.

OK, now the final part. Sometimes what you want to do is just move out of the way of the energy.

In this first strategy, you meet the energy, you absorb it, and take it down through your legs into the ground, to make you more rooted and stronger. You learn how other people's energy, whether positive or negative, can be received in a way that makes you stronger. I mirror it, feel the strength of it – as Campbell says, ultimately it's not good or bad energy, it's just energy. And I can use it to help ground me.

The second thing I can do is I can stay centered and move out of the way by turning to the side of the energy coming toward me.

SG: This is a classic aikido movement called *tenkan*. You're not running away from it, but you're also not blocking or getting crushed by it either. You're meeting it, blending with it by turning, then joining with it.

RD: The usual responses to perceived threat or aggression are the survival strategies: fight, flight, freeze. What we're doing here is learning a fourth strategy, called *flow*. As I turn to the side of it, I begin to turn a circle around it, so I'm close behind it, while walking with it in a safe and curious way. *(Robert demonstrates a few times.)*

(To Carmen) OK, I'll push you again, and you receive me, but as you do, let me go by, like a bullfighter does with a bull, by turning to the side, moving from your center. *(Robert moves toward Carmen, hands extended out. Carmen actually turns her back to Robert, thereby having Robert collide with her. Both Robert and Carmen laugh at the entanglement.)* That's a good learning! *(Both Robert and Carmen laugh.)* That's why we do somatic coaching. You've got to get this in the muscle as an automatic response, so that you don't have to think about it. Let's try again, this time move to the side of me, not in front of me. *(As they do it, Carmen turns in front of Robert again leading to another collision. Both laugh.)*

SG: Remember, Carmen, think like a bullfighter. Let the bull go by while you step to the side. Let me guide you. *(Steve steps behind Carmen.)*

RD: OK, I'm the bull. *(Laughter.)*

(As Robert slowly moves toward Carmen, Steve moves her to the side, showing the correct movement. Carmen smiles as Robert goes by.)

That's it! That's it. *(Applause.)*

OK, now we'll do it again, and this time I'll add the words. Are you ready? Get yourself centered, ready like a bullfighter to draw the energy toward you, then step out of the way as it goes by you. Let me know when you're ready. *(Carmen nods, Robert moves toward her.)* *I don't understand you. You don't make sense. I don't understand you.*

(Carmen elegantly sweeps to the side, letting Robert go right by. Robert looks surprised, Carmen is delighted. Audience laughs and claps with appreciation for Carmen. Robert smiles and congratulates Carmen.)

Interesting, yes? *(Carmen nods.)* Great, let's try it again. I'll approach you from different angles and directions. Just feel the dance of turning to the side, enjoying the flourish like a bullfighter. Step off the line, be in a place of safety and curiosity, sense how you can positively respond.

(Robert approaches from different directions. Each time, Carmen steps out of the way, turning so that she ends up slightly behind him and accompanying him as Robert continues in his direction. She is now guiding him with a feeling of confidence.)

See. Receiving "attacks" by stepping off the line can make you free and curious about how to join with it safely.

(Carmen is beaming, and looks very happy.)

Now, I'm going to ask you to put yourself back into that difficult situation in your company. Take a breath, close your eyes, keep connected to your center while you sense that old situation . . . from this new place of centering. *(Carmen looks very centered and relaxed.)* And notice, you don't have to think about anything or try anything. Just let your awareness sense how you can be in that situation in new ways.

(To audience) You probably can notice a big difference in her somatic state as she does this. *(To Carmen)* And, Carmen, what do you notice when you're here now?

Carmen: It is completely different. I have the feeling that I have something worthwhile to say, and people want to listen to me.

RD: *(In gentle voice) Yes, you have something worthwhile to say, and people want to listen to you . . . (To audience)* You can see this reprogramming happening in a very deep way right now. It's quite powerful to see that reorganizing . . . *(To Carmen)* Isn't it wonderful to know that you have another mind to take with you into that situation? And I'm just curious, Carmen, how would you express your calling, as you sense yourself now?

Carmen: *(In a strong, clear, congruent voice) My calling is to walk the path of communication.*

SG: Bravo. *(Loud applause. Carmen bows and leaves the stage.)*

RD: OK. Let's review the steps of the exercise. First, identify the challenging situation. Where is it difficult for you to extend your calling? Maybe the situation feels heavy, maybe turbulent. Share the details of the situation with your coach, then put yourself into it and relive it. We say in NLP, associate into the present state.

Then step out of it, and begin to do the active centering process. Remember to let your knees be supple. As soon as you lock your knees, you give your center away. As the coach moves toward you while you're centering, meet it, absorb it, reflect it back as you stay supple . . . receive, absorb, reflect back.

SG: Remember, receive it in a relaxed but centered state. If you meet it with aggression or agitation, you will increase the attacker's aggression. When you meet it with centered relaxation, it dissipates the aggression of the attack. This is a basic insight of aikido.

And by the way, when Robert says "meet it," we mean that you are extending your energy, radiating it out. You're not blocking it or clashing with it, nor are you passively collapsing . . . you're extending your energy beyond it, receiving it, reflecting it back like a dance. *(Demonstrates an aikido movement.)* If you see, my hands are open, I sense energy streaming through my fingers. My eyes are wide, I feel energy extending through them. My center is attuned and open. So I'm not in a "fight or flight" contraction; on the contrary, everything is in a "flow" state so that whatever comes in can be blended with and positively utilized. This gives me confidence and freedom and the capacity to translate negative energy into positive energy. We see this as one of the great skills and contributions of the hero on his journey.

RD: You don't need to run from the energy or fight it. Connect with it. Absorb it and take it down into the earth. Sit on your kangaroo tail. Keep the channel open. Remember: *Nothing into the body except relaxation. Nothing to cling to in the mind.*

We invite you now to explore the somatic skill of active centering as you explore the challenging situation. We're sure you'll discover some very interesting learnings. There will be some parts of the body that you will need to patiently coach to become more fluid; others will need to become more present. The process is unique for each person.

I was recently doing this process with a woman who was a vice-president of a bank. Whenever I touched the lower part of her back during the active centering, she would become very locked; she was holding this pattern of reactive vulnerability in her back. As she discovered how to allow it to stay relaxed and remain connected with her center, it really shifted how she interacted with others in her work environment. Interestingly, she was always worried about people at work doing things "behind her back" or people "stabbing her in the back." As she shifted to staying centered, these ways of relating changed in positive ways. So everybody will find different learnings and different improvements from exploring active centering.

When as the coach you feel that the client is able to stay centered when you are physically moving with them, then add the "negative hypnosis" words that go with the challenging situation. Have the client explore how to absorb and release the energy from these words in a positive way. Then shift from absorbing it into the ground while you stay rooted, to stepping out of the way. Move in circles, think like a bullfighter, enjoy the dance.

Then have the explorer close his or her eyes, breathe, center, and return to the original situation and notice what shifts in his or her experience of it. Invariably there will be significant positive transformations, as Carmen shared. The interesting thing is that the problem transforms without you consciously trying to think about changing it. *The problem transforms by your shifting the state in which you engage with it.* Then, finally, move to the very important final step of expressing "the call" as you stand in that situation with the new presence.

This coaching exercise typically only takes about ten minutes.

The Generative Somatic State

SG: Our focus in this section is how to develop a generative somatic state in yourself and others, so that your hero's journey may be realized. We're saying that whenever you need to create something new or transform or heal something, you need to be in a generative state. This generative state needs to show up in the three minds: somatic, cognitive, and field. To develop a generative somatic mind, we use the general principle of "aligning and centering." This allows a somatic consciousness that has equal parts relaxation, concentration, flexibility, openness, and sensual intelligence.

Another way of talking about centering is "mind–body unity"; that is, the cognitive thinking is united within the somatic base. To do this, you need to be able to think without locking your muscles. As soon as you lock your muscles, then you dissociate from your somatic base and deteriorate into a disembodied intellect. This capacity to think without muscular tension is an essential characteristic of generative consciousness; it is a basic element of practices such as meditation and generative trance, and high performance challenges such as sports, art (like music or writing), intimacy, or business. Any of these practices might be major parts of your hero's journey; all of them involve mastery of the challenge to "think outside the box," or create something beyond what's already been tried. So what we're looking at is how you can organize and train your consciousness to be in a place where you can do that.

If you're not in a generative somatic state, you'll be doomed to reacting with "fight, flight, or freeze." You'll be in a conservative state that can only produce more of the same. So when the challenge to create something new arises, as it inevitably will, you'll be consigned to "rearranging the deckchairs on the Titanic."

RD: Which is not going to be the way to stop the ship from hitting an iceberg.

SG: *(With twinkle in his eye)* Science has shown that the muscular patterns of the disembodied conscious mind are exactly identical to that medical condition known as constipation. *(Laughter.)* So you see people doing this *(Steve locks into a constipated-like posture)*, saying, "Can't you see I'm trying to think?" And all you can say is, "It sure looks like something else to me!" *(Laughter.)* Now from this tense, shut-down position, what do you think my chances are for transformation?

RD: Or creativity?

SG: Not very good. So we're saying that to operate at a generative level, you need access to subtle levels of consciousness. But when you do this *(moves back into "constipation" position)*, it's shutting down your access to the creative unconscious. It's sending a message to the nervous system: "Freeze that state! Shut down the flow! Don't allow anything new in!"

RD: We call it *neuromuscular lock*, which is a contraction of the channel.

SG: The body–mind loses its wholeness and loses its center, so you don't have access to an inner intelligence. The field contracts, so you don't feel connected to a space beyond the narrow confines of your ego-intellect. You lose access to an intelligence greater than your conscious mind, which you need to do anything interesting and generative.

How many of you have a voice inside that says: "You're not enough"? *(After a few moments, hands begin to lift.)* You can see that struggle going on – one mind saying, "Yes, that's right" and the other saying "Shut up, don't admit anything!" *(Steve demonstrates by lifting up one arm, then having the other quickly push it back down.)* *(Laughter.)* We are encouraging you to agree with that voice that tells you that you're not enough. Your conscious mind isn't enough – it needs to connect with the mother ship of deeper consciousness. *This is what generative consciousness allows you to do.*

Every time you do this *(Steve contracts his body)*, you're withdrawing from the larger consciousness, which is where all the good stuff happens. So mind–body centering is a way to train your base to stay connected with the deeper field of consciousness, by "yoking" your little mind with the big mind. When you can do this, good things happen; when you don't, bad things can happen easily.

Perhaps we can turn for a moment, in this context, to the great historical theme of "sin." We don't need to wait until Sunday to tell you that you're all sinners. *(Laughter.)* We're suggesting that, without negative connotation, what is called "sin" or in a different context, "neurosis" or "symptom," is a basic human state of consciousness that is trying to create something. What makes it a negative state is the negative human relationship with it; sin or symptom is a core human state without mind–body centering or other generative relational connections.

For example, let's consider the seven deadly sins – those old family favorites. Who can name any of the sins for us today? For instance, what did you do at lunch time?

Audience member: Gluttony. *(Laughter.)*

RD. That's good. Gluttony is one. What's another one? What's that "state of sin" that many of you are in at this late hour of the day?

Audience member: Laziness! *(Laughter.)*

SG: Great. You're enjoying the sinful state of sloth. What other sins have you experienced today. How about lust? *(Laughter.)* Greed? . . . Envy? . . . Pride? . . . Anger? *(Different hands lift, smiles and laughter are sprinkled through the audience.)*

You see, they are quite common experiences; so common that we suggest that they are the basic experiential states of human consciousness. But they are only half-human! They are the "deep structures" that the unconscious gives us to become human. To make them fully human, to make them generative and positive, *we* need to "humanize" them, to have creative and positive relationships with them. By bringing full human consciousness to them, they transform from their half-human states, where they have no generative human value, to their fully human states, where they have significant positive value.

Somebody asked me earlier, "Well, how do you use this generative somatic work with addictions?" Addictions, like other symptoms and "sins," are deep somatic experiences without a human center. If you center, the problem will come to be a solution.

RD: So to be clear – a symptom or problem is a deep somatic state without a center. When I work with people who have addictions – it can be a food addiction or a smoking addiction, whatever – very often the feeling is: "There is a black hole in me, and nothing will fill it." This a way of talking about not sensing one's center.

SG: So we're suggesting a formula:

Sin plus centering equals grace.

Or from a slightly different tradition:

Symptom plus centering equals resource / solution.

This is one of the major values of developing a generative somatic state – it allows you to transform negative experiences into positive ones. As a simple example, put yourself for a moment into a state of sloth. Let yourself arrange yourself into a state of deep laziness . . . *(Some shifting goes on in audience.)* It looks like many of you don't have to change anything! *(Laughter.)*

RD: But seriously, let yourself sink into that state. Let go of judgment, let go of trying to change it, just observe it with curiosity.

SG: And once you get a sense of that state, we'd like you to very slowly, from the inside out, let yourself find a state of centeredness. Just become curious about the subtle shifts in posture, in breathing, in orientation that allow you to begin to bring centering into the heart of that experience of sloth. Let go of the names, let go of judgment, just upgrade the state by adding the generative somatic experience of centering.

RD: And as you do, notice any shifts that begin to occur. The way you sense yourself . . . The way you feel things . . . The quality of your inner experience.

SG: And notice as you do that, what is the name for this state now? What is the best name for this state? Is it still "sloth," or has the name changed? Anybody like to call out what name you have for this state now?

Audience members: Meditation ... Attunement ... Deep awareness.

SG: Really amazing, huh? So just notice that, then let yourself come back out into the room ... Welcome back! We hope you can sense, even in that very brief experiment, what happens when you can bring somatic centering into a negative state. Its very nature begins to change! As we'll be exploring more of next, you can apply this with many different types of problems. Say a person wants to stop smoking. She says: "I don't want to smoke anymore, but something in me feels a need to have a cigarette."

RD: It's an urge in the body.

SG: So, as we'll be seeing in the next part of this program, you can approach that problem with curiosity. How do we find and support the positive intention in that symptom? We operate from the presupposition that *every symptom represents an attempt at healing or transformation, and that by bringing it into a generative state, it can be held and guided into its positive form.* So when you're slipping into a state of anxiety, or addiction, or anger, something in your consciousness is trying to heal or transform. *To realize its human "gift and goodness," you have to absorb it into a generative human consciousness.*

Centering is a vital component of that generative state. So when you work with a negative problem in yourself or another person, you don't need to try to get rid of it or treat it harshly. We're recommending instead that you develop a generate state, then engage the challenge.

For example, with smokers you might help them to get centered and develop a state of witnessing and curiosity. You then ask them to let their body express the basic somatic pattern of the problem over and over. For example, the smoker would, with eyes closed, be slowly repeating the behavioral pattern of lifting the cigarette up and taking a puff. As they do that repeatedly, you ask them to slow it down, to develop centering, to allow a graceful movement to begin to develop. To perform a problem with grace is a real transformational shift! As they repeat the problematic pattern as a centered, graceful dance, you ask them to hold a question like, "My unconscious is trying to bring something to me. What is it?"

By holding this question in a centered, rhythmic state, all sorts of helpful awarenesses can arise.

RD: Ironically, there are many people I've worked with who smoke where the positive intention of the behavior is to remind them to breathe.

SG: For others it's to have time for themselves.

RD: When I helped my father quit smoking, he discovered that smoking was the only thing in his whole life that he did just for himself. Not for his family, not for his job, it was the only thing just for him. And that's sad, if that's the only thing you do, just for you. But that was the realization he had.

SG: So if that's what comes up, you happily appreciate the positive intention and need: *It's really, really important for you to do something that's just for you!*

RD: Isn't that wonderful to know?

SG: And if you can appreciate that the pattern of smoking is trying to help you achieve something very positive, like taking time for yourself, you can use further centering to become curious about all the other ways that you can honor that need, without the behavior of smoking. Once you have the positive intention, you can generate many new ways to satisfy that important need.

RD: So you're connecting, centering, and then opening beyond the fixed forms of the problem.

SG: If you didn't have centering, you probably wouldn't be able to get a meaningful answer to the question of positive intention. What is my deeper consciousness trying to heal or create? And how can I create in other ways beyond the negative forms?

RD: I see many people trained in NLP looking for positive intention before they have developed a generative state for effective inquiry. They say something like (*Robert speeds up into an anxious state*), "What's the positive intention of smoking? What is it? I don't know what this intention is." (*Robert calms back down.*) We're saying that unless you have first developed a generative state, including centering, you won't be able to answer that question in a helpful way.

Once you've developed centering, you can invite the symptom into that generative space, holding the question of positive intention. In that way, the positive intention and the different other ways it might be expressed will come to you. You're holding the question in a centered state, rather than chasing the answer in an uncentered state.

Learning to Be with What is Moving through You

SG: So the road to your hero's journey goes directly through your body. That's the first mind you need to connect with in order to bring transformation into your life. We should probably emphasize that while centering is a simple process, it's often not an easy one. You might say: "Well, if centering is so great, why do so few people do it?" Partly it's a matter of ignorance: in a culture dominated by consumerism and fundamentalisms, finding your own center is forbidden. I mean, how many more televisions are you going to want to buy if you're deeply connected to your center? *(Laughter.)*

But another reason is that the road back to your deepest self is typically booby-trapped. That is, you will come across a lot of different experiences that are trapped in your center. In the hero's journey, Campbell talks about this in terms of crossing thresholds and battling with demons. But not to worry, because as we will see coming up, there are skillful ways that you can work with such obstacles. For now, we might just note that when we talk about centering, we're always talking about two different levels. The first level is a content-free, open space through which life flows. In Buddhist terms, it is empty and spacious; in neuropsychological terms, it is a transducer that brings information/energy patterns from one domain into another.

RD: Think of it as the open channel that we were talking about earlier. The center is the open channel that allows you to live in a free and creative way.

SG: The second level, though, is the content that is passing through the channel at any point in time. So we have this open channel – that's your center – and the stuff that is moving through it – that's your cognitive consciousness. One of the main tasks of generative consciousness is to differentiate these two levels. If you do meditation or centering you're practicing how to be present in a non-reactive way, just witnessing what is happening in each passing moment, as the river of life flows through you. You are learning how to "be with" something or someone without becoming them. You are then free to act in a creative, loving, positive way.

RD: The Buddhists talk about the relationship between the clouds and the sky. If I identify with the clouds, I can get lost in the confusing and stormy contents of my experience. But if I center myself and open to the field of the sky beyond the cloud formations, I can let the clouds or contents of my thoughts pass through my awareness without becoming disturbed by them. The sky is not trying to say: "I have to get rid of the clouds and have sunny days forever!" I can be aware of the all the clouds and let them pass through.

SG: So when we think about the center, we're thinking about this embodied and attuned core of awareness than can open to whatever is there, breathing it in, breathing it out.

RD: And if you don't have that, what happens is that you get caught up in whatever is happening. You start reacting to life, getting lost in "fight, flight, or freeze." So when negative energies come up – anger, fear, despair – you lose yourself in them.

SG: In an uncentered state, the problem absorbs the self. You lose yourself to it. When you center, the self can positively absorb the problem. You can invite it to tea, connect with it in a positive and intelligent way, then happily send it on its way, with all parties being helped by the connection. So with centering, we're developing a higher state of consciousness, a context or a sort of nest into which you can invite experiences that need transformation . . . and in doing so, transform your own consciousness in the process.

This important distinction between the context and content levels of the center is illustrated really well in one of the simple techniques used by one of our main mentors, Virginia Satir. When she worked with families, she would often ask two consecutive questions to family members if they started to struggle or shut down. She would first ask, "How do you feel about that?" She would then ask, "How do you feel about feeling that way?" The first question is the content question. To a coach or therapist, it really doesn't matter – it could be anger, or happiness, or fear, or whatever. It's the answer to the second question that really matters: What is your relationship to what you are experiencing? Are you OK with it? Or do you feel a need to treat it harshly and violently? It's that second level that determines everything that follows. *It's not the content that matters, it's the human relationship to the content that matters.*

RD: The second feeling determines your relationship with the first feeling. If I feel angry and I am afraid of the anger, or angry about the anger, or ashamed that the anger is there, then the anger becomes a problem.

SG: We can say this about anything really. No experience in and of itself is a problem; it's your relationship with it that makes it a problem or a resource. So if you have an intense fantasy of wanting to murder somebody, it's not a problem. *(Laughter.)* I'm serious . . . such feelings come and go in the river of life. But if you muscularly lock into that experience, or try to run from it, then it becomes a problem. But if you can be with it in a centered way, it becomes helpful information. So it's all in how you hold something.

I had a client who grew up in a family where the rule was: "Always be positive and cheerful." So this person would walk around like this *(smiling unnaturally and speaking in a loud voice)* "Hi, how are you?" *(Laughter.)*

RD: *(Smiling incongruently and shaking his head "no")* I'm just great, Steve.

SG: *(Loudly and inauthentically)* I couldn't be happier myself!

RD: *(Sarcastically)* Life is wonderful, isn't it? *(Laughter.)*

SG: And this family was the most miserable bunch of people I've ever met. *(Laughter.)* So we worked with her connecting to her center, the place "beneath and before" all of the ego masks of the conscious mind. And after a couple of sessions, she came in, and I said: "How are you?"

And she said: "I had the strangest week." If you do trance work, this is a very good sign. It means that the creative unconscious is bringing some new experiences into a person's awareness that are "strange" or "different" from the "ordinary box" of ego identity. Anyway, she further reported, "All week I felt so melancholy . . . and I don't *ever* feel melancholy . . . But the even stranger thing was, it felt so good to feel so sad." *(Laughter.)* She asked, "That doesn't make sense, does it?"

I said: "Of course it does. My ancestors are from Ireland, and it's the only feeling that the Irish trust. Because they know that no matter how good it gets, the English are always five minutes away . . . and they are coming to take everything!" *(Laughter.)*

But you can hear in that example that this woman was sensing the two levels of the center. In the content level, she felt sadness; but in the context level, she felt happy that she could finally allow those forbidden feelings to be there. This second mind is the basis for the generative cognitive mind. This is what we'll be exploring next.

RD: The organizing principle of this second mind is *sponsorship*, which is the term that Stephen used to describe this generative capacity to receive whatever is there, to create a holding environment that allows things to be, and then to connect with them in a creative and respectful way that allows them to integrate, transform, and creatively unfold their deepest positive potentials.

SG: What we've been exploring so far is how to create your somatic base, your first generative mind, so that you can be an attuned, centered human being, creatively engaging with each moment in a positive and intentional way. And we've been pointing out that if you lose this base, you start to reactively operate with fear or anger, blocking the life flow. This shutting down of the channel will move you away from the path of your deepest calling, getting you lost in the insignificant soap operas of the day, rather than unfolding on the great journeys of your life.

RD: So the hero knows that life can be difficult, but it's not a problem. *(Laughter.)* Isn't that nice to know?

SG: What we will do next is to build on this base of how to get a somatic wholeness, which, among other things, creates a nest inside of you, so that whatever comes in, you can use your mind not to control it, but to be able to open the positive intention and the goodness, the gifts that are inside of that experience.

Conclusion: Keeping Your Channel Open

RD: For the moment, however, we'd like to end this part of the program the way we began, with a little meditation. So get settled into a comfortable position. And notice how much you had to change your position to get into a comfortable position! *(Laughter.)* Scary, isn't it? That's good that you have moved from your uncomfortable positions into comfortable ones. We should have suggested this a long time ago! *(Laughter.)*

SG: *So let's take a few moments to settle in and settle down . . .*

RD: *And remember that ancient wisdom . . . namely . . . Relax . . . Find the inner space, the space inside.*

SG: *Let go of your performance self.*

RD: *Take a moment . . . to really become the sky . . . that can hold whatever clouds are there.*

SG: *And you can also become the earth . . . with roots that go deep into ancestral places.*

RD: *At the same time being the sky . . . where above the clouds there's a place where the sun is always shining. You are the light.*

SG: *And in that resting place . . . let us return to this core idea . . . of a hero's journey . . . that constitutes your life path.*

RD: And in closing I want to share a poem by an anonymous author entitled "Look to this Day."

> *Look to this day, for it is life,*
> *the very life of life.*
> *In its brief course lies all the truth of existence,*
> *the joy of growth,*

the splendour of beauty,
the glory of action.
For yesterday is but a memory,
and tomorrow only a vision.
But each day well lived
makes every yesterday a memory of happiness
and every tomorrow a vision of hope.
Therefore, look to this day!

SG: And on this day, we began to open the buds of the idea that your life can be lived as a hero's journey, a great opening of consciousness through time on a path toward generative transformation and healing of yourself and the world. And on this day, we touched upon some of the simple ideas of that hero's journey. That there is a consciousness beneath and before your ego-intellect, below your conscious mind. It has been here even before your thinking mind ever developed. And we call that original presence the unique human spirit that is you.

RD: That life force, that vitality that Martha Graham talked about . . . And we touched upon how the ultimate goal of the hero's journey is not to perform . . . but to look back over the day and be able to say, "That was a good day. That was a day well lived." To be able to look back upon a whole life and say, "That was a good life. That was a life well lived."

SG: And so you may sense from that place of gratitude and openness, as you look back upon this day, any learnings you had today that you especially want to appreciate and remember. Perhaps what you learned about your calling. What is the deepest path that wants to be lived from within you?

RD: And can you open your channel, open your heart and mind, to that path?

SG: And we talked further about how, as you begin to walk on that path, you will come up against thresholds; places where you feel called to take a step into a new territory, beyond where you've ever stepped before. That there will likely be many places in the days ahead where you'll find yourself coming into places on your journey where it's hard to take that next step . . . where you feel paralyzed, discouraged. These are predictable and inevitable parts of any significant journey. And at those times, can you sense how to return back home to your center? How you can remember to not give your mind to the problem, and instead bring your mind home, to join with the center of your inner being?

RD: So we wish you a night well lived tonight, and invite you to use it as an opportunity to periodically drop down into your center. Begin to calibrate to your center. Notice if you can begin to sense more and more, when and how do you get closer to your center? When and how do you become more distant from your center? How do you bring yourself back home to center . . . anytime, anywhere, any way that offers itself to you?

SG: And in the great tradition of Milton Erickson, we will just point out that each of you is going to have a number of dreams tonight. Science has shown that you'll have six or seven dreams tonight. And we're going to suggest that you feel free to use just one of them to have a deep meaningful dream about your hero's journey.

RD: You might think you should have two dreams about your hero's journey.

SG: But we think you should limit yourself to just one. *(Laughter.)* And we further think it *should be* the third dream tonight.

RD: You might want to resist and make it the fifth. But *we* really want it to be the third.

SG: Some of you will openly defy us . . .

RD: . . . and have three dreams about your calling . . .

SG: . . . but *we* think it *should* just be the third dream.

RD: And *we* think it should only be one dream.

SG: But I'm sure you'll show us who's boss . . . in terms of how many dreams you'll have tonight.

RD: And which one . . .

SG: . . . will be about your . . .

RD: . . . calling.

SG: But however many dreams you will have . . . and whichever ones they are . . . we deeply and wholeheartedly emphasize that you really can have a nice . . . deep . . . restful . . . sleep all the way through the night . . .

RD: . . . and wake up so very refreshed.

SG: So that when we begin again, you'll be able to bring all of your somatic mind to the next part of the journey . . . and all of your cognitive mind . . . and all of your field mind . . . to explore the mystery of the alignment of the trinity.

RD: So go forth into the world . . .

SG: . . . and spread the sacred word of the hero's journey.

RD: Go forth and center. *(Laughter and applause.)*

Day 2

Generative Cognitive Consciousness

SG: Good morning, everybody. We wish each of you a very, very good day today.

RD: And of course our main question is: Was it the third dream? *(Laughter.)* Or were you very resistant and had at least two dreams? *(More laughter.)*

Yesterday we began to explore this notion of "the call" to the hero's journey – the idea that there is a unique energy in you that is the gift that you bring to the world. We also pointed out that each of us, on our journey through life, becomes wounded or carries the wounds of our cultures or our families, and that the hero's journey is both about sharing our gifts and healing our wounds, and the wounds of others. So we want to start with a few readings, as usual. This first one, for me, relates a lot to what we will be doing today. It's a passage by Marianne Williamson that is widely cited as having been read by Nelson Mandela at his inauguration:

> *Our deepest fear is not that we are inadequate. Our deepest fear is that we are powerful beyond measure. It is our light, not our darkness, that most frightens us. We ask ourselves, who am I to be brilliant, gorgeous, talented and fabulous? Actually who are we not to be? You are a child of God. Your playing small doesn't serve the world. There is nothing enlightened about shrinking so that other people won't feel insecure around you. We are all meant to shine as children do. We were born to make manifest the glory of God that is within us. It's not just in some of us; it's in everyone. And when we let our own light shine, we unconsciously give other people permission to do the same. As we are liberated from our own fear, our presence automatically liberates others.*
>
> (A Return to Love: Reflections on the Principles of "A Course in Miracles", 1992)

RD: I think this beautiful prayer says something very important about the hero's journey, namely, may you allow your light to shine, liberating yourself and others from fear.

I have a second brief reading from D. H. Lawrence:

> *When we get out of the glass bottle of our ego,*
> *And we escape like squirrels turning in the*
> *cages of our personality*
> *and get into the forests again,*
> *we shall shiver with cold and fright*
> *but things will happen to us*
> *so that we don't know ourselves.*
>
> *Cool, unlying life will rush in,*
> *and passion will make our bodies taut with power,*
> *we shall stamp our feet with new power*
> *and old things will fall down,*
> *we shall laugh,*
> *and institutions will curl up like burnt paper.*

RD: So may we all leave our cages and get into the forest again today.

SG: Beautifully said, Robert. Today we're going to be exploring the generative cognitive principle of sponsorship. This principle is implicit in the work of Tibetan Buddhism, which emphasizes that perhaps the greatest gift of human consciousness is the capacity to transmute negative energy into positive energy – to be able to connect with a negative pattern and to transform it into something that has value for human beings. Do you believe that we have that capacity?

RD: Say "Amen," brothers and sisters! (*Laughter.*) Say, "I *believe!*" (*More laughter.*)

SG: And do you believe that it would make a difference in how you lead your daily life if *you* had a pretty good confidence that you could do that? That if you just gave yourself a little bit of time, and a little bit of attention, that you could open up to whatever is there and use this great gift of your human consciousness to transform what's there? The belief in this possibility underlies the process of sponsorship. You can hear it in this beautiful poem by Rumi, the great Sufi poet, from 700 years ago. Some say that he is the greatest poet of all time, and I don't argue with them. This poem is called "A Goat Kneels."

The inner being of a human being
is a jungle. Sometimes wolves dominate,
and sometimes wild hogs. Be careful when you breathe!
At one moment gentle, generous qualities,
like Joseph's, pass from one nature into another.
And the next moment vicious qualities
move in hidden ways . . .
At every moment a new species arises in the chest –
now a demon, now an angel, now a wild animal.
But there are also those in this amazing jungle
who can absorb you into their own surrender.
So if you have to stalk and steal something,
steal from them!

SG: So you can hear in this poem the very important distinction between two levels of the cognitive mind. Just as yesterday we were talking about two levels of the somatic center – the content, and the space in which the content is held – we say the same thing about the generative cognitive mind. In the generative somatic, we create a sort of "body of bodies"; in the generative cognitive, we open a sort of "mind of minds." It's adding another contextual level.

RD: In NLP you might say it's a "meta-mind" that includes and transcends the other minds.

SG: So in the generative mind, one's identity is at the level of the field that holds all patterns.

RD: As Gregory Bateson used to say, it's at the level of "the pattern which connects."

SG: This generative meta-mind level differs markedly from what we are calling the ordinary ego level of the mind, where identity is in one position or one part of the field. So if Robert and I are in a field together, the ordinary mind would say: "This is *me* here; and that's *not me* there. And my identity is right *here* . . . I'm *not there.*"

At this level of identity, when we have differences, which are inevitable, I will see his different perspective as threatening my identity. To therefore preserve "my self," I must therefore deal with these differences by obliterating "the other." *(Steve starts moving toward Robert like a zombied axe murderer.)* "I must kill, kill, kill." *(Much laughter.)* *(Steve is laughing, while continuing the movements.)* And somehow I must remove this horrible threat to my identity from the field, by whatever means necessary.

Now we're laughing, but the way this plays out in the world is usually not so funny. It's called fundamentalism, and unfortunately it is the most dominant ideology on the planet today. "My position is the one true position. And his is the position of the infidel. So he must be destroyed." *(To Robert, in a voice like a mafia hit man)* It's nothing personal. It's just business. *(Laughter.)*

RD: When we are able move to a generative level, a higher level than the ordinary ego identity, instead of being opposites, we become complements. Moving to a generative field level of identity, you could say that we have created a third entity that holds both of us and much, much more. It's a little bit like our earlier example of bringing two hydrogen atoms and an oxygen atom together and getting water. Water is not hydrogen, and it's not oxygen. But it cannot exist without their relationship. It's emergent from their interaction. And that's the generative state: it emerges from holding all the members of the lower level in a harmonious way.

SG: Of course, this applies equally with humans. If you've ever been in an intimate relationship . . .

RD: . . . or read about somebody who has . . . *(Laughter.)*

SG: . . . you can see that in the first stage of intimacy, the romantic phase, one plus one equals one. So love is thought of as "we merge, and live happily ever after."

RD: *(Robert hugs Steve in a dream-like fashion.)* Stevie, my love!

(Laughter.)

SG: And as Robert is showing, this romantic fusion is literally a drugged state. The brain releases chemicals that put you in the "oneness trance"; it is nature's way of drawing you into a trap. "Come here, my little pretty . . ." (*Laughter.*) Of course, all drugs wear off, so at some point you enter the second phase of intimacy where the differences become more salient than the oneness. All those things that used to be so cute in your partner, now bug the hell out of you! But for any intimate relationship, this movement to "two-ness" is an essential step. We are challenged to realize that even as we love each other, we have significant differences.

RD: Differentiation is necessary. It's essential.

SG: This differentiation allows a shift from identifying with a single position, to identifying with a field that holds many positions. This is the third phase of intimacy. To enjoy mature, creative love, we must grow a field consciousness, an "us" that includes but goes beyond "you" and "me." Our differences don't disappear – in some ways they become more clear – but there is an emerging space that is holding the differences. This field consciousness is a higher level than the "ego position" consciousness. It is the basis not only for interpersonal generativity – where the "us" holds and guides the "you" and the "me" – but also for intrapersonal generativity, where the meta-space awareness makes room for every part of my thinking, behaving, feeling, and being. This allows complementarity, not competition; it allows a "both/and" rather than an "either/or" relationship. As we shall see, this makes a huge difference for creating generative outcomes.

When we look at problems, we generally see a clashing between positions, where violence is attempted to get rid of one position in order to affirm a different position. One typical example is the large gap that typically exists between the "ego ideal" – as Robert was saying earlier, what I *think* I want, or what I think I *should* be doing – and what's actually happening. For example, I want to be healthy, but I'm eating 12 jelly doughnuts every day. That's a difference between the ego ideal and the actual!

The typical way that the ego identity tries to resolve this is by "getting rid of" the problematic actual state. Stop eating jelly doughnuts! Don't feel scared! Attack the person who disagrees with you!

RD: So you try to control it, try to minimize it, try to get rid of it.

SG: And if that works, great! Sometimes it will actually work to just ignore or say "no" to something. If that's the case, great, let it go and move on. But if the problem keeps coming back, then hopefully you realize this: I tried to get rid of it. That didn't work. What's my plan B? And plan B is what we call *sponsorship*.

Sponsorship

RD: Sponsorship is entering into the generative space of being able to safely and skillfully hold whatever is there, in a way that allows new, positive experiences and realities to emerge, similar to the metaphor of the sky that holds the clouds. And through that holding environment, transformation becomes possible. A core principle of our work here is: any energy that is not centered, sponsored, and integrated is a problem. A problem represents some energy that is disconnected, rejected, and not centered – in other words, a shadow.

If you think about any emotions that you struggle with, you can probably see that you're not centered in them. You don't like them and don't want them, and they're not integrated with any other energy in you. They're always in a pure, primitive form. So sponsorship is about welcoming what's there, centering in it in a way that allows you to hold it, and transformation happens as it becomes integrated with other energies and other aspects of yourself.

SG: Let me give you an example. I live near San Diego, in southern California. A couple of years ago, I had a Friday morning supervision group. About six therapists would come in for three hours and we would explore some of their difficult cases. One of my students worked right outside the big military base that is about 20 miles north of my office. She had a client, a 26-year-old Marine officer, who came in with the following story. When she was a girl, she and her sister were sexually abused by their next-door neighbor on a repeated basis. Each time it happened, the perpetrator would say, "If you tell anybody, I'll kill your sister." So she didn't forget, but she didn't feel free to report this guy. She was afraid of what he might do to her sister.

So she went away on her hero's journey, as many trauma survivors do. She joined the Marines, and what kind of speciality do you think she developed? She became a small weapons demolition expert. These are the little weapons of mass destruction that we thought were in Iraq. And it turned out they had been in the United States the whole time. *(Laughter.)* Who'd have thought? We were shocked! *(More laughter.)* Anyway, at one point she received security clearance to have access to these little bombs. And guess what kind of fantasies began to visit her? Peace and love and forgiveness? No, of course not . . . she had intense fantasies of taking one of these little bombs and paying a visit to you-know-who. Actually, *she* didn't want to do it. *She* didn't want to take a life – and she knew that, if she did, her own life would effectively be over. But the fantasies were very intense.

So she went to this clinic and started talking to her therapist (who was my student). When the therapist heard the fantasies, she became very tense and frightened *(Steve begins to act tense and frightened)* and *tried to suggest . . . relaxation. Please, just relax . . . think of a beach scene . . . anything but that fantasy! (Said in a very tense, unrelaxed voice to audience laughter.)*

Apparently she had forgotten the somatic centering exercises we've been talking about. And of course it made the client even more nervous. Luckily, the therapist had a support group where she could bring the case, and we talked about how she might proceed. After a little bit, the therapist, looking distressed, said, "I'm sorry. I wish I could handle this better, but I feel overwhelmed."

I said, "No problem. How about inviting the client into our supervision group? You and I can interview her together for a session, maybe two, and we'll see how things might go from there." She thought it was a good idea, the client thought it was a good idea. So the next Friday I met them in the waiting room. This woman appeared to be in a very interesting sort of dissociated trance state. By that I mean, a trance without a human center to ground it or guide it. She had very straggly hair, teeth missing, glasses with very thick lenses, and she had a strange sort of smile on her face. I thought, "Yeah, I think she could do it. I'm glad she's here." *(A little laughter.)* So we went into my office and got settled. I usually take a couple of minutes with the client to do some silent centering at the beginning of each session. I say something like, "Well, it sounds like you want to do something very important for yourself here today. So why don't we just take a few moments of silence to connect with the deepest part of ourselves." This gives the client a chance to settle in and settle down, and it gives me an opportunity to attune to "meditational mantras" such as, "Something's trying to heal here. Something in her spirit is trying to come into the world. May I sense, receive, and help that awakening."

RD: As we said: there's a positive intention behind the fantasy, behind the energy, inside of the symptom.

SG: Then the next meditational mantra I do is something like, "Whatever is there, I'm sure it makes sense." Don't ask me how it makes sense, because my conscious mind is the last to find out. But in sponsorship, you're accepting each moment of experience as "making sense" in terms of the unfolding of spirit into the world. So as I sat there, it didn't take long to feel that her homicidal rage was a good sign that the healing process had begun. If you had been tortured and a family member had been repeatedly raped, and you couldn't deal with it for many years for whatever reason, and then something shifted so that the healing process could begin, what do you think would be the first step? Forgiveness? *(Shaking his head.)* It would be a very healthy first step to realize, I want to kill the bastard! That makes sense, yes? And one of the key ideas of sponsorship, unlike what the Catholic nuns taught me, is that *to think it is not to do it.* That is, you can make room for the thought or feeling without having to act it out. By being able to "be with it without becoming it," which is a key aspect of the generative cognitive, you can begin to transform it into a positive experience.

RD: So you're sponsoring the energy, not the behavior.

SG: You're looking to create this energetic field, if you will, that can receive and hold it.

RD: So we're sponsoring the urge, not a specific behavior. In NLP we like to say: "Separate the identity from the behaviour." I will do everything in my power to challenge or stop a harmful behaviour; at the same time I will do everything in my power to support the identity and the positive intention that is giving rise to the behavior.

SG: So as I looked at her, I felt this rapport with her, and so I said in a provocative but gentle way: "I understand you want to blow some asshole up . . ." Her eyes opened wide with fascination and surprise. Then, predictably, she turned away, hiding her eyes like a shy child. Usually when you touch something in a person's center, there will be a couple of seconds before they have to disconnect from it. That's OK – when they disconnect, you don't. You stay respectful, relaxed, and connected. After a few moments, I asked her, "What do you think your best techniques might be?" (Some laughter.) She again looked very interested and her eyes started moving around, suggesting she was visually accessing different fantasies. When she seemed to become especially absorbed in one, I said, "Yes, *that* one! What is *that* one?" She looked at me, smiled for a few moments, then hid her eyes again.

By this time, I felt deep rapport with her, and began to notice my own fantasy images. (This suggests that the therapist/coach is starting to join the client's relational field. The point is not to get lost or fixed on these images, but to become curious about all the different ways that the creative unconscious might express the justified rage.) I picked one out and said, "How about a pipe bomb up his ass?" (Laughter.) This time, she looked at me and kept looking, very deeply absorbed. This is a way of her saying, *You are speaking my language, so my unconscious will give you full attention.*

RD: Remember that key step in the active centering exercise: *Meet the disturbing energy. Don't run away from it, don't oppose it. Meet it. Then see how out of that respectful meeting, you can join with it and redirect it so that new patterns and outcomes can emerge.*

SG: And this involves giving a blessing to the wound when you encounter it. For some primitive experience to become fully human, it needs a blessing. So I said, "I don't know all of the different images that will flow through you in the coming weeks. But I do know that something very, very wrong was done to you. And for whatever reason, you could not begin healing until now. But it feels like the healing is beginning to happen, and I say to that presence in you that is beginning to heal, *welcome . . . welcome . . . welcome.* And by the way, when you sense that presence that wants to kill the bastard, where do you feel that energy most in your body?" And she went *(intensely claps hand onto his belly)*. And I said, very sympathetically: "Yeah, that's where I felt it, too."

As I attuned to that presence in her center, sensing it as the source of her strength and wisdom, I continued: "*I really would like to say . . . to that presence inside of you: 'You speak with great integrity. There is a lot of rage – that's good to know. Inside of that is where all your power is. And I'd like to thank you for beginning to bring that into healing.'*"

Tears welled in her eyes, and her body relaxed as her wound was blessed and began to be dressed. I began to teach her how to center with that core feeling, as we explored yesterday, so that she could begin to create a safe space to hold and let whatever needed healing to heal. Thus began her journey of transforming the wound of dark rage and hurt into the human resource of protecting life, of saying no, of challenging social injustice and violence. Her connection to the belly energy became her anchor, her grounding, and her place of wisdom.

RD: We mentioned earlier the processes of centering, sponsoring, and then integrating. Whatever the energy is, however a problem presents itself, you center and meet it. Bring it into your center. Invite it to tea. Become curious about how your connection can help the both of you.

The piece we're exploring next is that of sponsorship. Not only do I meet it and either ground with it or move with it – I give it some sort of blessing. The philosopher Albert Camus said, "Until somebody has been seen and blessed by another person, they don't yet fully exist." So sponsoring is about seeing and blessing what is there. Usually people find that is easy to do with the gift. It's more difficult to see and bless the wound. And yet, for our hero's journey, this is a crucial challenge and skill: how to heal wounds and transform the "demons." Sponsorship is the generative relationship of healing, transforming, and awakening. This is what we're going to be exploring next.

SG: This process of sponsorship is the core process of art, of culture, and of becoming a person. Each involves bringing some primitive energy into its full human form. In sponsorship, you're looking to humanize whatever is there in the psyche.

RD: It's also the principle of good parenting.

SG: You will no doubt agree that children do not arrive into the world as full persons. It's a *long* process of sponsorship. Perhaps one of the greatest achievements of civilization is to help a child eat like a person. *(Laughter.)* My daughter is almost 16, and she's been receiving long-term therapy for this challenge. *(Laughter.)* Three therapy sessions a day, each day, 365 days a year, to try to help her learn to eat like a human being. And finally we're seeing a little progress. *(Laughter.)*

And whether it's eating or anything else, there are so many problems and disturbing energies on the path of becoming fully human. When a child is 1 year old, you will likely see her throwing her food around and wiping it all over her face with great delight. You remember those days? *(Some nods and laughter.)* And if you are the parent, you hopefully don't scream and yell, "You're such a bad baby. Why aren't you more like the other babies? If you were a good baby, you would completely eat like a grown-up!" You hope- fully don't do that. Instead you realize: Well, this is a work in proc- ess – this kid needs a bit of help in maturing. I'm happy to do that.

My daughter is a pretty fierce kid – she has good, positive warrior energy. When she was 3, she was in the backyard playing with a friend. The friend took away Zoe's toy, and Zoe responded by picking up a bat – luckily it was a plastic bat! – and clubbed this kid over the head. *(Laughter.)* This is one of those great parenting moments, yes? The question is, how do you sponsor that? How do you accept that in a way that further awakens the goodness and the gifts of your child? Do you say, "Oh, that's so wonderful that you're expressing your feelings! We all need to express our feel- ings spontaneously?" *(Laughter.)* Or do you walk over and shake her and scream, "We don't do those sorts of things in this family! That's bad, bad, bad!" Of course not. Again, the principle of spon- sorship is to sense and acknowledge the positive energy and inten- tion at the heart of the pattern, and connect with it to allow new possibilities to emerge. So you realize first, "Wow, she's got a really fierce spirit, this kid. It's a huge gift. But she needs work." Then you connect to bless that spirit and explore how she can express it in more humane ways. You don't get rid of the fierceness; you humanize it.

RD: A key to sponsorship is sensing the positive human value behind something. To do this, you need to be able to hold whatever this energy is, whatever this behaviour is, so that you can find out, how does this make sense? What positive outcomes are they trying to create? As an example, I can remember one of my own parenting moments with my son, when he was small. He got angry with his little sister, and began to become very aggressive with her, hitting her, pushing her down, and making her cry. As the parent, what do you do? Do you hit him and say: "Don't hit your sister. It's wrong to hit other people!"? *(Laughter.)* Instead, I decided to explore its positive intention. So I asked, "What do you want to get by pushing your sister? What does it do for you to do that?" And, of course, he looked at me as if I was a total idiot and replied, "I want to hurt her." *(Laughter.)*

Now this is the essence of sponsorship. This is a time when you've got to accept that energy and be with it a little longer. So instead of saying, "Well, then you are a bad boy" or "It is wrong to want to hurt her," I asked, "What does it do for you to hurt her?" "I'm getting back at her. I'm getting even." "And what does it do for you to get even? Why get even?" "Then it's fair. She took my toy, so I'm getting back at her."

So I said, "Ah, *fairness* – that's something important. That's something I really want to make sure that you have in your life. Let's explore the ways to get fairness. How can you use your words as much as your hands to get fairness? What does fairness look like? What does fairness feel like?"

From that frame, it becomes possible to explore how that very powerful energy can operate in the service of something that's humanly valuable. Your main interest is not in getting rid of anything, but in seeing how new possibilities can emerge by accepting and redirecting what is already there.

SG: A basic principle here is:

   In order to transform something, first stop trying to change it.

Most of the time when we're trying to change something in ourselves or others, we're giving the message, "You're not OK in your present state. You're not loveable as you are." This degrading of the human spirit, whether intentional or not, makes it harder for a person to change. So instead we're saying: "I'm sure what you're doing and experiencing makes sense. I'm sure wanting to hit your sister makes a lot of sense. And I'd really like to be able to support what's going on inside of that." You become curious how at the roots of "hitting my sister" is this deep interest in fairness, how at the heart of every symptom or problem is a jewel of human goodness. Sponsorship is the art of connecting with that intrinsic goodness and releasing it.

RD: And when we can release it, that's how humans grow. That's how you grow as a person. We appreciate that this process of sponsorship is probably a very different approach for many of you. For those with NLP training, when your clients encounter symptoms and difficult feelings you're taught to think, "Oh, this is a negative state! Here's a tool to fix it. Here's a tool to disassociate, to change it, to get rid of it." We're suggesting something radically different from that. Instead of saying, *Here are tools for the ego to control emotions that it doesn't like,* we're suggesting, *Here's a method for the soul to grow. For us to become more fully human.*

As Albert Einstein said, you can't solve a problem with the same thinking that is creating a problem. So if the problem is one of conflict, you're not going to solve it by strengthening one half of the conflict. The other side is going to rise to the occasion. Whether it's a conflict inside of a person, or a conflict between persons, or cultures, or countries. Using "power over" as your main approach creates an escalating conflict, not a new solution.

SG: Remember, we suggested that there is a fundamental difference between a hero and a champion. In a conflict or challenge, the champion is there to defeat otherness, to make one part of the system supreme against all others. The hero's calling, on the other hand, is to shift the relational dynamic and the relational field so the either/or of violence can open to the both/and of complementarity. You're looking to create more wholeness in the field, rather than one part of the field having unilateral control.

RD: So we're suggesting that in the hero's journey, the goal is not to defeat or destroy the difficult feeling or the negative energy. It is to humanize it by first becoming more human yourself. You start by centering, by opening the generative somatic level; then you add the generative cognitive process of sponsorship, where you're able to hold what's there in a way that allows new positive experiences and outcomes to emerge.

It is important to recognize that even if you did succeed in defeating or suppressing the problematic energy, then that energy is no longer available to you. If I actually succeeded in suppressing all of my emotions, I would become numb and without energy. So part of what we're saying is that contained within the problem are energies that you'll need in order to truly succeed at your hero's journey. The more challenging the journey, the more you're going to need every energy that's available to you. You're going to need the power inside of fear. You're going to need the power inside your critical judgments. You're going to need the energy inside of your grief and sadness . . . as well as the energy of your joy, and your excitement. Having access to all of those energies is what allows you to do the extraordinary. So from this perspective, when I defeat the enemy, I defeat myself.

Practicing Sponsorship

RD: In our next exercise, we are going to apply the process of sponsorship in order to more deeply understand and appreciate the path of your hero's journey within the larger context of your life.

SG: In this process that I developed, you're understanding a whole life, your own or another's, in terms of a hero's journey. It's really interesting and helpful to interview someone about the past, present, and future of his or her life journey, so that every significant part of it can be sensed in the positive light of their spirit's attempt to fully awaken in the world. We're going to demonstrate this process and then ask you to do it with a partner. The questions for the interview are listed below.

Exercise: Questions for Your Hero's Journey

1. What is your calling?

2. How would you know your calling has been fulfilled? (internal/external states)

3. When did you first hear the call? What were subsequent calls? ("positive transcendent" and "negative" events)

4. In what ways have you refused the call? What have been the consequences of the refusal?

5. What people are models/ancestors/sponsors for your call?

6. Which people are negative examples/warnings?

7. What are the demons that block your path? (inner states/ habits or addictions/external associations)

8. What are the resources that support/nurture/motivate your path?

9. What will allow you to deepen your commitment to your hero's journey?

RD: As we have emphasized in our previous exercises, the key to making this interview meaningful is not just asking the questions, it is also the space or container that you create for your client to answer the questions. Which means that more important than the questions is your presence. You could ask these questions and get very superficial answers from somebody's ego-intellect. What we're trying to do is to create the space so that the person can answer these from the soul. As a coach, as a therapist, as a parent, as a manager, it is your job to create and hold a space that can bring out the best in yourself and others. So before we start the interview and the questions, Stephen and I are both going to drop into that place of connection with our centers.

SG: It doesn't have to be anything wild and esoteric. We'll save that for this afternoon. *(Laughter.)* You can just begin by saying something like: "Let's take a couple of moments before we begin our conversation to settle in and settle down." *(Robert and Steve both slow down and begin a centering process.)*

Demonstration with Stephen

RD: So, again, I know the distance that I feel between me and Stephen will be the same as what I feel between myself and myself. *So I first want to just connect with myself . . . Relax . . . and bring my attention to my center . . .* As we practiced yesterday, once you drop into your center, you then open into the field to include your partner. Remember, *the greatest gift you can give to another person is the quality of your attention.* And so really sense and commit to bringing a high quality of attention to the interview.

SG: And from over on this side, when you are being interviewed, really take it as an opportunity to do some deep self-learning. Let go of trying to impress or please the interviewer, and gratefully accept whatever support they can give you to deeply connect with yourself.

RD: As before, when each of you feels centered and ready, give the "secret signal," the head nod . . . *(After a few more moments, both Robert and Steve nod in readiness.)*

Steve, as you reflect back on your life and also to your future, what would you say is your deepest life calling?

SG: *(Pauses in reflection)* Well, it's interesting . . . It's sort of hard to find words sometimes, because where I experience my response, it has no words. But I think for today . . . maybe the best way of saying it has something to do with . . . *always going beyond the given reality.* To do that with myself, but also with other people I come into contact with. To really help them get a sense that there's an infinite number of realities. And that each person has the capacity to access and live in so many different realities. *You don't have to be limited to any given reality – there's always something beyond . . .* I'm pretty sure my calling is around that notion.

RD: *(Slowly and gently)* So, Stephen, I really sense and feel that beautiful space where you say there are really no words for this calling. I also really hear that for today, it can be expressed in terms of helping yourself and others get beyond any limited reality . . . to see that there are many realities. And your calling is about helping people get to that place, so they can recognize that they in some way can choose realities.

SG: Mmmm . . . yes . . . interesting. I was just remembering . . . these very deep experiences I had as a kid.

RD: Yeah. I was just going to ask about when you first heard that call.

SG: *(Pausing in reverie)* Well, actually, there are different types of experiences connected to that . . . but one I was just remembering was being really so sad and confused about what a closed, dreary, depressed state I felt most people were in when I was a kid. So, I don't know, perhaps based on that I had this urge . . . sometimes I just wanted to shake people out of their trance . . . with this sense of, "Don't you realize there's more?"

And then there is a whole other class of memories that I have . . . *(Smiles.)* There were these times as a kid of having the most incredible, amazing experiences. I am remembering, for example, when I was about 8 or 9, and I had this very deep connection with my Italian grandfather. He was really such a positive sponsor for me, I loved him so much. We were at this big family Easter Sunday gathering. I was over in the corner, my traditional place, where I was just sort of trancing out and watching what was happening with people. I remember feeling this sort of telepathic connection with my grandfather. It was really such a pleasurable feeling to know that he loved me. It was at his house and he was gathering the hors d'oeuvre plates to bring them into the kitchen to replenish them. I remember feeling this really deep connection with him, and then he began to walk toward the hallway. Just before he was about to disappear from my sight, I had this horrifying realization, "I'm going to lose my connection with him!" So in that moment as a kid, I leaped out of my body and landed inside of his body, and thinking, "Wow!" *(Laughs a bit.)*

As he walked into the kitchen, I felt myself sitting right behind his eyes, sort of witnessing his whole consciousness. It was an amazing, amazing experience! But as he was cutting the vegetables, I had this astonishing awareness, *He wasn't aware of me at that moment. I didn't exist in his reality at that moment.* It was really a shock. But it was a shock that actually popped open this space . . . many, many experiences began to flash in a moment through my mind. I saw my family and me standing at the bottom of his stairs, later that night, as we were waving goodbye to him. I knew that we probably wouldn't see him for several months, and I just noticed all those moments of experience that he would be having during those months . . . *and I would not be in most of them!* It was a beautiful experience, to sense that there were countless realities beyond my own. And then I saw myself with a bird's eye view of his neighborhood in San Francisco, and in each house were people I didn't know and would never know, but each of them would be in their own experiential realities, moment after moment after moment. It was really an amazing feeling to sense that there were countless, ever-expanding numbers of realities in the world, and that I could spend my whole life exploring them, and never really have scratched the surface. I remember realizing at that moment, *I'm going to be exploring this for the rest of my life!*

RD: *(Pauses, breathes it in, then responds gently)* I feel really touched by that . . . I can feel that 9-year-old boy, and really relate with him. I can really sense that awakening . . . it's really strong. I can tell that it's a very key imprinting moment for you.

SG: Yes . . .

RD: Anything you can say about subsequent calls? Either from what we've been calling the positive transcendent kind of experiences . . . or intense struggles that set you on this path about helping people to get beyond any one reality to recognize there are many infinite realities?

SG: Oh, I certainly can remember a number of really deep positive experiences that were important openings in my consciousness.

RD: Mmmm . . .

SG: But it's interesting, I think that in those early days especially, getting to those places of joy and exhilaration required that I dissociate, that I would just cut off all the unhappiness that was happening in me and around me. And that strategy of dissociation – well, it had a lot of positive aspects, but it also had some negative aspects. I think I used the positive "transcendent" experiences to avoid dealing with my emotional pain and woundedness. Sort of a version of the idea that the gift is used to hide the wound.

RD: Mmmm . . . so it sounds like in addition to helping yourself and others to get to this place of recognizing infinite realities, there is something in your journey about also . . . staying with what is, or what is going on for you – somehow connecting the difficult energies.

SG: Yes, I mean that gift of seeing all the amazing realities is there – I think it would probably be there regardless of my history. Everybody is given a jewel, and I think that's the one I've been given . . . but as you know, that light can be used to mask or blind one from the dark . . . and I grew up in a very violent, alcoholic family, where there was so much that couldn't be dealt with. So looking back, it feels like I in some ways exploited the gift. I can appreciate it as helpful then, but also sense it as unhelpful now. So as we're talking, it's interesting for me to sense how the path has changed over time.

RD: So that brings up the question for me, when in your life have you refused your life calling, and what consequences has that had?

SG: *(Pauses)* I think there are at least two main ways that I've gotten off my path. One is any time that I found myself pursuing fame and fortune more than living the gift – it really got me into trouble.

RD: Mmmm . . .

SG: And the other is, following that Irish Catholic proclivity for sex, drugs, and rock 'n' roll. *(Robert laughs.)* But seriously, getting lost in that has occasionally moved me away from feeling that I was really living my calling. So these are two things that I have really learned that I have to pay attention to . . . partly because I know from experience how much pain it creates for me and for the people I love. I also know from experience how much pleasure and satisfaction really living more closely on my path brings to me . . . Also, as you know, I went through a very painful divorce three years ago, and I feel that was in no small way about having gotten away from living from my core. But these days I feel better really than I have in a long time.

RD: Hmmm. I can see that.

SG: It's great to sense what my calling is, and experience the happiness and excitement about being able to live it.

RD: Hmmm. So where do you perceive your growing edge today? Another way to approach this is the question, what are the demons that block your path?

SG: *(Pauses)* One of the demons . . . what just came up for me when you asked that is noticing some bitterness towards my ex-wife in terms of the divorce, and feeling that I really need to heal whatever bitterness or anger that is there . . . I'd say another demon is this sort of very young inner fear that sometimes comes up that thinks that nobody will ever love me. And that often gets me, for whatever reason, to work harder.

RD: Another question that's coming to me is, which people have been models, ancestors, or sponsors for your call? And at the moment, I'm wondering if any of these could be a resource for your healing the bitterness and fear you were just talking about?

SG: *(Pauses)* When I was younger, I think I had so many more sponsors. I mean, one of the greatest things about being in my twenties was that I had an amazing pantheon of great teachers: Erickson, Bateson, Satir, John Lilly, Grinder, Bandler, professors at Stanford . . . I could go on and on. And I've been noticing lately that I haven't connected with positive sponsors in a way that I need to or like to.

RD: Hmmm . . .

SG: But I have a real interest in Tibetan Buddhism, particularly some teachers like the Dalai Lama. Some of these people are really great models and teachers about how to do healing with inner anger and bitterness. It's really helpful to me, personally and professionally. But I really have sensed, partly from the work that we've been doing together, that I need to find some good sponsors for me in my present life.

RD: Mmmm . . . that really touches me a lot, and rings true to me. I can really relate to it, also personally. Which brings me to two key questions. The first is, what resources support, nurture, and motivate your path? And related to that is, what would really allow you to deepen your commitment to your hero's journey?

SG: I've actually been paying a lot of attention to that question. The answer, it feels increasingly to me, has to do with the core process of self-care, how to really feed myself when I have such a busy work life. So I really notice and I am trying to remember that reading is always one of the great resources that opens my imagination. It brings me back to a sense of wonderment, of entering a reality beyond my own and becoming curious about how that reality opens up.

And then my daily meditation and yoga practice. Those are really important. *(Pauses and smiles.)* And as you know, I've got a sweetheart, Grace, who *really* brings me back to my center. *(Robert and Steve laugh.)* Unfortunately, right now she lives in China and I live in the United States. But it's really such a core relationship, and we talk every day. Thank God for Skype! *(Robert laughs.)*

RD: I can really see how that also requires that you expand your reality! Which brings me to my final question – one about the future. How would you know your calling has been fulfilled? As you look to your future, how will you know that you're staying on that track? What is it that seems to be calling you now to it?

SG: Well, the response I notice inside was that I felt this radiant heart.

RD: Yes, a radiant heart . . .

SG: And I saw an image of me with my arms open like this *(extends arms open)*, with this great feeling of living free.

RD: *(With tenderheartedness)* I really see . . . and I honor that huge, open heart.

SG: Thank you, Robert. It's really great to receive your love and sponsorship . . . *(Robert and Stephen hug.) (Applause.)*

Skills of Sponsorship

RD: So one of the things we're exploring here is, how do you have a sacred conversation with somebody? How do you invite somebody to speak from the deepest part of their heart about their dreams, their truths, their callings, their life journeys? I know, when I'm coaching the CEO of a big company, that is precisely the quality of conversation that I'm looking for. It's the same when I am working with somebody who is struggling with a health problem. And, as I think you could probably sense, your commitment to that conversation can open this beautiful field that welcomes and supports the deepest truths.

It's very powerful, I think, to be on both sides of this conversation. For me as the interviewer, there were these waves of things that were touching me very deeply about what Stephen was sharing. It was not only the words that Stephen was using, but the place that he was speaking from, the energy that was coming behind those words.

SG: And for me it was just great, the way that Robert was supporting me. It may not have seemed like it, but half the time I forgot he was there – because his questions, and the way he was asking them, allowed me to dip into a very interesting space inside of me. And then it was a pleasure to come and see his radiant smiling eyes and to feel this sense that he was really excited about my journey.

RD: In Stephen's book *The Courage to Love* he outlines a number of skills of sponsorship. The first one is to be innerly congruent, connected with myself. The second is to be connected with my partner. And I noticed, as the listener here, there were times when I had to be careful of not becoming truly lost in what Stephen was saying, so that I could still be present for Stephen as I received it. So, I needed to continually manage my connection with myself, as well as my connection with Stephen.

The third and fourth skills of sponsorship are complementary skills as well. They are curiosity and receptivity. Curiosity is an expression of myself, of my own interests. But that needs to be balanced with receptivity for what Stephen is giving – what he wants to give, what he is ready to give. Because if you're only curious, you're just trying to satisfy yourself. And if you are only receptive, you are not present enough in yourself to create the space for this exploration to continue to happen. So when you're the listener or coach in this exercise, it is important to embody those four very powerful skills: your connection with yourself, your connection with your client, your inner curiosity and fascination, but also your receptivity to what the person is really needing and wanting to share or to say.

SG: So get together with a partner and do this exercise. Remember, the core inquiries you are making with your partner are: *Teach me about your hero's journey . . . its past, present, and future. Tell me about your demons, the guardians, the resources. Tell me about the deepest unfolding of your life.* You don't have to use all of the questions we listed earlier, but those are some of the questions that you can use.

RD: And you don't have to do them in exactly the order they are listed. You can add, subtract, or modify them according to how you sense the conversation unfolding.

SG: And when you are the interviewer, breathe everything the person shares deeply through you. Attune with the silent request: *Fill me with the beautiful trance of your hero's journey. I want to be an observer / participant at every level.*

RD: When I was listening to Stephen, there were moments that *(breathes in)* I was literally breathing in the beauty of that story. And in doing so, feeling a connection to the unique vitality, the unique energy of Stephen and his journey. That's a big part of sponsorship – feel and mirror back the deepest beauty of a person's unfolding spirit. It's like that Martha Graham quote – find and connect with the unique life force of your partner.

SG: *My client is on an amazing journey.*

RD: *This person is up to something big here. What is it? There's something big, right here.*

SG: So get a partner, then go where no man nor woman has gone before.

Dealing with Resistance and Refusal

SG: This exercise is one way to really see and sense the very best in a person. To see how all of their experiences – positive and negative – are part of a deeper unfolding of their hero's journey. You don't ignore the difficulties and sorrows of a life, but you can place them within this larger context. However big a person's problems may be, the space of the self is always much bigger. You sense that at the heart of every core experience, the spirit is trying to wake up, to heal, to grow.

RD: Once you have this general sense of your journey, it's possible to tune in to different parts of it. What we'd like to do next is explore some aspects of the *threshold* and the *refusal* of the calling. We often meet resistance at the thresholds of our journey, frequently because we know that we are going to have to deal with the demons and shadows that we will encounter on the journey. And the difficult news is that there is not just one demon, there are many demons.

SG: *(Playfully acting surprised and upset)* Oh, that's just great! *(Laughter.)* First you lure me on to my hero's journey, and it's only now you're telling me I'm going to be possessed by many demons!" *(More laughter.)*

RD: *(His hand on Steve's shoulder)* The good news is: it's not a problem. *(Laughter.)* As Stephen is playfully showing, there are often immediate resistances, second thoughts, and doubts about the journey when the topic of demons is raised. Yesterday, in the active centering process I did with Carmen, we were working with the "demons" or negative energies that come from outside of you. Now we're also including the demons that come from inside of you. So our next exercise, one that I developed, is called "Beginning the Hero's Journey." Or you could also say it's taking the next step on your journey. The following is a summary of what we will be doing.

Exercise: Beginning the Hero's Journey

When you have completed reflecting on your hero's journey, you can begin your journey by going through the following format with a coach or partner. One of you is to be the "client," the other will be the "coach." This process uses a physical timeline and the "as if" frame to help you identify and transform any resistances you have to crossing your threshold and beginning your hero's journey.

1. Create an imaginary timeline on the floor. Place the "calling" and the "demon" where they belong with respect to the future dimension of the timeline.

Past   Present   Future

Figure 2.1: A physical timeline can be used to recall the past and anticipate the future.

2. Have the client/hero stand in the present and get a felt sense of the threshold he or she must cross in order to successfully deal with his or her demon and achieve his or her calling. Ask, "What holds you back? Where is the resistance?"

3. Assist your client/hero by helping him or her to physicalize this resistance – interact with the client to create a physical metaphor for the feeling of resistance (e.g. holding/pushing the client back, dragging the client down, pulling the client off track). Role play various possibilities until you find one that the client intuitively feels is right.

Figure 2.2: The sponsor helps the client physicalize his or her resistance to crossing the threshold by role playing a physical metaphor for the resistance.

4. The sponsor and client then switch places, so that the client is in the role of his or her own resistance. From this perspective, the client considers the questions: What is the positive intention of the resistance? What are the resources I need to fulfill the positive intention in a new and more appropriate way? How can I change the physical expression of the resistance so that it becomes a guardian for me with respect to the positive intention rather than a limitation?

Figure 2.3: The sponsor and client switch places, so that the client is in the role of the resistance and can reflect on its positive intention.

5. The client leaves the present on his/her timeline and walks to the future, acting as if he or she were able to cross the threshold

and go to a place in the future that represents the calling. The client stands in the location representing the calling and gets a felt sense of being successful and centered.

6. From the location of the calling, the client/hero turns and looks back to the present, where he or she was struggling with the threshold. From this location, the client becomes his or her own guardian and self-sponsor, and offers a resource and a message to his or her present self.

7. The client returns to the present, bringing the message and necessary resources from the future position, and transferring them to the present. The client reflects upon how these resources help to further transform the former resistance into a guardian.

8. Taking these resources, the client again walks to the future location on his or her timeline that represents the calling.

RD: A key part of this exercise is a process that we call "self-sponsorship," where you become your own coach, your own guide, your own creative and compassionate leader. As with active centering, we're also going to be engaging the somatic mind. Because, as Stephen was saying earlier, your ordinary ego mind isn't enough for your hero's journey.

We're also going to be physicalizing aspects of your journey, by using a physical timeline to represent its path. The client will move to some place on their timeline where he or she feels resistances or doubts about being able to continue on the journey; a place where you feel there is something holding you back or stopping you. Not so much something outside of you, but something inside that's stopping you. We want to emphasize that these self-doubts and resistances are essential parts of every journey. Every hero has second thoughts. Jesus had second thoughts. "Is this really what I want to do? Are you really asking me to do this?" So we want to appreciate the presence of these doubts, and see how they can positively contribute to the journey.

SG: In his roadmap of the hero's journey, Joseph Campbell calls this "the refusal of the call." Nobody just walks their transformational path without major obstacles, internal and external. You're *supposed* to hit these places of resistances. You're *supposed to* hit these places of doubt. They are telling you that you're approaching a threshold, you're about to take a step to a point beyond where you've gone before. So look forward to that! But at the same time, train yourself to skillfully work with these inevitable points on the journey.

RD: These doubts are often not logical or verbal. They may appear somatically as body tension, contractions, or fears. Very often these doubts are not really clear, logical thoughts. They may arise as a felt sense in the body of something that is stopping you or holding you back. So we need to work with the resistances in the body as well as the mind.

Demonstration with Vincent

RD: So I would like to ask for a volunteer, someone who would like to explore how to transform these resistances. *(A number of hands list, Robert selects one man.)* What is your name?

Man: Vincent.

RD: Vincent, I'd like to have you start by telling us a little bit about your journey, your calling.

Vincent: I discovered in the last exercise that my journey began when I was around 11 or 12. I was in the Boy Scouts. I remember hearing the message of Baden Powell, the founder of the Scouts. The message was that we have to leave the world in a better place than we found it. That message really hit home for me, partly because I had seen a lot of injustice when I was a small boy.

RD: Yes. So you feel your calling is about leaving the world a better place than you found it? And promoting justice, and transforming injustice?

Vincent: Above all, being a role model; showing others how it's possible to live life.

RD: As Gandhi said, you have to be the change you want to see in the world . . . Good . . . I'm curious, Vincent, do you have a kind of a symbol for yourself, something that might represent this calling?

Vincent: Many.

RD: I'd like to ask you to select a symbol that most touches you. *(Vincent looks up and away, searching for the symbol.)* And rather than look up there, I'd like to ask you to feel into your body. Let the image come from within your bodily wisdom and intelligence. *(Vincent closes eyes, develops reverie.)* That's it. Feel what's there. What is your symbol?

Vincent: *(Opens eyes)* Can I draw it?

SG: Sure.

(Vincent draws a peace symbol onto the flipchart.)

RD: So, like a bringer of peace. What would be your name for this?

Vincent: Justice.

RD: Justice. OK. Justice is the calling. And are there specific situations, specific contexts where it's important for you to bring your calling?

Vincent: I think the most important is the day-to-day life situations.

RD: Yes . . .

Vincent: In everyday relationships.

RD: So, this part of your calling is about bringing peace, bringing justice into day-to-day relationships.

Vincent: Yes, through small acts.

RD: Through small acts. And for you to be an example, a role model for doing that.

Vincent: Yes, that's it.

RD: Good. *(To audience)* So we begin by identifying the call, and the contexts in which it is relevant. Next, we will identify the resistance to the call. What is the demon, or the threshold? To do that, we're not going to ask the ego-intellect to talk about it. Instead, we're going to create a timeline.

(To Vincent) I'm curious, Vincent, when you think about your past and your future, would your future be that way *(pointing to the left)* or that way *(pointing to the right)*?

Vincent: *(Pointing to the right.)* That way.

RD: Your future is to your right and your past is to your left.

(Vincent nods.)

So I'd like to have you stand in your present and face your future. *(Vincent positions himself accordingly.)*

(To audience) And now as the coach, the sponsor, I want to help Vincent put himself into his experience of his hero's journey. *(To Vincent)* So in front of you is your calling . . . the calling represented by that peace sign *(pointing to flipchart)*. The calling is to bring justice and peace into the world, to the small details in everyday life.

And behind you is your past, including the injustices you experienced as a child. They are part of what brings you on the journey. We also know that journey ahead will probably have challenges – the demons and also the thresholds. So that in order to fully live your calling, you will sometimes be challenged with experiences that carry some discomfort, unfamiliarity, or uncertainty. And even though I know and I can see that you are deeply called by this vision, there may be doubts or resistances. *(Vincent nods.)* I see that you recognize that. So I am curious, how do you sense these doubts and resistances? Do you have a felt sense in your body?

(Vincent pauses, looks deeply absorbed.)

What can you share about your experience of those resistances? How and where do you feel them somatically?

Vincent: Here. *(Touches shoulders.)*

RD: Here? *(Robert touches Vincent's shoulders.)* OK, I'd like to ask Stephen to join us now, and his role will be to become that resistance for Vincent. Vincent, you'll have to teach Stephen how to become that resistance. So, for example, would he be pushing on your shoulders? *(Stephen presses down on Vincent's shoulders.)* Or would he be pulling on them? *(Stephen pulls Vincent by the shoulders.)* And as you sense each particular way that he engages with you, notice whether it fits or not to how you actually experience it. So you may say, "No, not quite like that . . . a little more like this . . . yes, that's it!" Your body will now teach both you and Stephen how you experience the resistance. So Stephen will become your demon, in the service of your journey. And don't worry, he's really good at this! *(Laughter.)*

SG: I've been serving as Robert's personal demon for many years. *(Laughter.)* But seriously, Vincent, would I be in front of you or behind you?

Vincent: *(Pauses.)* Behind me.

SG: *(Stepping behind Vincent)* And would I be pressing down like this? *(Stephen starts pushing and pulling Vincent in different ways.)* Or like this?

Vincent: Yes, like that! And push harder down with the thumb! *(Some laughter.)*

RD: It's a little funny to do this, but it's very interesting to discover that your body knows exactly how it feels.

(To audience) So this is the first step. Teach your partner to take on the resistance for you, so it's differentiated from you.

(To Vincent) Now the other thing I'd like you to attune to is, would Stephen be saying any words to you as the demon. Perhaps "Stop!" or "No!" or "You're not allowed." What message does the demon give you?

Vincent: Many.

RD: Yes. What kind of messages?

Vincent: Impotence.

RD: Yes, something about impotence. What would the actual words be?

Vincent: "You can't do this by yourself!"

RD: Yes, the message is, "You can't do this by yourself!" So now I'm going to ask Stephen as the demon to apply both the physical expression of pressing down on your shoulder from behind, while adding those words.

SG: *(Presses down on Vincent's shoulders) You can't do this by yourself! You can't . . . do this . . . by yourself . . . You can't do this by yourself!*

RD: OK, let's stop for a few moments. Does that feel right, Vincent? Is that what happens to you?

Vincent: Yes. And what happens is I resist very strongly.

SG: This is the typical thing that happens for each of us when we encounter the demon. We forget what our deeper intention is – in Vincent's case it is, "I really want to bring peace and justice into the world" – and lose ourselves to the negative energy. We lose our deeper vision, and everything becomes, "Can I destroy this part of me or is it going to destroy me?"

RD: This presence that's trying to stop you is what I called yesterday "the internal terrorist." In Stephen's self-relations model, it's called "possession by aliens."

SG: Which means the presences that alienate you from your center.

RD: Now here's the next step. What I'm going to ask you to do, Vincent, is to change places with Stephen, and you will become your own resistance. So, now you get to torture him for a while. *(Some laughter.)*

SG: And really make sure to step into this fully, become the resistances so you can begin to understand them from within.

RD: So, as Stephen is you, you will hold him down, and say in that harsh tone of voice, "No! You can't do this!" Really sense and become the energy of the resistance.

Vincent: *(Steps behind Stephen and places hands on his shoulder, pushing down.)* You can't do it by yourself! You can't do it by yourself You can't do this by yourself!

(Stephen shows discomfort.)

(To Stephen) Are you OK?

SG: Yes, I'm just interested in feeling what this is like from this position. I'm OK, you're doing great.

RD: OK, Vincent, I'm going to ask you to continue to do this, but this time in a slower, more centered way. We're going to see what the positive intention of the demon is by adding centering and presence to the resistance pattern. Remember our formula yesterday: *symptom plus centering equals resource.* It applies to the demons as well. When you can become your resistance and shift it into a centered state, its expression will begin to become more positive and helpful.

OK, Vincent. Do you understand? Are you ready?

Vincent: Yes . . . *(Becomes more centered, more gentle, as he connects again with Stephen.)* You can't do it alone! You can't do it alone . . . *(Stephen sighs deeply and relaxes.)* . . . You can't do it alone.

RD: Good, let's pause again. And Vincent, as you do that to "Vincent," what do you sense as the intention of this demon?

Vincent: *(Looks touched)* Connection.

RD: Connection. It's very interesting – even though this resistance looks very negative, it's trying to make a connection.

SG: That's so very interesting. That's exactly what I was feeling during that time. I felt like I was getting the best massage I've had in some time. *(Some laughter.)* And you heard me take that sigh . . .

Vincent: Yes, it's very interesting to me.

RD: Remember what we said: uncentered energies are problems; centered energies become resources and solutions. So we're going to do one more step here. Stephen is going to stay here, still representing Vincent in the present time of his timeline. And I'm going to ask Vincent to step into his future. *(Robert walks Vincent to a future space on the timeline.)* And Vincent, as you stand here in your future, I'm going to ask you to again connect with your life calling. *(Vincent smiles and nods.)* And notice that you, as represented by Stephen, are still back there in the place representing the present moment. From here in your future, let yourself become the symbol of peace that you identified earlier. *(Vincent breathes deeply.)* That's right. Just like in the exercise yesterday, let yourself breathe deeply and become the full realization of that calling. *(Vincent seems deeply absorbed in the process.)* So here in your future, you are already fully living your calling.

Vincent: *(Smiles)* It's a great feeling . . .

RD: I can see this touches you very much. That's a really great thing to allow to develop deeply inside of yourself. And as you do that, I'm going to ask you to become your own sponsor. And looking back through time, seeing yourself back in what is the present today, including the resistance that we were just exploring, what is the message and what is the resource that you need to bring back to yourself and to that resistance?

Vincent: As for resources, I would say the ones we explored yesterday in terms of flexible energy and relaxation. I need a lot of relaxation.

RD: Mmmm . . . so you need flexible energy and lots of relaxation for yourself. That's good to know. And what would be your message to the resistance that is trying to make connection?

Vincent: Hmmm . . . gratitude for what it has done for me . . . and a sense that I can continue my life without it.

RD: Without it? Or can you transform it into something else? Because its intention is to keep you connected.

Vincent: *(Tears in eyes)* Yes . . . yes . . . yes.

RD: Yes, it's very important.

Vincent: *(Looking touched and a bit confused)* You mean, I can live with that?

RD: Yes, I think so. Because if you try to get rid of it, you could also lose its intention and power to keep you connected.

Vincent: *(Strong emotion of release, breathing deeply)* Yes.

SG: So, you can see what's happening for Vincent is the transformational shift where a person realizes, *What I always saw as my problem is actually a crucial resource!*

RD: The demon becomes a guardian. The resistance becomes the guardian of connection. But to become that, it needs another way to express itself. And that's what you can bring from the future self. *(To Vincent)* You were saying that part of the resource is relaxation. Is there another resource that you could bring to the resistance that actually helps it to become a guardian of your connection?

Vincent: I began aikido recently. And I'm going to continue . . .

RD: What's the biggest resource from aikido that you have learned?

Vincent: That of transforming negative energy into another, more positive form.

RD: Yes, good. So what I'd like to ask you to do from this future space – where you are your own sponsor and feeling that sense of your calling – is to see if you can bring that message back in time to the resistance, and be curious about how you can give that resource to the resistance. To see if you can transform that negative energy into a guardian. Make sure the resistance keeps the intention of connection even as it transforms into a guardian. OK?

Vincent: Yes.

RD: So go ahead and center and then really sense the positive intention of the resistance and the resources of flexible energy and relaxation. Bring these resources back across time to the part of you that had been expressing itself as resistance. *(Robert and Vincent walk back to where Stephen is standing, representing Vincent in the present.)*

And as those positive energies and intentions become absorbed by that resistant part, notice how it begins to change that part. *(Vincent steps back into the location in which he had been acting out his own resistance.)*

And from that transformed place, go ahead and connect with Stephen again, who is representing you in your present. Notice what you would do differently in terms of connecting with yourself there. With what energy do you touch him?

(Vincent gently places his hands on Stephen's shoulder. They both connect with deep non-verbal rapport.) And as you feel that new connection as a guardian, what are the words that come? Do you still say, "You can't do it alone," or are there different words that are there to be spoken?

Vincent: *(Deeply absorbed with Stephen)* You can relax. I am with you now.

RD: Yes, it's OK now. You have connection.

Vincent: Be patient. It's OK to be patient.

RD: Great. That's really beautiful, Vincent.

Vincent: Yes, it is.

RD: Now we're going to switch again, and Stephen is going to take on this new role of the guardian, and you be in the place of yourself in the present. And just let yourself receive and absorb the sponsorship from Stephen as he becomes what used to be the resistance that has transformed now into a guardian.

SG: *(Places hands gently on Vincent's shoulder, both are deeply absorbed.)* It's OK, Vincent . . .You can relax now . . . You don't have to do this alone. I'm with you now . . . And I'm here to support you every step of the way.

RD: *(With gentle voice) You can be patient, Vincent.*

SG: *You can be calm, Vincent. You can be patient.*

(Vincent breathes deeply, integrating the guardian messages.)

RD: And now, Vincent, I'm going to ask you to go to the very beginning of your timeline. *(Stephen and Vincent walk slowly to the beginning of the timeline.)* And I'm going to ask you to very slowly, very mindfully, walk through your whole timeline, bringing that presence and connection to every point on your hero's journey. And Stephen will walk with you every step of the way, in the role of your guardian, to help you connect to relaxation and self-love at every point. You may feel like stopping briefly at certain points, where you sense you really can be helped by integrating the resources you are bringing from your future into any past events in your life.

(Vincent and Stephen begin to walk together, Stephen's hands gently on Vincent's shoulders. The journey through the timeline takes several minutes, with Vincent periodically pausing at points to integrate resources into that point of his life.)

(To audience) And as I think most of you can see, as he continues on his path, Vincent is going deeper into his connection with his resources and his calling. So hopefully this gives you a sense of how you can transform your demons into guardians, your resistances into resources. And you can see how inside the demon or resistance is something very, very important for a person's wholeness; it just needs to be centered, sponsored, and integrated. It would have been a terrible thing for Vincent to have dissociated from that part of himself. As he continues on his journey, he's really going to need that part – no longer a demon, but transformed through centering and sponsorship into a guardian. This is one of the major challenges on the hero's journey.

(Stephen and Vincent complete the journey through the timeline.)

Vincent: That was great. *(Nods very strongly.)*

RD: And just to complete the exercise, I'm curious, Vincent, what is it that you have really learned the most in this exercise? What is it that you most want to remember about this learning?

(Vincent looks deeply absorbed, without words, still integrating.)

Anything you would say?

(Vincent breathes very deeply, has big smile.)

Ah, yes, breath is one thing. Thanks for sharing that. I like that.

SG: Anything else?

Vincent: I think it is very, very deep feeling I have . . . I am without words, it is such a deep experience.

RD: *(To audience)* I think you can obviously see that there is an incredibly different energetic quality in Vincent now. Earlier on in the process, there was a big difference between the energy of the calling and the energy of the resistance. Now there is a beautiful integration. The resistance has shifted from a negative sponsor to a positive sponsor.

Thank you, Vincent, for sharing a piece of your hero's journey with us. We need your help for this calling of creating a world to which people want to belong.

(Vincent exchanges hugs with Robert and Stephen, then receives thunderous applause as he leaves the stage. As he goes back to his chair, some friends jump up and deeply embrace him with great excitement. Laughter and more applause fills the room.)

Summary: Transforming Inner Resistance through Self-Sponsorship

SG: So you can see Vincent is discovering more guardians on his journey almost immediately. *(Laughter.)* We hope you can see in this exercise one of the major points of the Generative Cognitive Self, namely, that opposites or polarities are always part of a deeper unity. But when you initially encounter them, they may be in an adversarial relationship. The typical response is to label one "good," the other "bad," and then you take sides, thinking, "Well, this is the good side – he just wants to get on with his hero's journey – and this part is bad, bad, bad!" And when you lock them into a violent opposition like that, you immediately lose the possibility of Generative Self, because violence can never be a generative solution. It destroys, rather than creates.

RD: In fact we can see that consciousness actually degenerates when we split the self into these oppositional parts. You can see how much energy is lost in the self fighting itself. All the life energy you need for your hero's journey gets drained away in this fight against the "inner enemy."

SG: And if you are labeled as the "bad self," you feel completely unacknowledged. The sense is, "I'm bad, I shouldn't be there." And you begin to act accordingly. So just by shifting to sensing "the other" with curiosity and positive intention, and dropping into a centered somatic state, you can begin to explore, *what is this part trying to balance in me? What is it giving me that I'm needing or leaving out?* Carl Jung used to say that "the unconscious is always compensatory for the biases of the conscious."

RD: Which means that it's always trying to balance the conscious mind, often by bringing in the opposite or complementary energy. We could see with Vincent, where the resistant part was bringing a mature guardian presence to complete the beautiful childlike energy that he was first standing in. But because that complementary energy was not centered, it became expressed in a negative way.

So to review the exercise, you are creating a physical timeline for your life. It represents that you are on a journey – you are on this great life path. Then you stand in your present and sense the way in which you are you presently experiencing resistances or doubts on your journey; that is, anything that is holding you back, trying to stop you from achieving your calling. Sense it in terms of its somatic energies: Do you feel it in your shoulders? Is it tense, or pushing, or blocking? Just notice how the resistance is expressing in your body. Then the coach is going to help you to physicalize the resistant energy by becoming the resistance.

SG: As the coach, you are saying, *teach me how to be this resistance for you, so that you can learn from it.*

RD: After you teach your coach to physically be your resistance, add the words that go with that resistance.

SG: What's the core negative internal dialogue? What are the hypnotic inductions that put you into a deep negative trance, such as: *You have no right to this. People are going to destroy you. Who the hell do you think you are? You're not good enough! You're going to fail!*

RD: Once you have established the "demon" pattern, then the client switches positions and enters the energy of the resistance, becoming his or her own resistance.

SG: These are the core pieces of sponsorship. Accept the negative pattern, join it, hold it with a curiosity of, *I'm sure this makes sense. I'm sure that it has a positive intention. I want to find out what it is.*

RD: Once the client has taken on the demon energy in its negative form, then the client centers and attunes to himself or herself before doing it again, this time more slowly and with presence. Let it become part of a creative dance that you're exploring, in order to discover the positive intention of the resistance. It's strange, but very often the expression is actually creating the opposite of its intention, because they're very often expressed initially in their negative form, such as, *Don't get hurt. Don't fail. Don't think you can do this by yourself!* Or the non-verbal tone is negative, even if the verbal message is positive. In both cases, the somatic mind receives a negative energy or suggestion. It's an old principle from hypnosis that the unconscious doesn't process negatives very well. I mean, if I was trying to non-verbally communicate to you, "Don't fall down," how would I do it? *(Robert starts shaking his head "no" and falling down. Laughter.)*

SG: Sometimes this can be really funny. I was on a meditation retreat in India a month ago, and for one particular meditation it was emphasized that there should be complete quiet, like you could hear a pin drop. Well, one day, a new woman was giving the instruction, and she was a bit authoritarian. She said rather strongly, "There will be no coughing in the room allowed at any time! You must not cough! If you cough, you must immediately leave the room." Guess what immediately began to happen? A coughing contagion began to break out. Each time, she would turn to the new transgressor and shout, "You! No coughing! You must leave immediately!" So they drag out this person, but the people around started coughing. It quickly reached a breaking point! *(Laughter.)*

RD: So you can see the positive intention was to develop quietness, but paradoxically, the opposite result was generated. So in order to realize a positive intention, you need to have a positive version of the statement. That's what you're discovering by entering into the state of the resistance.

Then you're going to become a self-sponsor by stepping into your future (on the timeline), and sensing that you have realized the calling already in that place. Take a few moments to sense, what is the resource and the message you can bring back to your present, especially to your "resistance"? As you do that, notice what begins to transform in the resistance, and in your relationship with it. When you return to your present self and the resistance, you are first bringing the resource as well as a new positive message to the resistance in order to replace the old negative form.

You then step back into your present self, and the coach becomes the resistance that has now transformed into a guardian. You will be able to feel in yourself how this core internal relationship now becomes positive. All of the energy that has been fighting and resisting, on both sides, now becomes integrated and available for the more important task of living the journey. Finally, the coach goes back to the beginning of the timeline with the client, and you slowly walk through your timeline, bringing these new awarenesses and resources to every part of your life.

Find a partner and practice this now.

Integrating the "Shadow"

SG: We hope you can begin to sense that this process of transforming your resistances and your shadows is one of the greatest challenges of the hero's journey, and one of the most important skills of the Generative Cognitive Self. This involves the ability to sense the resource inside the problem, the jewel inside the disturbance. Again, we want to emphasize that perhaps the most important gift of human consciousness is the capacity to transmute suffering and sorrow into happiness and wholeness.

RD: The key to this process is to start with centering. Before you trust your cognitive mind, make sure you are fully connected to your somatic intelligence. When we lose our centers, it is easy to become overwhelmed and "possessed" by negative energies. Negative fields can be very powerful.

I found it really interesting, for example, that when the American soldiers who had tortured inmates at the Abu Ghraib prison in Iraq were put on trial, their attorneys brought in many people who knew these soldiers – parents, childhood friends, old bosses, or teachers. And each of them would say, "He's not a bad person," "He was not violent or sadistic as a child." And I suspect that these testimonies were true. So it becomes an interesting question: How can a seemingly normal person become a "monster"? We would suggest that if you get into a situation where you lose your center, the bigger archetypal energy of the field can easily take you over. And if that energy is negative, you can end up doing some really nasty things.

The center is the important counterbalance to the field. If you can keep your center, then the energy of the field becomes humanized through you. But if you lose your center, it's easy to get lost and consumed in playing out the confusion or violence of an uninte-grated field. And it's "not me" that's really doing it; I'm a pawn in a half-human field that's playing out. But when you can keep your center, you can maintain your human presence and begin to positively influence the field.

SG: Another way of talking about this is that when we center, we are free to let go of rigidly holding on to fixed frames, so we can have more clarity, flexibility, and wisdom in our experience and behavior. A center gives you, among many things, a stabilizing of consciousness, so you can stay open and curious. And until we can let go of rigid attachment to our linguistic frames, we will not be able to sense and realize the deeper underlying positive energies in a problem pattern. You'll only be able to see it and respond to it as a problem. What we're exploring here is how to sense the positive seeds of goodness and gifts within a disturbing energy, and then be able to interact with it in order to make that transformation.

I had a guy come to see me. He was a prototypical engineer – living from his neck up. His wife was a lawyer and had the same approach to life – complete dissociation from somatic energies. He said, "I have a confession to make. I'm a sexual pervert." I said, "What does that mean?" He said, "I watch internet pornography for five, six, seven hours a day." When I share that with people, there is usually a kind of emotional jolt like that's a "socially illegal," "bad" energy. And so how could you possibly even consider accepting that? How could that possibly be a resource, an expression of goodness and human gifts?

Well, if you're looking at it just from the surface form, it's impossible to see it as a resource. When I first heard his description, I lost my center. So when he asked, "What should I do?" I found myself possessed by Father McCarthy, who was my old, alcoholic Irish Catholic parish priest. *(Laughter.)* And the good Father was urging me, with veins popping out of his neck, to tell this client that he must take five cold showers a day, and say 100 Hail Mary's and 50 Our Father's every time he felt an urge. *(More laughter.)* I tried to explain that my client was Jewish. *(Laughter.)* But it didn't matter – Father McCarthy has the same intervention for everybody.

So that's a time to say, "I can't get out of the negative box. I need to center so I can take a fresh look." That's where we center, then organize our cognitive process around the questions: What's trying to wake up here? What's trying to heal? With the pornography, it became very clear: his conscious mind was insisting that life be lived from the neck up, but his unconscious was insisting that things were much more interesting than that!

And of course, many people will say, "Well, you just can't accept and encourage his perversion!" Father McCarthy lives deeply within each of us! *(Laughter.)* But again, we're not encouraging the surface structure of watching pornography; we're interested in the generative goodness of the deep structure of his sexuality. And in sponsorship we realize that if we can connect with that deeper structure, many new and more positive surface structures can emerge. The basic appreciation is: *Wow, this guy has intense sexuality.*

And for 40 years he has tried to get rid of it. But it hasn't worked . . . isn't that great! So let's see how we can positively sponsor it so that additional ways of experiencing and expressing it can emerge.

So I said to him, "I don't know exactly how I can help you, but I know there is no psychotherapy in the world, no hypnotic trance that will take away the fact that *you have an amazing sexuality.*" He looked startled and interested, and said, "Yes, but I'm ashamed." So here's where you begin your sponsorship. You center, receive that energy deeply and without judgment, give it a place inside of you, wipe away any negative conditioning, bless it, then mirror its positive form back to the person.

(Steve speaks in a very gentle, intense, focused way) Yes, I see that as a sexual being, that you have a lot of shame . . . I see that, and it's OK . . . It's good to know that that's there . . . And who else are you as a sexual being?

He flashed a shy smile and said, "I'm really horny!" I responded in the same way: center, absorb it, give it a place of honor, wipe away any negative conditioning, bless it, reflect it back. *Yes, I see that as a sexual being, you are really horny . . . (Pause) . . . And who else are you as a sexual being?*

We did this for about seven or eight rounds. Each time he responded with a different dimension of his sexual identity: *I'm scared . . . I like to look at naked pictures . . . I'm confused . . . I'm a man* . . . Each time I received it and fed it back in that same way. At some point, this amazing shift occurred. Perhaps you have seen this in people, when they really touch something deep inside of themselves – a beauty begins to radiate from them. I could see it. I could feel it. I was touched deeply by it. This indicates he's found his center – he's no longer dissociated from the energy. So I said to him: *Why not close your eyes for a few minutes and just let yourself go on a healing journey, allowing your deepest wisdom mind to integrate all of these important dimensions of your sexual identity into a new, more satisfying pattern.*

This was a great experience for him. When he returned the next week, I asked: "How's it going?" He said, "Well, it was a really strange, interesting week! I didn't have any urges all week to watch pornography. But all week, my wife and I fought . . . *(Laughter.)* And the thing is, we never fight!"

They had been living, literally, on opposite sides of the house, icebergs passing in the night. And all of a sudden they were coming together with heat and passion. You can see the sexual energy is now being redirected from the pornography to the marriage. And so I said, "It sounds like it would be a good thing to invite your wife in so the two of you can work this out together."

He replied, "Oh, I'm sure she wouldn't come."

I said, "Just tell her that I said we are going to discuss the future of her sexual fulfillment." *(Laughter.)* She came. *(Laughter.)* And I did the rest of the work together with them as a couple, seeing how that passion and sexual energy could be expressed between them in positive, satisfying ways.

Transforming "Good Self" and "Bad Self" into Positive Complementarities

SG: So in thinking about this case, we can see that we started with a conflict between two sides, just like we were exploring in the last exercise. He presents with this pattern: his presenting self is a logical, "in the head" engineer. That's his ego ideal, what we are calling here the "good self." We put these in quotes, because we're not saying that this side is actually "good"; it's the way it's being framed by the person. And yet he has this other self, which is presenting with the form of "addiction to pornography." And this self is presented as the "bad self." The usual request is to get rid of the "bad self" so the "good self" can live happily ever after. What we're saying is that these two selves are two sides of the same coin, that each completes each other, that they are part of a deeper unity. One of the main challenges in the hero's journey is to create a space so that these complementary parts can move from a mutually exclusive clashing to a mutually inclusive balance. To do that, we need to get out of the head, get down into the center, and then open a field beyond the opposites that will allow an energetic sensing of the complementarity.

This is what we were doing in the last exercise, and we're looking now to generalize into a model of how "good self" versus "bad self" can become a Generative Self of positive complementarities. So again, you can transform the inner fight that sucks up all your attention and energies to an inner harmony that realizes a deep intelligence and openness to the greater journey of creative living.

Exercise: "Good Self / Bad Self" Identity

SG: To give you a sense of this transformational model, Robert and I want to demonstrate and then have you practice a simple but very powerful exercise. It's called the "Good Self/Bad Self" exercise.

1. Partners non-verbally center, extend into relational connection.

2. Partner A says, "What I want you (or the world) to see is that I am (good self)_____."

    "What I don't want you (or the world) to see is that I am also (bad self) _____."

3. Partner B listens, gives non-verbal sponsorship, then says:
    - I see that you are (good self).
    - I also see you are (bad self).
    - I see you are both.
    - I see you are much, much more.

4. Partner B speaks two statements, and A feeds back.

5. Partners alternate three to five rounds, taking time to speak, touch, make visible, and release each truth.

Demonstration with Stephen and Robert

(Robert and Stephen sit down opposite each other.)

SG: In this exercise we will be exploring: Where is the wholeness of the self split? As long as a split occurs, the hero's journey will be impossible, for the journey requires wholeness of being.

RD: To begin the exercise, we are going to do what by now is hopefully becoming an ongoing practice for you: center, and then open into the field to make a connection with your partner. So each of us starts to *drop in our center . . . and relax . . . in order to bring the mind and body into alignment.*

SG: *And as we settle in . . . settle down . . . and connect to center . . . we then open outwards . . . while maintaining the center . . . get a sense of connection with our partner . . . while remaining equally connected with ourselves. And as before, we'll each nod our head when we've completed that hook-up to self and* other . . . *(Steve and Robert both nod their heads.)* Next, Person A, that will be me, is going to make two simple statements: *What I want you to see about me is that I am _____.*

RD: And just let a statement come up which expresses your "good self" or "ideal self."

SG: Don't think about it beforehand. Don't break connection to think about it. Stay in this connection and see which identity part comes forward. So I could say: *Robert, what I want the world to see about me is that . . . I'm an accepting person.*

RD: And I am receiving these words, letting them touch me and creating a space to hold them.

SG: Then I make a second statement: *What I don't want the world to see about me is that I am . . . also critical.*

RD: And I also receive that, and hold it equally with the other; without judgment, without trying to fix anything, without needing to assure my partner of anything. Just be with them both, holding them both with respect and kindness. To do that, you need to receive them into your center. Make room for them to rest within you, as guests of honor. Only when you feel you have experientially received them, then you're going respond with four statements. First, I say: *Stephen, I really see, I really sense that you really are an accepting person and I honor that.*

SG: And I take that in, breathe it in as deeply as I can.

RD: And then I say: *And, Stephen, I also really get, I understand that there are times when you're quite critical. (Stephen takes a breath and nods.)* Then a third statement: *Stephen, I see that you are both an accepting person and a critical person.* And then a fourth statement: *And Stephen, I see that you are much, much more.*

So those four statements are: *I see that you are X, I see that you are Y, I see that you are both X and Y,* and *I see that you are much, much more.*

SG: In an important sense, these represent the four points of attention in a conversation for change. They are (1) the goal ("good self"), (2) the problem ("bad self"), (3) the relation between them, and (4) the generative field beyond them.

And one of the main skills in coaching and therapy is sensing which to focus on in any given moment. A generative conversation flows among these different focal points.

RD: So after we do it one way, then person B, that's me, will say: *Stephen, what I want the world to see about me is X. What I don't want the world to see about me is Y.* And then Stephen will mirror that back in the four statements.

SG: That would be one round of the exercise. We'll demonstrate two rounds here, and ask you to do it for 4–5 rounds. It often takes a few rounds to slip deeply into it. And remember, when you're speaking, the point is not to transmit intellectual information; it is to access and share the experiential energy of each identity statement. This is a practice for touching the center of a core identity, then lifting it from its center into a field of connection.

So if I say (places hand over mouth, looks away and mutters), *Robert, I don't want the world to see that I'm critical* . . . That's not the exercise. That might access the energy of it, but keeps it stuck inside. It's only when you can release what is in your center into the field, that healing and potency occur. Who was it that said, "Wherever two or more are gathered in my name, healing shall occur?" Was it George Bush, or Robert Dilts? *(Laughter.)* OK, it was Jesus, but Jesus actually modeled his life after Robert. *(Laughter.)*

RD: I don't know if Stephen was speaking from his good self or bad self there . . . *(Laughter.)* But maybe we should find out. So let's settle back in . . . and take a few moments . . . and then Stephen will begin whenever he's ready.

SG: *Robert, what I want the world to see about me is . . . my happiness. What I don't want the world to see is . . . my hopelessness.*

RD: *Stephen, I really see . . . it's wonderful to see . . . your great happiness. And I also really acknowledge . . . and am really touched by . . . your hopelessness. I see that you are both . . . happy . . . and hopeless. And I see and sense that you are also so much more at the same time.*

(Stephen closes his eyes for a few moments, breathes deeply, hand on heart.)

And Stephen, what I really want the world to see about me is that I am . . . an open, capable spirit. And Stephen, what I don't want the world to see about me . . . is that . . . I can be lost . . . like a child.

SG: *Yes, Robert . . . I see . . . your spirit is open . . . and highly capable. And I see . . . the younger presence that can sometimes feel lost. And it's really nice to be able to feel both of them, at the same time. And also to sense this amazing space in you . . . that's beyond those parts.*

(Robert closes his eyes for a few moments, breathing deeply and touching his center.)

And Robert, I want you to see my love . . . And I don't want you to see . . . my pain.

RD: *Stephen, I really see your love . . . It's very beautiful. And Stephen, I also see . . . and I'm very deeply moved by . . . your pain. I see both the love and the pain, existing at the same time. And I also see in you . . . so much more . . . Much, much more.*

(Pause as Stephen closes his eyes and receives.)

Stephen, what I want you and the world to see in me . . . is a big, generous heart. And what I don't want you and the world to see . . . is the hurt that I've brought to people that I love . . . by following my heart.

(Pause as both Robert and Stephen breathe together in rapport.)

SG: *I really see . . . the open, generous heart. And also . . . that presence in you that's connected to others feeling pain . . . from your behavior. And I really see and support both of them . . . at the same time. And I feel and see that much larger space . . . within you and around you . . . that is able to hold both of them . . . and much, much more.*

(Stephen and Robert connect silently, then place their hands together to bow with respect and love toward each other. The audience is very touched by the exchange.)

OK, that's the exercise. You can see, it's a very simple exercise. What makes it deep and meaningful is your willingness and ability to touch and share and bless the deeper energies underlying the words. Notice how slow we went, how much pausing we allowed to let the non-verbal energy of the words open.

RD: We did two rounds. Go ahead and find a partner and do four or five rounds. Remember, do the centering and relational connecting first. Then let the words ride the waves of breath and feeling. Touch it, speak it, release, allow it to be held, receive it back from your partner. Let that take you deeper into a sacred space within yourself.

Sponsoring Archetypal Patterns of Transformation

SG: Doing this exercise, you can feel how you can fairly quickly find these core parts of your identity, and how they may be opposing each other needlessly. To be generative, you need to let go of the fixed "good" versus "bad" distinctions, and instead sense the challenge as sponsoring all the different aspects of the psyche, humanizing them into a sort of "mandala" of self, where each part belongs to a larger whole. It's the wholeness that makes for the Generative Self, and that wholeness cannot be realized if you have locked some parts of you into the "bad self" camp. This is one of the critical points we are making.

So one of the main tasks of sponsorship is to awaken some not-yet-human energy or pattern into a full human consciousness. Again, the notion is that what the unconscious gives you is only half human. It takes human presence to fully humanize it. That's where you come in! This human presence is originally outside of you – family, teachers, significant others – but as we mature, our capacity for self-sponsorship becomes more available. Without your presence, you'll stay lost in the unconscious, never becoming fully human.

In making something fully human, we distinguish two parts of an experience – the *archetypal* and the *personal*. The archetypal refers to a ancestral pattern developed over many generations, which is a deep structure for human beings in a given challenge. For example, we each face the challenge of learning to love, to find communion with someone or something beyond ourselves. Luckily, we are not the first to face this challenge. *Every human being throughout time has faced such challenges.* So your grandparents, and their grandparents, and their grandparents, all the way back, have faced this challenge to create communion. The idea of archetypes is that each time a person has such an experience, a very faint trace of that experience drops into the generative field. And over a long period of time, the many, many different traces begin to constellate into a general pattern that represents the ancestral "deep structure" or "blueprint" for achieving communion. Then, whenever a person faces this challenge, especially when it challenges them beyond where they've been personally in their individual journey, the generative field accesses this archetypal pattern as a resource for you to meet the challenge.

But as we are emphasizing, the archetype itself is general and could be individually expressed in an infinite number of ways. You can experience and express communion in an infinite number of ways. So the challenge of the individual is to attune to the archetypal patterns that are active, and then humanize them by expressing them in a unique way that is best for that individual person. If you don't do this, you will either live without the energy and intelligence of the generative ancestral intelligence, or you will be overwhelmed and governed by these patterns, losing your individual self in the process. Jung called this "inflation of the archetype."

So we hope you can sense from this, there is a difference between the archetypal level and the personal level. And one of the tasks of the generative cognitive mind is to sponsor the archetypal patterns, translating them into personally helpful and meaningful forms. This is what we'd like to explore in the next exercise.

Exercise: Moving through Archetypes of Transition

The following exercise applies the systemic NLP processes of spatial sorting, somatic syntax, and the concept of characterological adjectives to some common archetypes, and is drawn from the work of Carol Pearson (and Judith DeLozier) as a way to examine key stages in our development. It can be used to help track and manage the cycles of transition which make up our lives. It is organized around the archetype of the "dragon," which represents something huge, largely unknown, and potentially dangerous. Some common dragons in the life path of our species would include issues such as death, adolescence, old age, menopause, career change, retirement, loss, and other major life transitions. The other archetypes involved in the process symbolize the various stages of our relationship with the mysterious and dangerous dragon.

1. Define the dragon. Identify the life transition issue you are confronting. This can include key elements of the context or environment relating to the transition, such as the reactions of significant others or problematic details concerning the circumstances surrounding the transition.

2. Create a spatial anchor for the dragon and spatially sort the following archetypes around the dragon in a circle:

   a. The Innocent (doesn't know the dragon exists)
   b. The Orphan (overwhelmed or consumed by the dragon)
   c. The Martyr (persecuted by the dragon)
   d. The Wanderer (avoids the dragon)
   e. The Warrior (fights the dragon)
   f. The Sorcerer (accepts the dragon).

3. From a state of objectivity (meta-position) notice which archetype of transition you currently occupy in relationship to the dragon (Orphan, Warrior, etc.), remembering that in some cultures the dragon represents good luck.

4. Associate into the location representing that archetype and explore the body posture and movements (somatic syntax) associated with that space.

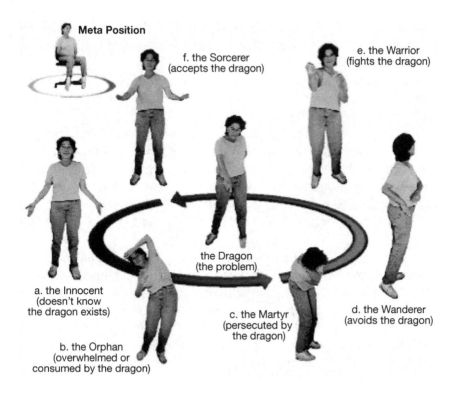

Figure 2.4: Landscape for archetypes of transition.

5. Begin to move through each of the remaining positions in the cycle toward the Sorcerer space (acceptance). For each space, explore the body posture and movements (somatic syntax) associated with that archetype. End the process at the space which feels most appropriate for you to be in at this time in relationship to the dragon. Notice that you can do this having full knowledge of the next steps in your cycle of transition.

6. Return to the meta-position and reflect on what you have discovered and learned.

RD: To do this exercise, you are going to need a little space to make a circle that you'll be moving through. This is an exercise for you to somatically explore, and then cognitively sponsor, your responses to some significant challenge in your life. We will refer to this challenge as the "dragon" that you are facing in your hero's journey, and we will be exploring how you are responding to it at present and how you might respond to it differently. We will be emphasizing different archetypal patterns as typical modes of response.

SG: The archetypal patterns are shown in Figure 2.4. The first is the Innocent, who doesn't know the dragon exists. The second is the Orphan, who is overwhelmed or consumed by the dragon, losing everything. Next is the Martyr, who is persecuted by the dragon. Then the Wanderer, who avoids the dragon and goes somewhere else. Fifth is the Warrior, who opposes and fights the dragon. And finally is the Sorcerer, who is able to accept and transform the dragon into a resource. These archetypes were suggested by Carol Pearson in her book, *The Hero Within: Archetypes We Live By* (1989).

RD: One of the main processes we will be using is called *somatic syntax*, a process that Judith Delozier and I developed. *Soma* is the Greek word for body, so somatic obviously means body, the somatic mind. *Syntax* has to do with language, but not so much the words of the language as the order. Somatic syntax has to do with identifying and exploring the somatic patterns that are being used in a process, and then seeing how their order can be shifted in different ways.

To do this exercise, you move around a circle. In the center of the circle is the dragon, which represents your challenge. Arranged in a circle around the dragon are six spaces for the different archetypes of transition.

So let's first start with the dragon. Create a space where you can, in a moment, step forward into the dragon's lair . . . *And as you sense that space, ask yourself: Where is the dragon at present in your hero's journey? Is it in your intimate relationship? Is it in your job?*

SG: *Is it in your physical health?*

RD: *Is it in your relationship with your children? With your family? Is it in your relationship with your culture?* What is the thing that really frightens you or overwhelms you? When you have identified your challenge, step forward and put yourself into that energy. Then when you're ready, take another step forward into the place of the dragon and feel the energy of the dragon. And as you feel that, let your body take on a physical expression . . . a posture, a gesture, a movement . . . that represents the dragon. Really feel that energy.

Let it not just be an abstract idea – let it be a felt sense. When you really feel it, just anchor it there in that spot, leave it there, and then step back. Breathe, let it go. Move your body a bit, shake it out.

Now we're going to explore how you are relating to that dragon, that challenge, in terms of archetypal responses. As we go through each archetypal pattern, just notice where you are with it at present. There's no right or wrong response, nothing to judge.

So let's start with the archetype of *the Innocent*. Innocence is being unaware, or acting unaware, of the presence of the dragon. Really allow yourself to get that energy of innocence, that childlike energy. How do you sense that in your body?

SG: What and where is the feeling? What posture? What movements? What internal processes go with innocence?

RD: And you might notice whether you are centered or uncentered in the experience of innocence. And what is the relationship between that state of innocence and the dragon? Maybe there is none.

SG: Notice if you are using it in the negative form of dissociating from what you fear. Or in the integrated form of finding a deeper place of openness and non-cynicism.

RD: And if there are any sounds that go with it, it's OK to make those sounds. Just let yourself fully feel into that archetypal pattern, and how it's playing out for you in relationship to this challenge.

When you're ready, you can let go of that. Shake it out a bit.

And go next to the place of *the Orphan*. The Orphan is one who is on his or her own, not belonging anywhere. Find the place inside where you can experience the Orphan. The Orphan is overwhelmed by the dragon. Access that place in you. Let yourself explore and discover the body feelings . . . the posture . . . the movements . . . the basic thoughts and images of your Orphan pattern. If and how you feel abandoned . . . or overwhelmed . . . or lost.

And let yourself explore any movements that go with it, let your body show you. And if there are any sounds, it's OK to let the sounds come out . . . Just become that pattern, letting yourself know it from the inside out.

And then when you're ready, you can let that energy go. Shake it out, shake it off, breathe it out. Brush it off.

The next energy is the archetype of *the Martyr*, the presence that feels persecuted by the dragon. So let yourself open to the experience of the Martyr within you. Let yourself completely feel into that place, that energy. . . The feelings . . . the thoughts . . . the images . . . the posture . . . the movements . . . the verbal phrases . . . the sounds. What is your pattern of martyrdom in relation to this dragon? Just let yourself sense deeply into it, getting to know it.

Perhaps you feel like a victim, but you're angry about it. *It's not right that this should be happening to you!* Sometimes there's a sort of righteous indignation . . . sometimes there's self-pity. Allow whatever is there to awaken into your body . . . and discover, what is its somatic syntax? Sometimes it might be something like pouting . . . sometimes in the form of complaining how you've been misunderstood or mistreated . . . Whatever it is, notice your pattern of responding to the challenge as a Martyr.

Then let it go . . . And again, you can move around . . . Brush it off . . . Breathe it out . . . Come back to center.

The next archetype is *the Wanderer*. The Wanderer avoids the dragon. Pretends it's not there.

SG: Just takes off . . . Goes the other way . . . Goes far, far away.

RD: So really let yourself become the Wanderer. Step into it, sense how it feels . . . How you respond to the dragon from that place . . . feel the posture, the movements, the basic somatic and cognitive patterns associated with it.

SG: You may feel that as you enter a particular archetype, elements of others start to creep in. Just notice that, and keep coming back to attuning to the one in question. Become one with it on a somatic level, while witnessing it on a cognitive level. In generative consciousness, we're always looking for the fluid "both/and" of being both a participant and observer at the same time, each completing the other.

RD: Give it space, allow it expression in you now. What are the movements? What are the sounds? What is the somatic syntax of your Wanderer pattern? And again, when you've really been able to experience and honor it, then you can let it go. Shake it out, brush it off, release it.

The next character is that of *the Warrior*. The Warrior wants to fight the dragon, to defeat the dragon, to aggressively control the dragon . . . to kill the dragon . . . to get rid of it. So find that place of the Warrior within you in respect to this dragon that you've chosen. There might be a movement as well as a posture. There might be a sound. *(Some participants shout "Huh!" "Pooh!" "Shh!" "Ha!" etc.)* OK, there is some good Warrior energy in here. I like that. Now let that Warrior energy go as well, let that flow on through you.

The final archetype in this cycle is *the Sorcerer*. So get access to your magic . . . your ability to transform . . . your ability to receive and accept . . . and to use your alchemy. The Sorcerer accepts the dragon and in doing so transforms the dragon. The Sorcerer is also the shapeshifter. Feel into your capacity to shift from one form to another . . . the movements, the feelings, the energies . . . of the Sorcerer.

And then once again, when you've really been able to access the current relationship of that energy with respect to the dragon . . . then let it go . . . breathe it out . . . free it . . . Come back to center . . . Let go.

OK, that's the first movement through the archetypal circle. Now we're going to make a second trip around the circle to make sure that you sense and claim the gift, the value of each archetypal position.

SG: Again, any pattern, especially an archetypal one, can be equally a problem or a resource, depending on the quality of your relationship with it.

RD: That's why in this second round, we're going to add centering, so you can more deeply sense the value of each archetype, and then see how you can integrate each value into your deeper sense of self. Even now, as you reflect back on the journey you have just made, you may have a sense of the particular archetypes in which you felt more centered, and those where you felt more disconnected or uncentered. Again, any pattern, especially an archetypal pattern, has its gift and its shadow.

SG: Reflect upon which of these archetypal energies you have used most to dissociate from yourself. When faced with your challenges, maybe you just take off as the Wanderer? Or it may be that you pretend that these challenges don't exist? Or perhaps you drown yourself in sorrow with drink, or drugs, or self-pity, or complaining? This first round was an opportunity to witness the typical ways that you abandon yourself. The second round is an opportunity to sense how you can use each archetypal pattern as a resource for transformation.

RD: And in transforming yourself, you of course transform the dragon. So let's begin by centering . . . Breathe . . . feel the soles of your feet . . . your connection to the earth . . .

SG: . . . your kangaroo tail . . .

RD: Loosen your knees . . .

SG: . . . and find your spinal alignment . . .

RD: Allow your breath to be deep and free . . .

SG: . . . and feel the relaxation developing in your muscles . . . even as you relax into centering . . . and then feel your energy opening *from* your center . . . so your awareness also begins to expand outward . . . like you have an energy field all around you . . . even as you settle deeper into a restful presence of center with you.

RD: Feel that sense, as Martha Graham says, that your channel is open in that unique energy that is you . . . here in this room. No need to perform.

SG: As you allow that energy field to open . . . from your center . . . to let it extend all around you . . . realize that you're opening a space . . . that the dragon cannot invade . . . Opening the space within you . . . opening the space all around you . . . So that each of these archetypal patterns . . . can be able to expand your sense of presence . . . pass through your center and bring you more fully into the world.

RD: And then when you're ready and you feel centered . . . allow yourself to move easily into the place of the Innocent . . . and begin to take on the somatic syntax of the Innocent . . . all the time staying connected to your center.

SG: You actually may invite the energy patterns and the information patterns of the innocent to come right through your center . . . as if it is a wholly human passageway . . . where you can indeed . . . *find innocence again.*

RD: And receive the archetypal gifts of the Innocent . . . all of the ancestral learnings and wisdom of innocence . . . the openness to possibilities . . . the childlike wonder and curiosity . . . the fascination with the world.

SG: Welcome it as a gift from beyond . . . receive it through yourself . . . and let it heal you . . . Let it help you regain your wholeness in relationship to this dragon.

RD: It's not an innocence born of ignorance. It is an innocence born of spirit that cannot be damaged or poisoned.

SG: Innocence that comes from self-purification . . . the always present original knowing.

RD: Feel that pureness of your soul, your spirit. And then, as you stay centered, bring the gift of innocence into the place of the Orphan. Allow yourself to move easily, flowingly, as the Orphan. Allow yourself to open, to discover the generative somatic syntax of the Orphan. Feel its gift, its power, its wisdom, its value. Find the gift of the Orphan.

SG: At one important level, you are truly alone in this world. Can you receive the gift, the freedom, of your aloneness?

RD: Find that place of softness, of compassion.

SG: You can feel deeply within you that the first layer of innocence is still there . . . Even as you discover this second field, this second layer . . . I am an Orphan in this world . . . I walk alone . . . I do it with my center and my deepest connection . . . Feel a sense of gratitude . . . toward the dragon . . . for allowing you . . . to deeply connect . . . with this archetypal place . . . of aloneness . . . that now you carry with an openness.

RD: The poet Hafiz wrote:

> *Don't surrender your loneliness*
> *So quickly.*
> *Let it cut more deep.*
>
> *Let it ferment and season you*
> *As few human*
> *Or even divine ingredients can.*
>
> *Something missing in my heart tonight*
> *Has made my eyes so soft,*
> *My voice*
> *So tender,*
>
> *My need for love*
> *Absolutely*
> *Clear.*

SG: Allow the self to again feel the dignity of your aloneness. A beautiful . . . trembling . . . open . . . aloneness.

RD: And then bring that gift of your innocence, the gift from the Orphan, and with it allow yourself to begin to flow gracefully into the place of the Martyr.

SG: Staying deeply connected with your center . . . opening to a field beyond it all . . . welcome this third wave of energy. *I can receive the suffering of the world and stay centered and open to a place beyond.*

RD: Sensing the desire for the commitment to justice and fairness.

SG: And again, feel the dignity . . . feel the dignity of the Martyr . . . the higher form, the higher consciousness of it.

RD: The willingness to open and sacrifice.

SG: The Buddhists like to say . . . *your heart is meant to be broken* . . . again . . . and again . . . and again . . . cracking like a shell . . . to a deeper tenderness . . . And as you feel the dignity of your broken heart, connecting deeply to the human center that is deeper than even that . . . allow yourself to feel free in this world . . . Let your tears fall freely to the earth . . . and water the seeds of new life.

RD: When you have been able to center yourself in this energy, breathe it in, breathe it down, breathe it through . . . then let yourself begin to open to the next archetypal station . . . the great archetype of the Wanderer . . . bringing the gifts from each of the other archetypes to deepen and widen your experience of this position.

SG: Letting the waves of the Innocent flow through you . . . Letting the waves of the Orphan flow through you . . . Letting the waves of the Martyr flow through you . . . and letting the waves of the Wanderer begin to enter you.

RD: Experience all of the gifts of the Wanderer: to set out for new worlds . . . to explore unknown places . . . to leave behind what doesn't fit for you . . . to walk away from a bad situation . . . to discover new spaces and possibilities you never imagined.

SG: Visiting many, many places. Moving beyond the dragon . . . beyond your family . . . beyond your old beliefs . . . The freedom to go anywhere . . . in the world of living consciousness . . . to know that and claim that right, that need, as your birthright.

RD: Letting go and becoming free . . . there's so much more in the world than the dragon.

SG: Free to wave goodbye . . . free to realize, *I've got my own journey, my own path to take.*

RD: Free to let go and leave behind what is no longer necessary.

SG: On the search, on the path of the hero's journey, something deep inside will wander the fields of consciousness . . . in the great adventure . . . of becoming a human being.

RD: And then, bring the gifts of the Innocent, the Orphan, the Martyr, and now the Wanderer into your centered state, and integrate those resources into the energy of the Warrior.

SG: As if an energy begins to pulse through you . . . awakening in you a place . . . to protect the sacredness of life . . . to be able to say, *no* . . . to be able to claim a space in this world . . . and to defend it. *You have no right to hurt me . . . neither my body nor my heart shall be violated.*

RD: *I will do everything in my power to bring my gift to the world . . . to bring healing to myself and others.*

SG: Breathe in all of this . . . feel the pulse of it. Open to the energy of it . . . these energies come from an ancient mind of great courage and self-love . . . that you can open to . . . a generative mind forged by the hero's journey of all living beings that have gone before . . . *I will protect this life that has been given to me . . . I will respect this body that has been given to me.*

RD: And when you're ready and you feel that sense deeply within your center, make the final transition to that place of magic and transformation.

SG: Some say it is the highest of the human energies. Remember . . . feel your center . . . let the energy come from deep within, through your center . . . The energy of the Sorcerer, the archetypal healer . . . Let it first touch and heal all of your personal wounds.

RD: Let it awaken you and transform you.

SG: There are some traditions that emphasize a body deeper than the wounded body. There is a heart in you that is not wounded. There is a body in you that is not wounded . . . unbroken . . . unstruck . . . whole. Let that healing presence bring you back to your true nature of unwounded wholeness.

RD: Find that source of magic inside of you . . . magic that makes miracles . . . magic that can reach beyond into the mystery. When I was a young man and I first went to meet Milton Erickson, at one point he showed me a card. It had a little man on it standing on a little planet in the middle of a vast universe. And it said: "When you think of how huge and how mysterious the universe is, doesn't it make you feel small and insignificant?" And when you opened the card, on the inside was written "Me neither!" *(Laughter.)* Because when you feel part of that larger mystery, you're not small and insignificant. You're big and mysterious just like the universe, connected to the larger mind that comes through you . . . to make you magic.

SG: And as you feel all of that, let yourself feel an even deeper sense . . . through your center and within every part of your being . . . feel the presence of innocence . . . through your center . . . emanating from every part of your being . . . feel the aloneness of the Orphan . . . through your center, radiating into the world . . . the brokenheartedness, like a radiant fire, of the holy Martyr . . . through your center.

RD: Feel the spaciousness and freedom of the Wanderer . . . through your center.

SG: Through your center and opening into the world . . . feel the sacred vow of the Warrior.

RD: Feel fierceness and commitment.

SG: Through the center, opening into the world . . . feel your power to heal . . .

RD: Feel the creative energy of the Sorcerer and the possibility to transform.

SG: And with those waves within waves within waves, you may want to look once again at the dragon from *this* place.

RD: Bringing all of these gifts . . . all of these energies . . . and most importantly, that place of your centering . . . And step back into the dragon now.

SG: And enjoy the human capacity to bring full transformation . . . full healing . . . from this place within you and all around you.

RD: Meet that energy of the dragon . . . absorb it . . . let it flow through . . . and as it does, let the transformation happen.

SG: Bring the dragon into the transformational light of your full human being. This is your legacy . . . this is your gift . . . this is your calling as a human being. Whichever dragons you encounter on your great journey through this world . . . let them connect you ever deeper . . . with the centers of human consciousness that can transform the dragon and transform you. *This is the path of the hero's journey.*

RD: This is the path of your evolution.

SG: So may you say to this path, in the coming days ahead . . .*Yes! I bring it all through me into this world. Yes! I call into the deepest places of my ancestral energies . . . help me . . . come with me . . . as I walk my hero's journey. Yes . . . every day in a thousand ways . . . I will say yes to my hero's journey.*

RD: *I now open my channel.*

SG: *Yes! . . . Yes! . . . Yes! . . . A thousand times, yes.* Because now you can see what turning away from your center brings . . . And what breathing through it brings . . . The stakes are indeed high . . . *(voice louder, speaking directly to audience)* so will you say yes?

RD: Say yes quickly . . .

Participants: Yes!

SG: I can't hear you . . .

Participants: *(Louder)* YES!

RD: What did you say?

Audience: *(Laughing with enthusiasm)* YES! YES! YES!

RD: OK. It can be useful after an experience like this to take a few moments and reflect on what happened for you in the exercise. What did you discover? What happened for you on this journey? You can either write it down or find a partner.

Closing: Sweet Darkness

SG: We hope you were able to get a feel for what a difference it can make if you stay present when the archetypal, the creative unconscious, opens. The archetypal can be helpful or not, depending on your degree of centeredness, presence, and your relationship with it. Remember, *you are the difference that makes the difference!* You have choice about whether to fall into life, rather than turn away. This is the difference that makes a difference.

So in closing this part of the program, we have two poems we'd like to share. I want to share part of a poem by Rainer Maria Rilke, called "Ripening Barberries." I dedicate this to all of the work that you have done here today because, as Rilke says:

> *The man who cannot quietly close his eyes*
> *certain that there is vision after vision inside,*
> *simply waiting for nighttime*
> *to rise all around him in darkness –*
> *it's all over for him, he's like an old man.*
>
> *Nothing else will come; no more days will open*
> *and everything that does happen will cheat him.*
> *Even You, my God. And You are like a stone*
> *that draws him daily deeper into the depths.*

SG: So my great wish for all of us is that many times each day, each of us can close our eyes, indeed certain that there is image after image opening all around us in the darkness. And speaking of darkness . . .

RD: . . . and the images that emerge from it . . . my reading is a poem by David Whyte, called "Sweet Darkness."

When your eyes are tired
the world is tired also.

When your vision has gone
no part of the world can find you.

Time to go into the dark
where the night has eyes
to recognize its own.

There you can be sure
you are not beyond love.

The dark will be your womb
tonight.

The night will give you a horizon
further than you can see.

You must learn one thing.
The world was made to be free in.

Give up all the other worlds
except the one to which you belong.

Sometimes it takes darkness and the sweet
confinement of your aloneness
to learn

anything or anyone
that does not bring you alive

is too small for you.

© Many Rivers Press, Langley, Washington

RD: So we wish you tonight some sweet darkness.

SG: *(Tempo increasing)* And so to complete this day, let us remember the words of the great Martin Luther King, Jr., "Free at last, free at last! Thank God almighty, we're free at last!" So, live as free people! We look forward to seeing you tomorrow morning.

(Long applause and cheering.)

Day 3

The Generative Field

SG: Good morning, class! *(Audience responds in kind)*. We wish you a very good day today. In the next part of our exploration of the hero's journey, we're going to focus on the important tool of living in the generative field mind.

RD: This is a mind that is created by relationships between multiple minds. Gregory Bateson said that the individual mind is a subsystem in a larger mind. We're saying the individual mind is itself a field and is a subsystem of a larger field – that there is a knowing that happens beyond the individual mind. If you look at the creative work of any genius – whether it's Mozart, da Vinci, Disney, or Einstein – there really is a kind of a tapping into a bigger mind, where they say: "It's not me that is doing the creating – it's something coming through me."

SG: Someone once asked the great Russian dancer Nijinsky, "How is it that you can jump so high?" Apparently, Nijinsky was the Michael Jordan of his day – he could jump higher than science thought was possible. And Nijinsky said, "It is not me that could answer that question, for it is not me that jumps like that. I don't know who it is; but you can't ask me, because it's not me."

RD: Mozart said: "I can't force my music to come. I can put myself into a state in which I receive it – in which it begins to flow." His description of the creative process was that it took place in a "pleasing, lively dream."

SG: So we're just suggesting the idea that all creativity comes from beyond your conscious mind. And if you're really totally caught in your conscious mind, you have contracted from the creative field.

RD: We're going to be emphasizing that, as with the somatic and cognitive minds, you can have generative or non-generative, even degenerative, versions of the field mind. Just as we have pointed out can happen with the first two minds, you can lose your center in the field mind, with negative consequences. Sometimes, when I'm doing business consulting, I walk into a company or organization and immediately feel a negative field that's operating. You've probably all had experiences like that. It's not in the color of the walls or the size of the building; it's in the energetic field that's operating. And it can be creative, or it can be oppressive.

SG: It's easy to lose yourself to the field. For example, the experience of addiction is getting lost in a field without your human center.

RD: Or the example we were giving earlier of the American soldiers at the Abu Ghraib prison in Iraq. You can get trapped in a field of fear, of anger, and of violence that effects your behavior. So part of operating at a generative level is opening to the dynamic field that is in effect, but then opening to a space beyond that. It's the space of awareness that can be with something without becoming it. For example, one important field to experience around your body is the energetic awareness of what we might call "second skin."

SG: To become a full person, a complete human being, requires that you develop this second skin. You don't have it at birth, it's something that slowly grows over time. Children don't have it. We've all seen young children playing freely, until a stranger walks into the room. And what typically happens? They freeze. You've all seen it happen, right? And when the youngster freezes in the presence of a stranger, where is the first place they look? Mama or papa. Mama and papa, family and community, they are the second skin for the child.

I remember when my daughter was 3 and I was taking her to swimming classes at the YMCA. It was the middle of the day and I happened to be the only dad in the class, so afterwards we had the whole men's locker room to ourselves to shower and change. I was on one side of the locker and Zoe was playing near the entry door on the other side. Just then the door swung open and this big guy enters. He seems like a very nice guy, but he's big with a big energy. And to make matters worse, he says to Zoe in a friendly but very loud voice, "Hi there, little girl! How are you?" *(Laughter.)*

And Zoe, naturally enough, freezes in fear and looks over to me in desperation. And I say, like any parent would, "It's OK, honey, Daddy is here." And she runs over, grabs onto my leg to put me between her and the stranger. *(Robert runs over and grabs Steve's leg, audience laughs.)* And we've all seen that, right? That's an example of what we are calling a "second skin." The space around you that allows you to be visible without feeling overwhelmed or invaded. And it's one example of what we are calling a generative field.

RD: In terms of the archetypal journey we were exploring in the "Moving through Archetypes of Transition" exercise, moving from the Innocent to the Orphan, the Martyr to the Wanderer, and finally to the Warrior and the Sorcerer, part of that journey involves the development of a second skin. This generative second skin is different from an armor or wall. As with physical skin, a second skin can give and receive information and energy. You feel through your skin; you can connect through your skin. And it is also selective, a sort of a filter that can be very helpful in terms of creating both communion and separateness. Of course, a generative consciousness has both at the same time – connected with itself, and connected to something beyond simultaneously.

I was working with a guy a little while ago who was a very high level manager in a well known international technology company. His division was the most profitable for his organization worldwide. We were talking about leadership, and he was saying that, for him, leadership was essentially the process of bringing positive energy into the field of a system. Regardless of whether it was his team, his organization, a particular meeting – he saw his job as being to bring positive, proactive energy. And, of course, to do that you need to deal with the inevitable negative energy that will surface. You need to be able to transform negative energy in a field. One of the things that he did as an ongoing practice was that every morning before work he would drop into his body and feel his energy, carefully measuring it by sensing his body. He would measure it as a space between his hands. Then, he would make the commitment to come home to his family with the same amount of energy at the end of the day.

This manager's ability to sense, set, and sustain a positive level of body energy requires an attention to what we're calling "field" – both within himself and within his environment. So this idea of a second skin becomes very important because there will be stress and pressure in any challenging or intense experience. You can imagine, for this manager, that the demands of his work and the people around him relying on him could suck his energy, depleting it and turning it into a negative form. So it becomes very important to have these skills to manage those field dynamics.

SG: So an important distinction we're making regarding generative field consciousness is that there are two levels of field. The first is the many dynamic content fields that we operate in; the second is the meta-level, content-free space in which we hold and work with these dynamic fields. The first is the content level, the second is the context level. Regarding the first level, we are always operating within multiple dynamic contexts or fields. The space around your body is a field. This room is a field.

RD: The space between you and another person is a field.

SG: Your personal history is a field. Your family is a field. Your culture is a field. You may work in the field of therapy, or the field of coaching, or the field of business. Your country is a field, as is your home. So there are many coexisting dynamic fields that we move around in. Of course, not all are equally active; there is a constantly shifting set of active contexts within which we navigate our lives.

RD: So there are many different dynamic fields operating at any given point. The second issue then is whether a field is generative or not. A field can be positive or negative, depending on the human presence within and around it.

SG: And the third basic idea is there is a field beyond fields, a meta-field that is beyond any content. We're describing that as the generative field – a "field of fields" that holds and positively imbues whatever fields are operating. Lest you think this is a hopelessly esoteric distinction, we want to point out that one of the basic principles in the martial art of aikido is, *never give your eyes to the attack (or attacker)*. This is a very practical principle: if you violate it, you'll get locked onto the attack and probably defeated by it.

So if some aggression is coming at me – it could be a person, but it could be a negative thought, or traumatic memory, or a feeling of fear from within – the question is, how will I respond with my attention? The untrained mind usually locks onto the negative threat. *(Steve demonstrates by tensing, locking eyes, withdrawing.)* In aikido we call this "giving away your center." At that point, I lose myself to the field of the attack. You all know that experience, right? You just get locked into the problem, forgetting about everything else, disconnected from all your resources. So this notion of a generative field means, in this case, responding to a challenge by opening your awareness beyond it. You allow your perceptual awareness to get wider, not more constricted. You open to a space beyond the problem, so you can be with it without becoming it. This is a main focus of our work in this next section of the program.

RD: We've been suggesting that the ordinary response to challenge is to close down, moving into survival strategies: "fight, flight, or freeze." You respond to challenges by contracting, dissociating, trying to control it, or get rid of it. We've been suggesting that for extraordinary results, you need to operate in the space beyond problems. You need to make room for it, but not be limited by it. In the generative somatic, this is done by centering. In the generative cognitive, this is done by sponsoring. In the generative field, this is done by opening beyond.

SG: As an introduction to this work, here is a beautiful poem about the generative field. It's from a Native American perspective. For some Native American tribes, the forest is a primary generative field. The forest is the deeper mind, the deeper wisdom, the deeper intelligence. This is a poem by David Wagoner, called "Lost."

Stand still. The trees ahead and bushes beside you
Are not lost. Wherever you are is called Here,
And you must treat it is as a powerful stranger,
Must ask permission to know it and to be known.
The forest breathes. Listen. It answers,
I have made this place around you.
If you leave it, you may come back again, saying Here.
No two trees are the same to Raven.
No two branches are the same to Wren.
If what a tree or a bush does is lost on you,
Then you are surely lost. So stand still. The forest knows
Where you are. You must let it find you.

SG: Contrary to traditional Western thinking, we are exploring this radical idea that every part of the universe has consciousness, that consciousness is actually the generative field that creates the forms and energy of the world. This consciousness operates as a unified field that implicitly connects everything within the field. If you withdraw or disconnect from these larger fields, you're in big trouble. Because you can't do it just from yourself. It is necessary to hook your mind, align it, yoke it to a larger mind.

It reminds me of a story about an old rabbi who walked around town in a long black overcoat, his hands stuck deep in the pockets. Finally, someone asks, "Rabbi, what's with the hands in the pockets?" And he pulls out his hands, revealing a strip of paper in each. "Oh, it's just a little something I practice," he says. "This strip of paper," he replies holding his right hand up, "says, 'I am the divine, I am everything, I am the universe.'"

"And this other paper," he says, holding up his left hand, "says, 'I am but a speck of dust, I'm so small; ashes to ashes.'"

"Why both strips?" someone asks.

"Well," he says. "Both are true, but I think the important trick is knowing which to remember at which point in time."

So this sense of connecting to one's self and also to the larger field is one of the challenges for the hero's journey.

RD: This is a skill that you need to practice. We are going to explore some of those practices today, but it's important to recognize that each person must find the practices that work best for him or her. Some years ago, I interviewed the founder of the second largest shipping company in the world. We were talking about solving a particularly challenging type of organizational problem. I asked: "How do you solve this kind of problem? What do you do?" I was expecting him to give me some kind of sophisticated analytical strategy, so I was surprised when he said, "Well, the truth is, I ride my bicycle." Riding his bicycle was the practice that, by engaging his somatic mind, put him in a place where he could connect to this center and then open beyond into the generative field. Later on in the interview we touched upon another challenging problem that his company faced and I jokingly said, "Oh, I bet you have to ride your bicycle on that."

He shook his head and with complete earnestness said, "Oh no! You cannot ride your bicycle on THAT problem. You have to golf on that problem." *(Laughter.)* In other words, this business leader had very specific practices to open beyond the field of the problem. He saw these activities as a major reason for his success in business.

SG: And by the way, when we do coaching, this is a very simple, important practical question:

> *When you need to get back to yourself, what do you do?*

It's a very simple question to find out how people get out of their head and into a more open, attuned field. You can then use that same experiential process to help them open a generative field to explore a challenging situation in a totally unrelated context.

RD: For some people, it's a physical activity; for others, it may be a poem. So here's a poem that for me says a lot about opening and closing. It's by E. E. Cummings.

> *somewhere i have never travelled,gladly beyond*
> *any experience,your eyes have their silence:*
> *in your most frail gesture are things which enclose me,*
> *or which i cannot touch because they are too near*
>
> *your slightest look easily will unclose me*
> *though i have closed myself as fingers,*
> *you open always petal by petal myself as Spring opens*
> *(touching skilfully,mysteriously)her first rose*
>
> *or if your wish be to close me,i and*
> *my life will shut very beautifully,suddenly,*
> *as when the heart of this flower imagines*
> *the snow carefully everywhere descending;*
>
> *nothing which we are to perceive in this world equals*
> *the power of your intense fragility:whose texture*
> *compels me with the colour of its countries,*
> *rendering death and forever with each breathing*

161

(i do not know what it is about you that closes
and opens;only something in me understands
the voice of your eyes is deeper than all roses)
nobody,not even the rain,has such small hands

RD: To me, this poem speaks beautifully about the dynamic process of opening and closing to a field. In the same way that you will not be centered all the time, you're also not going to be open to the field all the time. There is a rhythmic cycle of opening and closing that is part of the larger generative journey, a natural rhythm of going inside to connect to yourself, then opening outwards to connect beyond yourself. In this way, the individual center and the collective field balance and complete each other.

Practices for Connecting to the Field

SG: So we want to do a number of exercises today to give you an experiential sense of a generative field, especially in terms of how to sense them, create them, sustain them, and creatively utilize them for transformational change. The first exercise is pretty straightforward; it's a group experience we will guide you through. It has its basis in several traditions. In traditional hypnosis, it's called the "magnetic hands" technique. In Eastern mind–body traditions such as Tai Chi and Qigong, it is known as "the energy ball."

RD: In these traditions the whole notion of the chi or the ki is the energy or life force that permeates everything, including the human body (kind of like "the force" in the *Star Wars* movies). So in those traditions, you're practicing how to attune and work with this subtle energy as a source for good health and intelligent action.

SG: As we guide you through this process, please do not think of it as a process where we're somehow hypnotizing you, or where you're being passively controlled. Think of it as your own "experiment in consciousness." It's your learning experience, you're in charge. Use our coaching to help you explore your own possibilities.

RD: And to do that, you'll be needing to let go and discover another intelligence within you that can open up and guide you. To

sense and work with fields, you can't be dominated by your conscious thinking and ego control. Think of it like playing a musical
instrument, or doing art, or thinking creatively – you have to tune
into a deeper process and let it be the lead system. This requires
that you develop a felt sense of your consciousness, as this is the
experiential basis for experiencing a field.

SG: So we're asking you to just witness and support your own
experience. In all of these processes, you are simultaneously a
participant and observer, which requires that you cultivate the balance point between good concentration and complete relaxation.
If you're concentrated but not relaxed, the experience of the subtle
field cannot open because your tension is blocking it. But you can
also have too much relaxation, like if you're watching television
or sitting at a bar. So think like an artist or an athlete in terms of
relaxed absorption, curious how that can open you to a deeper
experience.

RD: Another term for this balance is *presence*. Be present in all parts
of yourself. So to begin the exercise, get into a comfortable position.

SG: As you settle in and settle down, let yourself begin to attune
to your center. Whatever way you're discovering is best for you,
let yourself begin to let go of everything else, and gently begin to
return to center.

RD: This is always the first step. Before you open to the field, find
your center, because uncentered consciousness creates negative or
unintegrated fields.

SG: Let yourself bring your awareness through your body. Drop it
through your body, then let it open beyond your body. In aikido we
say: *Drop into center, open into field. Drop into center, open into field.
Drop into center, open into field.*

RD: And in doing that, you can feel so comfortably grounded, feeling the soles of your feet gently but firmly rooted in the earth.

SG: And as you explore that process, you can let our voices become
secondary. Our voices can be voices in the background.

RD: Your first attention so deeply absorbed in your center.

SG: And as you do this, make sure your hands are spread apart, resting on your legs. And take a few moments to align through your spine . . . Letting yourself breathe . . . up and down . . . slowly . . . up and down through your spine.

RD: You can imagine a thread gently pulling the crown of your head up, relaxing the muscles but stretching the spine.

SG: One nice way to do this is through a simple process called the Celtic Cross. As you settle in a bit, take your hands and bring them to your center. Very slowly, so slowly it may seem like you're not moving your hands, even though they are moving. And when they come to your center, let them open through your vertical axis.

RD: One hand lifts up, and the other moves down, as if you're opening something.

SG: Very slowly, again, as if your hands are not really moving, but they really are. One hand lifting up . . . opening up through the vertical axis . . . lifting that golden thread . . . up through your crown chakra . . . all the way up to the heavens. At the same time, the other hand moving down . . . moving down . . . moving down . . . through your vertical axis . . . opening through the spinal passage to the earth below . . . And as you move one hand down, you can also very sensually, very slowly . . . move the other up.

RD: And your awareness can move all the way up the vertical axis, into the heavens.

SG: And all the way down . . . dropping to the center of the earth . . . at the same time . . . opening through your vertical axis . . . attuning your awareness through the spinal consciousness.

RD: Letting your hands open the vertical axis of the cross, the north and south of consciousness, the heaven and earth of your awareness.

SG: And then when you're ready, when you feel you've opened the vertical axis . . . come back to center . . . and begin to open the horizontal axis . . . touching into your center with both hands slowly . . . almost as if your hands are not really moving . . . even though they are.

RD: Opening one hand to your left . . . the other hand to your right . . . slowly . . . rhythmically . . . repetitively.

SG: Letting the energy flow through your fingers. Feeling the energy open through your fingertips, extending to the infinite dimensions of the east and west . . . right and left . . . the horizontal axis of consciousness . . . energy flowing through you, opening to the east and west.

RD: Unfolding . . . unzipping . . . opening the horizontal axis of consciousness.

SG: Beginning to extend . . . through the horizontal axis . . . to infinity . . . the mind stopping nowhere . . . energy flowing infinitely . . . And once you feel the horizontal axis opening . . . you can begin to shift back and forth with your hands . . . opening the vertical axis . . . the hands moving up and down . . . and then opening the horizontal axis . . . the hands moving to the east and to the west. You can let the hands move on their own, feeling a deeper presence beginning to awaken. In many traditions this is called "opening to the four directions." Letting your consciousness open from your center . . . into the four directions. North . . . south . . . east and west. It's a very sweet, sensual . . . opening . . . opening to a field . . . enjoying how all of your muscles can relax. There is a deeper presence than your muscles. A subtle energy that can flow up and down, left and right . . . all four directions.

Creating an Energy Ball

SG: And then in that field that you have opened, you can experiment with creating an energy ball.

RD: And to do that, you can let your hands extend out in front of you facing each other . . .

SG: . . . just like you're holding an energy ball . . . A ball that is pulsating, that is made of energy, that is vibrant . . . And as you feel the hands extending in front . . . imagining yourself holding that energy ball . . . not too tight . . . not too loose . . . let your arms relax. Let your shoulders relax. Let your elbows relax . . . and just sense your attunement to that energy ball. You may notice that it has its own subtle energy to it. So you can notice, for example, that as you breathe in, the ball expands just a bit . . . and as you breathe out, the ball gets a little bit smaller.

RD: And within that pulsing of your hands, you can feel the presence of the ball . . . feel the presence of the space within the energy . . . feel the presence of the space around the energy ball . . . all at the same time.

SG: Discovering just what very subtle, pleasurable adjustments you can make to become more attuned . . . tuning in to yin energy . . . the experience of being receptive, of being open, of being a space to hold whatever is there . . . exploring the mind–body possibilities . . . an experiment in consciousness . . . tuning more resonantly . . . deepening the connecting . . . breathing in and out.

RD: Feel that energy between your hands as if it's radiating from your center. Radiating out through your arms from your center . . . through your hands . . . to the space between your hands.

SG: Again, just give your hands and your arms permission to move as they would like . . . Give them the opportunity to move without your conscious control . . . creatively.

RD: Enjoy feeling the unique sense of the life force . . . your own vitality . . . your energy.

SG: And you might experiment with where your mental attention is oriented. What happens when you orient your attention beyond the ball . . . so the ball is only in your peripheral awareness? What happens when you attune again to the four directions –north, south, east, and west – to the Celtic Cross . . . and sensing the energy ball and your hands within that field of awareness? It's amazing to sense how your experience can change by virtue of where you place your attention. Just let yourself explore some of the possibilities.

RD: You can notice how if you begin to go into your thoughts, how that affects the ball. Does it begin to disappear? Is it more difficult to feel? But if you bring your presence fully back through your body, opening from your center beyond your body, you can feel a very different sense of the field.

SG: So this ball represents a simple version of a field . . . a space that can hold many different experiences. And what happens to the field when you begin to bring certain experiences in is one of our main curiosities. So we're going to add another piece to the experiment now, one of introducing an unintegrated energy into the field. My voice is going to shift in a few moments . . . to an unintegrated pattern . . . and we're going to ask you to just notice what happens to your energy ball when you experience the unintegrated pattern. Just watch with curiosity. Here goes . . .

(Steve shifts into an angry, aggressive voice.) I don't know what the hell is going on here . . . I think this stuff is a bunch of bullshit . . . None of it means anything.

(A brief pause, then Steve shifts back into a gentle voice.) And just notice what happened to your ball. Did it disappear? Did it get smaller? Did it get colder?

RD: Did it get brighter or thicker?

SG: Just notice what happened for you. This is an example of what happens to the field of your creative unconscious when you receive unintegrated patterns and for whatever reason can't sponsor them.

RD: So now we move to seeing what happens when we *can* sponsor them. So take a breath, let yourself release any tension, let yourself reconnect back with your center. Center yourself fully.

SG: Again, nothing to cling to in your mind. Nothing to do in the body except relaxation. Sensing your center again, and then sensing the ball fully.

RD: Feel the energy radiating from your center. Feel that sense of holding the energy ball . . . an amazing space that can hold whatever needs holding, whatever needs sponsorship.

SG: Sense the ball as a resilient, gentle sanctuary that can safely, absorb whatever needs healing . . . whatever needs transformation. Good. Breathing in the mind–body unity that allows an attunement to the energy field of the ball . . . And in a moment we're going to return to that unintegrated pattern . . . but this time around, don't give it your first attention. Don't give your focal attention to the negative voice. Instead, give your first attention to the energy field ... how to hold it, how to keep it alive, how to allow it to become stronger. So sense the negative energy being absorbed into the ball, curious about how to absorb in a way that gives it a safe space ... safe for you ... safe for the negative energy. Let your attention stay wide to the peripheral field of the ball, beyond the negative "problem" of the voice.

RD: Just like the active centering process, where you learned to absorb something into your center. Here you are absorbing something into a larger field.

SG: Exploring how to wrap the field around it ... using a field as a sanctuary to make it safe both for you ... and for whatever you're connected to. Keep the field alive. Don't give your mind to the problem. Let your mind rest in the generative field beyond the problem.

RD: Also tuning through your vertical axis to your center. Be present in your body, even as you open to the field beyond the problem.

SG: OK, so take a few moments to center and attune to the field. Good ... and here we go again.

(Steve returns to the angry, belligerent voice.) I can't stand this bullshit. It's a bunch of crap. There is no such thing as an "inner self." Lots of crazy people, if you ask me ... Argghhhh!

(Steve pauses and returns to a gentle voice.) OK. Just notice what happened that time. Breathe ... witness ... learn. Were you able to connect with the energy? Receive it, absorb it, move with it in a different way? Did it make your ball stronger? Brighter? Bigger? Were you able to feel compassionate? Curious? Calmer? This is what developing a generative field can do for you: it can allow you to sense a deep awareness that surrounds you, a presence that is bigger than any problem that may be challenging you. And in opening and sustaining a field, you can find the safety and the skill to be with whatever is there, without falling into it. So this is the first of a number of exercises we're going to explore today to help you to know how to deal with all of this.

Before you return, just sense your relationship to your inner field. Notice anything you just experienced or learned that you want to remember for later. And if there is a simple vow or promise, a commitment that you would like to make to yourself, about connecting more deeply, every day, with the energy field of your Generative Self, go ahead and do that now.

RD: Think of the vow of that manager I was mentioning earlier – the vow to self-care for the field of his personal energy throughout the day; how to notice it, how to care for it, how to preserve it, how to use it to help others. And when you're ready, we'd like to ask you to take a couple of minutes . . .

SG: . . . to slowly return back into the room . . .

RD: . . . and allow your hands to come back into the room . . . allow your legs to come back into the room . . . and last but not least, allow your whole being to return into the room.

Accessing the Field Mind through Presence

SG: Welcome back. Hopefully you got a sense of how in order to tune into a subtle field, you have to find this balance between attentional energy that is extending out and energy that is receiving. You're trying to find the balance point of yin and yang. That's where Tao, or "the way," opens up – which is another way of talking about a generative field.

RD: We also suggest that this kind of field is essential to the quality of your interactions with others. Your presence, your energy has an influence on the experience of your clients. We're suggesting with this idea of a field mind that there are certain types of experiential thoughts and awarenesses that will show up when you're with certain people. It's not a mechanical reaction to what they're saying or how they look – it's a reaction to "their energy." We can use this in a positive way: we can open a generative field so that people are able to do and say things they normally wouldn't. They might make connections and create ideas that would not happen if they were just by themselves. Maybe you've had someone say something to you like, "I really like who I am when I'm around you," which relates to the field you shared with that person.

SG: In coaching and therapy, there is often the question of whether the change comes from the client or the coach. We would say both and neither: the generative change comes from the relational mind created by cooperative relationship between the two. The creative unconscious is not inside of a person, it is a field that opens beyond the person. The field allows the "space between" to allow ideas to come from "nowhere" to create something totally new and needed.

But paradoxically, this field "beyond" needs to be created and sustained by the parts or members of the field. So you can't just be passive and "trust the field" to do it. You sometimes get this infantile idea in hypnosis, where the unconscious is somehow supposed to save you from yourself. Nor can you dominate things and force the creative process. Again, we're trying to find the balance between yin and yang, so that you can create something beyond yourself and then keep it alive by letting it give to you.

I sometimes call this balanced attention the "Errol Flynn principle." As you may know, Errol Flynn was one of the great swashbucklers of the silver screen. It turns out that he was actually an accomplished swordsman in real life. So someone once asked him, "Say, Errol, how do you hold a sword?" And he said, "Oh, that's easy. Whenever I'm holding a sword, I imagine I'm holding a bird." If you squeeze too tight *(Steve make squashing noise)*, whoops, no more bird. *(Laughter.)* But if you hold too loose *(Steve looks a bit spacey, and points to an imaginary bird flying out of his hand)*, also no more bird. As with birds, so with swords. And as with swords, so with fields and all other generative connections. We're saying that experiences of a generative field are emergent properties of this kind of attentional balance. They only awaken when you attune to a high quality of your attentional state.

RD: It's generated through the presence of who is there.

SG: And the great news is that *you can do this. It is within each person's capacity to creatively sense and work within a generative field.*

RD: I was recently coaching a woman who was working as a consultant in an organization. She would open to the field there but without holding and extending her center, as we've been teaching. She would get into such a receptive place, just taking everything in, that the unintegrated energies in her workplace would really overwhelm her. She would come home each day totally drained. It got to a breaking point when she looked in the bathroom mirror one morning and couldn't recognize her own face. It was as if this field was turning her into somebody else. So we did an exercise that we're going to be demonstrating to you now about building a "second skin." Building a second skin, as we discussed a bit earlier, is a form of generative field that is vital to your hero's journey.

SG: The second skin is what allows you to be visible without being exposed.

RD: It allows you to be present without being overly vulnerable or fragile.

SG: In order to live your hero's journey, you must be willing and able to step into the world and say: "This is where I stand. This is my truth. This is my experience." How well can you do that? Do you say *(Steve shifts to very incongruent and shaky presence)*, "Well, this is my truth . . . kind of . . . I think . . . kind of . . . maybe . . . well, not really"? *(Laughter.)* "Maybe I won't mention it." *(More laughter.)* Of course, the opposite is the hard core pounding of the "truth" into the world *(Steve shifts into "tough guy" pose)*: "This is the absolute truth and I'll kill anyone who argues with me." *(Laughter.)* So again, to speak your truth, to share your presence, requires this balanced energy field that is neither too soft nor too hard. That's where the second skin allows you to open safely and confidently into the world, both giving and receiving of your deepest self as you make visible who you are.

Your "Second Skin"

RD: People frequently say things like: "If looks could kill" or "That person is throwing daggers through their eyes." These are descriptions of energetic attacks. A major challenge for the hero's journey is how to receive these attacks skillfully and work with them positively. We practiced this on a somatic level through active centering; now we turn to how to do this at a field level. And in particular we're going to look at the field you create around you and how that affects your connections with the world. Sometimes when I watch coaches at work, I see their energy field dominating their clients. On the other hand, I also notice how if the coach's energy field is too weak, there is nothing for the client to push against, to feel that there is a presence there with them. This notion of the energy field through which you inter-connect with the world is what we are calling a "second skin."

The following is an overview of the exercise we will be demonstrating.

Exercise: Developing a "Second Skin"

1. Identify a context in which you became overwhelmed, lost, or assaulted by a disturbed or "shadow" field (i.e. a situation in which you felt caught or in the spell of some type of negative energy or vibration, such as fearfulness, aggression, sadness, depression, fatigue, etc.). This does not have to be connected with any specific behavioral content or expression. It may be a sense that you pick up in that context.

2. Select a location in front of you, step into it, and put yourself into that situation, imagining that you are there now, seeing what you see, hearing what you hear, and feeling what you feel. Take an internal inventory of what it is like subjectively. How do you experience the impact of this negative energy? How do you feel? What happens to your thoughts?

3. Step out and away from the situation and shake off the state. Center and ground yourself, becoming fully present in your body. Rub your hands together in order to make them warm and sensitive.

4. Hold the palms of your hands facing one another so that they are almost touching. Bring presence and awareness into your hands and let them become so sensitive that you can feel the life force energy of your body between the palms of your hands. Imagine that your grounded center is an energy generator. Imagine the energy from your center moving out of your arms and through your hands. Feel the presence of this energy in the space between your hands.

5. Move your hands a little further apart until they are about 3–4 inches (8–10 cm) away from one another. Keeping your

awareness in your hands, continue to sense the field of energy between them at this distance. Moving your hands very slightly toward and away from each other can help you to get a better sense of this field.

Note: Stay present and in your body. If your mind begins to wander or leave the present you will not be able to feel the field.

6. Continuing to feel the presence of the field generated from your center, slowly allow your hands and arms to move into a position as if you were about to embrace someone. Notice if you can feel a sense of embracing the field of energy emanating from your center and your body. Also become aware of any energetic sensations on the backs of your hands and arms (on the outside of your embrace).

7. Holding the sense of this field in your hands and arms, bring it around the you who has been caught in the difficult situation identified in Steps 1 and 2. Imagine that you are sculpting and creating a second skin around that you. The metaphor of skin is important here. It is neither armor nor a force field. Skin allows you to be both connected and selective at the same time. The skin of your body both protects your delicate internal organs and also connects you in an intimate way with your environment. This energetic skin will do the same thing with respect to the field. Take extra time to make sure this second skin is in place at the areas over your body where you have felt most vulnerable (heart, stomach, throat, etc.).

Note: If it helps, you can add other representational systems as well (e.g. visualizing the skin as an energy field or a certain color of light).

8. Step into the you who is now surrounded by this second skin and use your hands to be sure that you can feel the presence of the energetic skin around you. Feel the sense of both safety/selectivity and connection with the environment around you. As you re-experience the problem context and situation, notice how it is different for you.

9.   Future pace by imagining the next time you will be in that situation, being inside of your second skin.

If you are guiding someone else through this process, center yourself and generate a field with your hands as you are guiding your partner. As you are explaining and demonstrating what to do, you can sculpt and create an additional second skin for your partner as well.

Demonstration with Eva

(Eva volunteers to do the exercise.)

RD: Hi, Eva. Welcome to your hero's journey. As we begin the exercises, I'd like to ask you to share a little bit about the challenging situation you're facing.

(Eva looks a bit anxious and laughs nervously.)

SG: OK, great, so the first part of the energy field is a bit nervous. Would it be OK to take another full minute to let yourself be nervous? *(Laughter. Eva relaxes a bit.)*

RD: One of the things we sometimes do to get rapport at this level is a type of energetic mirroring, so that our fields can attune to each other. Eva, what I'd like to suggest is for us to face each other and let our hands extend toward each other's, not quite touching but sensing the energy between them. *(Robert and Eva place their hands close together, not quite touching.)*

And what I'd like to try to do is just feel your energy and mirror it, receiving it and supporting it. *(Robert and Eva begin to explore the energetic connection between their hands.)* It's important that my energy is not weaker or stronger than yours, but just connecting and blending and receiving and mirroring . . . That's good, thank you . . . And you can also feel mine . . . Mirror mine . . . Yes, that's good . . . So we can begin to sense a field opening between us that can still be here even when we turn and face the audience. So there is a nice comfortable field that we can be in as we explore this process together . . . and when you're ready, share what you can about that situation.

Eva: *(Looks much calmer and centered.)* As we did that, I remembered a time when I was doing a very lovely project with myself. I was in a creative trance – it was very nice. I was very happy in the trance . . . *(Smiles.)* It was as if I knew myself better than ever – who I was, and what I wanted. It was a very beautiful moment for me. And then I tried to express my experience to others, with language, and it was more difficult and confusing. *(Laughs a bit nervously.)*

RD: Yes, I hear you.

Eva: *(Moved)* And no one understood me. They got worried about me, and took me to a doctor, and I ended up in a hospital. At first I felt fine, because I had found myself. I knew who I was. I gave myself time. I was accepting my challenge. I had expressed myself, even though I hadn't been understood. After a while, though, it got more difficult, and I started to feel lost. *(Looks very sad.)* I began to lose my strength, I began to doubt myself. Everybody was looking at me like something was wrong. I felt they didn't understand me, so why express myself? So I began to think I wasn't worthwhile and felt incapable of getting back to the world. *(Cries.)* And now I feel whole again. But that feeling back then, it is still inside of me . . . and that's what I'd like to work with.

RD: Yes. You are on a very powerful hero's journey – bringing your gifts into the world, and also knowing there are others out there who may not quite understand. I almost get the feeling that in the moment where you really are yourself, then the connection to others disappears – it's just you. And if there are others there, then you lose yourself. So it gets very interesting.

A child has to learn that, too. If I am just fully expressing myself, there are other people around that I might be bothering, or hurting, or disturbing, or challenging, or confusing. So it's very important that you have this kind of second skin that allows you to hold yourself and be yourself, and still connect to others. So that you can feel your gift, and also can share it with others.

SG: I just want to point out that this sequence that Eva is describing is very typical for the hero's journey. *This is supposed to happen.* That is to say: the hero begins to feel her call, and she brings herself out into the world. It's really great for a while, and then she runs into a demon. The demon does what demons do – it cracks the field of the hero, and Eva falls into a sort of negative regressive trance. But she keeps returning into the world, responding to this call to know herself and share herself in the world. So we really want to appreciate that she's deeply on the path of her hero's journey. This allows us to become curious as to which resources might help her to stay connected with her center and her generative field as she encounters some of those predictable demons again.

RD: It's the very basic notion that when you awaken, it's not always going to be in a way that others can receive. It is a very interesting challenge to fully be yourself, yet also be with others. You don't want to be punished or put into a hospital because you're disturbing people, even though you're in your *own* truth, right? So, how do I be me and stay me, in contact with others who are different than me, or in a culture that feels different from me? It's not about giving yourself up or passively submitting.

SG: We really have to accept the fact that there are many people and presences in this world that don't want you to wake up. *(To Eva, with a smile)* Isn't that great to know? *(Eva laughs.)*

SG: But they don't want Robert to wake up, either. So I hope that you can accept the sponsorship of Uncle Robert and Uncle Stephen as guardians on the path. *(Eva laughs again.)*

RD: So, again, the important thing about any type of skin is that it allows me to connect to others. I have to be able to connect to the others that are out there. At the same time it is also selective about what comes in. So let's find a situation, recently, where you really recognized this challenge where you were disappearing because of the looks of others. Let yourself sense such a time, and let yourself step forward into that situation and relive it for a moment. *(Robert points to a space in front of Eva.)*

(Eva steps forward, closes eyes to sense the experience.)

And just first notice what happens. Put yourself into that situation . . . and notice what you feel in your body in that situation. *(Eva looks crestfallen.)* What do you feel in your body, and where? What is this sensation?

Eva: My body trembles. I have no desire to live. I don't feel capable of anything.

RD: Yes . . .

Eva: *(Crying softly)* I have nothing here. Everything I dreamed was madness. Nothing has meaning, I feel so rejected.

RD: And, Eva, please notice the energy that is overwhelming you. Let yourself become aware of the energy that puts you in this place. Do you feel it coming into some place in your body, or is it around your body?

Eva: It is as if it's crushing me.

RD: Yes, crushing you . . . From the top?

Eva: Yes, also from the front.

RD: It's good to begin to notice that the energy is coming from outside of you. What I'd like to ask you now is to leave the situation, step back to your original position, really step out of it, and let it go.

(Eva takes a step back, opens her eyes, breathes deeply, and blows her nose.)

OK, welcome back to the room. *(To audience)* You've probably all been in those situations that feel crushing and oppressive, overwhelmed by other people's judgment and disapproval. It's what we are calling a negative field, where you are under the influence of negative sponsorship messages. Her feelings were all coming from negative sponsorship. Positive sponsorship messages are: *You exist. I see you. You are valuable. You are unique. You have something to give. You are welcome.* You can notice here that the exact opposite type of messages are active in Eva's situation: *You don't exist. You don't deserve to exist. Who do you think you are? You're not special. You don't count. You don't help with anything. You're not welcome. You might as well die. You might as well not be here.* That is the opposite state of positive sponsorship.

Eva: I didn't believe it was actually me they wanted to negate. It was as if they wanted me there, as long as I didn't believe in the values I was connecting to. They weren't upset so much with me, as with all the things that have meaning for me. It felt like they needed me to give up all my values. But without those things, I don't have any strength or happiness.

RD: Yes.

Eva: It wasn't against me as a person. It was everything I believed in.

RD: Albert Einstein said: "Great spirits are always opposed by mediocre minds . . . including our own." *(Some laughter.)*

SG: In the language of fields, Eva is talking about how she falls into somebody else's negative field. So what we want to do in this exercise is explore: How do you attune to your own generative field, so that you don't fall into other negative fields? Because negative fields are all over the place in this world.

RD: What you can see here is the exact opposite of what we have described as the Ericksonian approach. Erickson emphasized accepting and honoring what is there, so that it can be sponsored and integrated. Eva was getting the exact opposite advice. "Get well. Get over all these things. You have to get rid of that crap. You have to get rid of that stuff, and you'll be fine." Erickson didn't say to the guy who thought he was Jesus Christ: "Get rid of that belief, then you'll be well." So sponsorship is key, and it all starts with self-sponsorship.

(To Eva) One of the things that's going on here is a susceptibility to what Stephen calls "aliens" or what I call "thought viruses" – external negative ideas about yourself that you take on and get overwhelmed by. Then you can no longer see yourself. Does that fit? *(Eva nods.)* So what I think would be helpful here is to see how we can support you in creating a second skin that allows you to stay connected with yourself and open to the world. Stephen and I will both be sponsors and guardians, but the first sponsor is yourself.

Eva: OK.

RD: *(Gentle voice)* We'd like to ask you to start by grounding and centering yourself. Stephen and I are doing the same, right along with you. *(Pause.)* And when you're ready, bring your hands in front of yourself, facing each other ... Feel your own strength ... You may find it helpful to give yourself some simple positive sponsorship messages: *I exist. I am. I am valuable. I am unique. I have something to contribute. I belong here* ... And breathe those messages in. And when you're ready ...

SG: ... you can let your hands extend out ...

(Eva extends her hands.)

... and let your palms face toward each other ... We're just beginning to attune here ... as you relax and feel the energy between your hands ... to the possibility that there is some simple, deeper healing presence ... that's already within you ... to begin to allow energy to flow between your hands.

RD: An energy that has both the capability to support your gift ... and to heal your wounds.

SG: An energy beneath your thinking ... that you can allow to develop so that you can use it to nurture ... and surround yourself ... with the deepest part of your wholeness ... Can you feel that energy between your hands now?

Eva: *(Nodding head)* Yes.

SG: Good.

RD: And in just a moment, Eva, we're going to ask you to begin to move your hands around your body, to begin to sculpt, to create a second skin ... not actually touching your body, but opening the field around your body ... beginning to allow an energy body to gently envelop your physical body.

SG: When you're ready, move your hands very slowly, very gently, very kindly ... to form that second skin around your body ... Let yourself begin to sculpt a second skin. Begin to create a lovely aura around your physical body ... with that lovely, deep, resilient energy between your hands.

(Eva begins to slowly move her hands around her body, sculpting an energy field.)

That's good . . . that's good . . . a resilient energetic sheathing that begins to awaken all around your physical body.

RD: You can use your hands . . . all the way over your head, down to your legs, so that it really surrounds you.

SG: That's good . . . that's it . . . that's it.

(Eva looks deeply absorbed in the very slow movements of her hands around her body.)

RD: Your hands will intuitively know how close to come to your body, or how far the second skin should be.

SG: That's good . . . creating a generative space for yourself . . . that's good . . . that's it.

RD: And make sure the hands open the space behind you too.

SG: And it really is an amazing thing . . . isn't it . . . how the deep inner wisdom of your being has a mind of its own . . . and can help you to feel that generative space safely opening all around you . . . a healing space . . . a safe space? Creating a protective field around you.

RD: And you can even make sure it's all the way down to your feet. Feel your feet and your legs, protected by the second skin.

SG: That's good . . . that's it . . . Feeling this important birthright of each human being . . . to experience a deep space of calm centering, of a safe space to be.

RD: And the field in the back of you . . . let yourself sculpt that.

SG: That's good . . . that's it . . . an amazing second skin . . . a deep protective field beginning to awaken all around you.

RD: *(To audience)* And as the coach, I'm noticing where her hands are sculpting, watching to see where and how she creates the second skin. This way, I can also mirror what she is showing me with her hands. *(Robert moves his hands around Eva, at a distance from her.)* Where I sense her second skin, I look to reinforce it, blend with it, deepen it.

SG: Your own special space.

RD: And in doing that, I'm sponsoring it. I'm not trying to add anything. I'm not adding my energy – I'm just mirroring back Eva's second skin.

SG: Just for yourself . . .

RD: I'm sponsoring her second skin. I'm seeing it. I'm receiving it, and reflecting it back.

SG: Learning how to trust deeply your own healing body . . . that's good . . . breathing in the self-wisdom . . . that's it . . . that's good . . . feeling yourself in a beautiful space . . . surrounded with a gentle clarity and calm . . . sometimes feeling it like a shroud . . . sometimes like a veil . . . sometimes like a vibration . . . There is a space around you within which you can walk freely.

RD: *(To Eva, gently)* There is a space around you where you can sense what is happening outside of you, and remain calm.

SG: That's good . . . That's great . . .

RD: Sensing those deep messages of self-love . . . *I exist . . . I am unique . . . I have something to give . . . I belong here.*

SG: And from that place . . . you can sense other presences . . . other people . . . at just the right distance . . . far enough away to be safe . . . close enough to be connected . . . and just enjoy learning from your inner wisdom the proper distance to sense the other presences . . . the other people in that situation.

RD: As you sense the proper distance . . . and feel the second skin . . . you can learn to stay connected to yourself and also feel those other people, those other energies . . . . and engage them . . . as you stay connected within yourself . . .

SG: . . . discovering the proper distance.

RD: And just let the parts that are appropriate to be let in, come in . . .

SG: . . . at the proper distance.

RD: Discovering how your second skin can filter what's coming in and what's going out . . .

SG: . . . at the proper distance between you and the others.

RD: Selective.

(Eva takes a deep breath, signaling some completion.)

SG: That's good . . . that's it . . . A deep breath of integration . . . a beautifully earned sense of healing and wholeness.

RD: And so when you're ready, Eva, you can take this generative field of a second skin with you as you step back into that situation . . . allowing yourself to be guided and protected within the energy field.

SG: You may feel . . . in a very curious way . . . that it is the generative field that is guiding you . . . You're just walking within the guidance of that field, the deeper wisdom of that space . . . the protection of your second skin . . . You can let the second skin be your lead system. Good.

RD: You can move into that place always keeping your own space. No matter where you are, you have your own space.

SG: So when you're ready . . . you can allow yourself to step forward . . . now with the presence of the energy field . . . and notice the differences this time . . . your first awareness resting in the second skin.

RD: Taking a step into the next part of your hero's journey.

(Eva steps forward.)

SG: Let your connection to your center and your field be the first attention. You may need to use your hands at any point to really sense the generative field in which you operate.

RD: And as you fully sense the connection within and around you, you can also sense in your awareness the other people in that situation.

(Steve and Robert pause to allow Eva to explore the experience. She looks radiant and peaceful, a great contrast to the first round.)

SG: That's good . . . that's good . . . whatever you are connecting with, that's really good . . . And as you connect with yourself, just notice that those people can be all the way over there.

RD: But you are here . . . with yourself.

(Eva is nodding, a gentle smile on her face, continuing to look radiant.)

SG: All the way over here . . . with yourself . . . your own field.

RD: And you can meet those energies over there . . . with your own energy . . . and stay centered . . . discovering how you can be close with some of them, further with others . . . Just notice whatever feeds your second skin, whatever makes you more attuned to the second skin.

SG: Just allowing yourself to shift . . . from reacting to them . . . to being with yourself.

(Eva takes a deep breath. Robert and Steve are quiet, allowing her the space to integrate. Then Robert speaks in a slightly reorienting voice.)

RD: So, I'm curious. From the outside here, you look amazingly different.

SG: And not only do you look different, the space around you, the whole room feels so different. (Audience members, who have been in deep rapport, nod.)

RD: So when you're ready, we'd like to invite you to bring that presence with you when you return back out here with us.

(Eva orients outward. She looks touched and radiant, open hearted with tears in her eyes.)

It looks like you just had an amazing experience. *(Eva nods.)* Just let yourself stay connected with yourself . . . and feel all the amazing energies out here in the audience . . . and in your life . . . that are not you . . . but you can engage with them, and stay yourself in the process.

(Steve notices how touched the audience looks, and calls Eva's attention to it.)

SG: And by the way, you might find it really interesting to just take a few moments to look around in the room . . . and look at people, see what's in their eyes and hearts.

(Steve gently points Eva's attention to the audience. She seems deeply touched and surprised at the depth of presence in the audience.)

And what do you see?

Eva: Love . . . I see love in people.

SG: And really sense all of that, and what they're reflecting . . . because what you see from them . . . is you. They are accurately mirroring you.

(Eva tears up, looks happy and a bit surprised.)

RD: And you might like to say, "Wow, this is the best seat in the house!" *(Laughter.)*

(To Eva, gently) It's nice to see you . . . to feel your presence. Welcome home . . . So nice to see *you!*

(Robert and Eva hug.)

SG: And what's really good to know is that whenever you need to get back to this place, all you have to do is click your heels together three times, and say "There's no place like home." *(Eva laughs.)*

There's no place like home . . . There's no place like home.

(Steve and Eva hug. Audience breaks out into loud applause, many people with tears in their eyes.)

RD: As I was saying to you, that is *also* an energy that you can let in or not. May you keep learning this amazing capacity you have to stay with yourself even as you connect with others. And may you continue to successfully move along the path of your hero's journey. *(More applause.)* So is this a good place to stop, Eva?

Eva: Yes, definitely.

RD: Thank you for sharing this part of your journey with all of us. I am curious if there is anything that you can say about what the experience was like with your second skin.

Eva: The biggest difference was how centered and whole I felt in my space, especially when you had me imagine the other people. Before, when I sensed other people's energies, it felt like they were coming directly into me, and really had a big impact on me. I felt their anxiety, their fear, and it really disturbed me. But when I felt my own space, what got through was their desire for me to feel good. I could feel their good intentions and their questions, but fear, anxiety, despair – all that stuff stayed outside. I could see it. I could see it in the others, but it didn't reach me. Nor did it arouse in me anything, because it wasn't part of me – that desperation was not mine.

RD: That is a really powerful thing to know: their energy is not yours. They have their energies, you have yours. That's what a second skin can allow you to know – what's yours and what's not yours. May you continue to know this very important distinction for your hero's journey.

SG: *(Smiling)* The Force is with you, young Skywalker.

Eva: *(Laughs.)* Thank you so much!

(Audience applause as Eva leaves the stage.)

RD: Now it is time to go out and practice this with a partner.

SG: First, identify a situation where you fall into a negative field. Step into it, sense what's happening, step out. Next, center, ground, attune to the energy field of the second skin. Finally, step back into the situation, this time with the second skin. These are the basic steps.

RD: As a coach, your role is to help your partner create his or her second skin. You are in the position of a sponsor – and the main goal of the sponsor is to see and to bless. Not to fix or rescue, but to bless, reflect, and sponsor. In doing this, your presence is your deepest resource. We suggest, before you actually start the exercise, that you face each other and hold your hands with your palms facing but not touching your partner's hands. Then create rapport at the field level by mirroring each other's energy. *(Robert and Stephen demonstrate the mirroring with each other.)*

What I've seen happen in NLP exercises is that people think that they are in rapport because they've mirrored each other physically. If energies aren't attuned to each other, however, there is a whole other level of connection that is missing, and which can really make a difference.

SG: By attuning, what we're talking about is extending and receiving equally. I extend my energy; I receive Robert's energy equally. I'm trying to find the balance point.

RD: And you're doing this from a centered state. It's similar to active centering – if I'm not centered and somebody pushes me and I push back, there will be a clash of force that is going to drain our energies.

SG: When you are centered and energetically mirroring each other, however, it is a very pleasurable experience. It will get you out of your head and into the mind of the relational field.

RD: So begin by attuning your energies. Then, during the phase when the client is sculpting his or her second skin, the coach can sponsor it by using his or her own hands to mirror it; like an outside, second coating. *(Steve begins to model sculpting his own second skin, and Robert traces with his own hands the movements, offering his support.)* Remember, you're not creating it for your partner – I'm not creating this for Stephen. I'm receiving and feeding back his energy, honoring and blessing that presence he's unfolding.

SG: If you're going to do this, it is usually important to get permission. You can simply ask, "Is it OK if I support you by reinforcing your second skin?" And then pay attention to both the verbal and non-verbal responses. If somebody contracts when your hands are near to them, that obviously is not a helpful thing. You want to feel what in aikido we call *ma-ai*, which translates from the Japanese as "proper distance" – close enough to connect, far enough to respect and give space. You want to find and honor the *ma-ai* in each moment of connection, whether in this exercise or any other.

RD: That's why it is helpful to the energetic mirroring at the beginning. It allows you both to attune to the relational field holding and guiding you both. Your eyes can be closed, and you may still feel this space. And you're using that to find the best way to connect with yourself and your partner.

Archetypal Energies: Tenderness, Fierceness, and Playfulness

SG: We hope that this exercise, as well as the "energy ball" process we did earlier, begins to give you a sense of the generative field as a content-free space within which you can absorb whatever is there and be with it, without identifying with it.

Incidentally, we want to apologize if some of the language about generative fields seems a bit esoteric. When we talk about any of the generative levels, language becomes very awkward, because we're talking about experiential contexts, not "things." So we start sounding like we're from California, which of course we are. But our point is that everybody starts sounding like they're from California when they address the generative field level! *(Laughter.)* In this program, we are frequently using metaphorical language in order to point at something beyond the limitations of literal language.

RD: As we said at the beginning of the program, language relating to the field is going to be poetic. Metaphor is a deeper, more basic language than literality.

SG: We'd like now to demonstrate another exercise about the field. This one is about bringing a goal or problem into the energy ball, then circling around the ball to see the challenge from multiple perspectives, while also feeding different archetypal resources into the ball.

The following is a summary of the process.

Exercise: Energy Spheres and Archetypal Energies – Creating Transformational Futures

1. Identify transformational goal (problem to be changed/future to be created).

2. Center and develop energy sphere (energy ball).

3. Move goal into sphere, maintain first attention "to and beyond" sphere.

4. First revolution: walk slowly around sphere, bringing tenderness to self in sphere, noticing new possibilities at different perspectives.

5. Second revolution: walk slowly around sphere, bringing fierceness to self and noticing new possibilities.

6. Third revolution: walk slowly around sphere, adding playfulness to self in sphere and noticing new possibilities.

7. Fourth revolution: walk slowly around sphere, mixing all three archetypal resources and noticing new experiences.

8. Integration: allow all experiences to integrate into a new "mandala of identity."

9. Sense presence of new patterns and orient to their expression in future.

10. Self-appreciation, vow, and commitments.

11. Reorient and discuss.

SG: In the first step, the guardian (coach) helps the hero to identity a transformational goal. This typically can be one of two things. The first is a future that you want to achieve. For example, it could be, "I want to have this book written," or "I want to be in an intimate relationship," or "I want to make more money." Just attune to whatever you sense is a main calling in your life right now. Pick one that vibrates in your center.

RD: A step in your hero's journey.

SG: The second possible goal, in some ways complementary to the desired future, is changing an undesirable present state. That is, "Something is happening now in my life that I want to transform."

RD: *I want to heal something.*

SG: *I'm having a difficult relationship with a loved one.*

RD: *I'm struggling at my work.*

SG: *I'm getting caught in an emotional wound.*

These are possible undesired present states that may be the goal of transformation. So you can pick either something you want to create in the future, or something you want to change in the present. Just feel which has the most resonance for you.

RD: Either "away from a undesired state" or "toward a desired state," as we say in NLP.

SG: Once the goal is identified, you will return to your old friend, the energy ball. The coach will help the client center and attune to the energy ball. Once the client signals that this has happened, the coach asks the client to take the transformational goal and drop it inside the energy ball. In other words, bring your intention inside of a generative field. This will give two levels of experience: the content that you're working with, and the field in which it is held.

The main task for the exercise is to keep the field alive, even more important than attention to the content in the field.

When the generative field is active, good things will happen; when it freezes and contracts, bad things will happen. We can't say it any simpler than that.

Once the goal is in the energy ball, the coach will ask the hero to begin a series of very slow rotations around the ball. So you'll be standing up, holding the ball, and slowly walking around the ball. Most people do this with their eyes closed. As you walk around, you'll be sensing the challenge from multiple new perspectives, sometimes pausing to see things from a new perspective. But as you rotate around, you'll also be bringing resources to yourself inside the ball. The ones we'll be working with today are *tenderness*, *fierceness*, and *playfulness*.

RD: These three resources are the fundamental resources needed to successfully complete a hero's journey. These are "archetypal energies," that is, patterns and energies that come from the history of consciousness, from many generations of experiences regarding how to become a human being. The first basic archetypal resource is tenderness.

SG: If you're going to live a hero's journey, if you're going to do any generative sponsorship, if you're going to meet any deep challenge in life, you'll need to be connected to tenderness. It's what allows you to touch and be touched, to soothe, to calm and be calm, to feel empathy and sensitivity, and so forth. Your mother probably told you that without these energies you won't get very far as a human being. *(Laughter.)* So in the first rotation around the ball *(Stephen begins to model holding a ball and very slowly walking around it)*, you'll be witnessing what's inside the ball, creating a space for it, being curious about it, and gently dosing it with tenderness. Don't rush, let it be very, very slow. Notice, as you give tenderness to yourself in the sphere, how it shifts the way you experience or respond to the situation.

Once you finish the first rotation, coach, you can suggest the hero take a deep breath of integration and then begin a second rotation, this time bringing the resource of positive fierceness.

RD: Like all of the energies that we have talked about, there is a shadow side and a resource side to each archetypal pattern. So, negative fierceness or uncentered fierceness comes out as aggression, violence, and so on. Positive or centered fierceness comes out in the form of determination, clarity . . .

SG: . . . strength, courage, commitment . . .

RD: . . . boundaries . . .

SG: . . . having a good "bullshit detector," seeing through the games and seductions . . .

RD: . . . protecting life, your own and others.

SG: These are some of the crucial qualities of positive fierceness. To take on any major task, you have to be able to have a fierce commitment – a deep, intense focus. That's the positive Warrior energy. In aikido we ask, how do you hold a sword? Which means, how do gather all of your life energy into one point – your center – and then extend it through your instrument of connection into the world, and keep extending it from a relaxed, focused center. So you bring your commitment and intention through your center – that's positive fierceness. If you had negative fierceness, you would be tense and blocked and probably angry, and then you'd clash with lots of things and be stopped, one way or another.

RD: You would actually trigger aggression against you. So instead, you're going to bring the positive quality of fierceness into your situation.

SG: Once the hero completes the second revolution, the coach invites the hero to take a breath of integration, then the third revolution begins.

RD: In this third round, you will bring the archetypal resource of playfulness to yourself in the ball.

SG: Your mother also probably told you: to succeed on the hero's journey, you must have a lot of playfulness! How many of your mothers told you that? (*Many smiles, but no hands lift. Steve smiles,*

191

with twinkle in eye.) Well, they should have . . . *(Laughter.)* Life is much too serious to not have a sense of humor!

RD: To be generative, you cannot be only serious. You've got to be able to play. If it's really serious, it's necessary not to take it too seriously. Otherwise you end up in that narrowing, constricting field. Playfulness is about creativity, new perspectives, getting outside of the box.

SG: It's about being fluid, being able to shift, to sense things in many ways. When I'm working with someone, there are different points in a session where I can see that person get much too serious. You can notice the typical signs – tense muscles, furrowed brow, emotional constipation. *(Laughter.)* This is the kiss of death, because nothing new can be created from that state. So that's usually where I bring out humor in some way, to pop the bubble of the over-serious trance. As a coach, it's your responsibility to keep the person from rigidly attaching to any particular point of view for too long. To be creative, you need a good quality of playfulness.

RD: There is a healing quality to laughter. If you've carefully observed our demonstrations . . .

SG: . . . you may think it's one big joke. *(Laughter.)*

RD: You'll notice actually that there's a particular point in the session, a turning point, where the client starts to laugh or smile. It's a type of laugh of awakening. The shift happens, the consciousness releases into a laugh, and boom, they're out of the box. So laughter can be a beautiful opening to a generative field.

SG: One of our main points, then, is that in order to live the hero's journey, you will need connection to all three of these archetypal energies. You will need to bring to yourself and to the world tenderness, kindness, calmness, sweetness, gentleness. But if that was all you had, you would be too soft and sentimental.

RD: The shadow side of tenderness is weakness, co-dependency . . .

SG: . . . listening to music like Barry Manilow. *(Laughter.)* We call it "schlock" – overly sentimental music.

RD: So in addition to tenderness you need fierceness.

SG: And what we're looking at in terms of the center is a place where you can integrate opposite energies. So, what does fierce tenderness look like?

RD: Or what does tender fierceness look like? One way to think of these energies is that they're like the primary colors – red, yellow, blue. You can mix them in many different proportions. They're elements that mix together in an infinite number of ways.

SG: So, after the third turning, where you bring in playfulness, you will do a fourth and final turning where you bring in all the energies at once.

RD: In an integrative and centered combination.

SG: So this is a way of thinking about the resources needed to support yourself on your hero's journey, or the resources needed to translate a problem into a solution. To demonstrate the exercise, I'm going to ask Rosa to come on up.

Demonstration with Rosa

(Rosa comes up onto the stage.)

SG: So, Rosa, I want to thank you for volunteering to explore your hero's journey.

Rosa: Thank you.

SG: *(Motioning toward the audience)* How does the group look so far?

Rosa: Well, very happy, and excited.

SG: So it's great being up here?

(Rosa nods.)

Let yourself feel all the support in the room for your process. And even though you will do this process with your eyes closed and likely forget consciously about the presence of the group, you can continue to draw upon that support for your process.

Rosa: OK, good.

SG: I hope you can use this time as a great opportunity for yourself for a deep learning. I want to express to you my deep commitment to support you in every way that I can, so that you can experience a deep, positive transformation for yourself. Part of what that means is that as you do your process, I'll care for the external space, making sure all is safe out here. If you feel me gently touch your shoulder, it's just to keep you within a safe space so you don't bump into anything out here. So my commitment is to hold the space so you can release your spirit.

Rosa: Thank you.

SG: You're welcome. And so to start, I'd like to ask you if you have a sense of your goal for this process, either something you want to create in your future or change in the present.

Rosa: Yes, I want to write a book . . . in the name of and on behalf of my mom. It's about transformation. *(Smiles.)* Can I add something?

SG: Of course, sure.

Rosa: I want to thank you for the work you introduced yesterday, because I really learned something deep in the process. It was about my mother, and my relationship with her. I learned I had an addiction and didn't even know what it was. I had been living overseas and I came back here about five years ago because she developed Alzheimer's disease. And as her disease progressed, I developed an anxiety about connecting with her, and went on a long journey with her. Yesterday, I was working with this, and decided it would be really good for me to write a book about my experience with this.

SG: Great, let's just take a moment to breathe with that . . . because I know as you breathe, you can begin to connect with the deepest parts of yourself . . . parts of you that are below the thinking mind that can be able to help us here today on your journey. Parts of you that are beyond intellectual thinking. And it's nice to know as we just take a few moments to breathe into some of them, that our field . . . can be able to welcome . . . all of those creative presences . . . And then, Rosa, what I'd like to ask you to do is to sense what image begins to arise from within you that would represent that future . . . it could be a literal image, it could be a metaphorical symbol. Just notice the image that your creative self sends up.

Rosa: *(After a few moments, nods.)* It's a butterfly.

SG: A butterfly. *(Pauses to breathe deeply.)* That's a nice thing to experience with you . . . That presence of a butterfly . . . and all that it represents . . . about your future . . . I want to thank your creative mind for sending us that image and helping us in the process here today. And I'd like to support you here today in finding how you can open a deep space within you to allow that future, that butterfly, to develop in your world. If you want to open your eyes now, you can . . . *(Rosa keeps eyes closed.)* Or really enjoy keeping them closed so you can continue deepening your space . . . Good . . . And from this space I want to ask you to shift your attention to creating your energy ball. Were you able to do that in the exercise this morning? *(Rosa nods.)* Great. So let yourself shift again into that process. Take all the time you need in the next moments to really enjoy sensing that ball.

(Rosa holds her hands out, as if holding a ball.)

And as you begin to feel your hands tuning and sensing, you can begin to feel the vibration of that energy ball . . . and who really knows how big it will get? You can allow your inner creative self to develop that ball, noticing its colors . . . textures . . . translucence . . . all the different experiential qualities so amazingly developing . . . Allowing a space, a sanctuary, a nest within which your future can unfold . . . That's good . . . That's good . . . That's good . . . And when you feel that you have developed that energy ball, you can just let me know by nodding your head.

(Rosa nods.)

Good. And just allow yourself to deeply concentrate on that ball . . . relaxing . . . but deeply concentrating . . . so that whatever else we're doing . . . whatever else you become aware of, you can remain deeply absorbed in the creative space, the comfortable sanctuary of that generative field that you have opened. Different thoughts can come through . . . different feelings . . . and you can remain with your first attention connected with the ball. You can just witness whatever else comes and goes.

You have come to this space today . . . to really find your future . . . within this timeless creative space of *nowwww*. So as you sense and enjoy that energy ball, when you're ready, I'd like to invite you to sense again that image of the butterfly, and just allow that image of the butterfly to drop inside your energy ball. Give it a home within the center of your generative field. And when you feel that again you can let me know by nodding your head.

(Rosa nods her head.)

That's good . . . That's great . . . And you can enjoy allowing that image to remain in the center of the field, even as we move around it. Your future can remain in the center of the ball, as you add wonderful resources to nurture it and allow it to grow. Your future can remain in the center . . . receiving . . . opening . . . ripening . . . like a beautiful flower.

And so when you're ready, Rosa, I'm going to ask you to begin a very, very slow rotation around the ball. Let your body move as it wants to move. It may move clockwise, or counter-clockwise . . . Just be curious as your creative self begins to move around your future . . . And as you do so, on this first circle you can bring to yourself, bring to your future, resources of kindness and tenderness . . . and as you do so, I will be completely holding the space all around you.

(Rosa very slowly begins to rotate around her energy ball. Steve is gently behind her, protecting the space and supporting the movements.)

That's good . . . slow down . . . slow down . . . slow down so your deepest self can awaken within . . . and as you circle around . . . you can bring from deep inside of your heart–mind . . . a tenderness to yourself . . . to feed yourself with tenderness . . . to feed yourself and your future with tenderness . . . to bring the presence of tenderness as a resource . . . and really enjoy and sense how it may begin to transform . . . to form trance . . . in the center . . . of your own future self . . . creating a sacred circle around your self . . . seeing your future from multiple perspectives. Bringing to it that sense of tenderness . . . watching, experiencing, shifting perspectives . . . and how much your future self . . . a woman . . . a butterfly . . . can drink in . . . the healing waters of tenderness . . . turning round slowly . . . turning round . . . slowly feeling the first revolution, the first transformation of the butterfly . . . as you move round . . . that's it . . . breathe . . . then the things move from the superconscious mind . . . through your body–mind . . . fulfilling the need for tenderness . . . fulfilling the longing for tenderness . . . receiving the support of tenderness . . . for your future self . . . a book of time . . . a relationship between mother and daughter . . . a butterfly dreaming a future . . . as you continue to turn round . . . the first revolution. *(Rosa completes the first rotation.)*

That's good . . . and taking a deep breath of integration, you can let all the learnings of the first revolution begin to move even deeper within you . . . *(Rosa breathes deeply.)* That's good . . . And when you're ready, you can begin the second turning. Just letting your body rotate . . . That's good . . . And in this second turning of the self . . . round and round . . . shifting and turning, widening and deepening . . . you can again circle round the future self . . . a butterfly . . . a woman writing . . . a new creative calmness . . . And as you circle again, you can bring to yourself in the center of your future . . . the resources of deep, positive fierceness . . . sending a beautiful Warrior energy to yourself . . . *I support you . . . I bring my sense of commitment . . . I will protect you and support you* . . . And noticing how the presence in the center of the field begins to "trance form" . . . as you bring it the gifts of positive fierceness . . . round and round . . . and round you go . . . where you stop, nobody knows . . . bringing round . . . positive fierceness . . . round . . . through "no mind" . . . bringing in those resources . . . feeding into that presence . . . deep, intense . . . beautiful . . . positive . . . fierceness . . . feeling the second turning . . . the second transformation . . . the second revolution . . . and feel how this amazing future can reach back into your past . . . and connect to the present . . . that feeds the future . . . as you turn round . . . feeling the sense of moving round. *(Rosa completes the second cycle.)*

When you arrive back at the beginning . . . again now . . . you can take a deep breath . . . feel the integration . . . of positive fierceness . . . into the field . . . into the center of the field . . . of your future self. *(Rosa takes a deep breath, then begins the third rotation.)*

And now as you begin the third transformation . . . what a nice thing to know . . . that you can bring the resources of playfulness to your future self . . . discovering how your body naturally turns toward the future . . . in the unfolding spiral of your journey, all of the different perspectives turning . . . different ways . . . different experiences . . . body moving . . . playful experiences . . . bringing all the spirits of play.

(Rosa spontaneously begins to move into a more non-linear slow dance. At the same time, Steve begins to speak more playfully, adding confusion and mischievous rhythms and tones.)

Turning . . . tuning . . . lifting . . . flying . . . two become one, one becomes two . . . all become themselves again . . . that's it . . . things falling apart sweetly . . . things coming together deeply . . . turning . . . tuning . . . a butterfly flies through the wind, landing on the future happiness of a book well written . . . that's it . . . that's it . . . that's it . . . a beautiful sense of play infuses . . . defuses . . . reuses in new ways . . . a butterfly's wings . . . freedom to tell your story . . . that's it. *(Rosa completes the third turning.)*

And as you complete the turning of play, you can take a nice breath and let these new awakenings migrate to all the relevant places in your life. *(Rosa takes a deep breath and then begins the fourth round.)*

That's good. And as you begin the fourth round . . . the fourth transformation . . . you can find that all of these different resources . . . like different notes of music . . . like different colors of the largest palette . . . can begin to move together . . . bringing to your future self inside . . . tenderness . . . fierceness . . . playfulness . . . and much, much more. Turning round . . . round and round . . . feeling at the very center of the turning . . . the very center . . . still moving . . . unfolding into a butterfly of your future self . . . it's your future . . . you can feel it . . . you can give birth to it . . . seeing it supported with . . . infused with . . . a beautiful tenderness . . . a deep fierceness . . . a wonderful freedom to play . . . you can see it with your own eyes of your eyes . . . you can feel it with your whole body of your body . . . you can know it with your whole being of all your becomings. *(Rosa completes the fourth cycle.)*

That's it . . . That's it . . . .That's it . . . And just enjoy a nice breath of integrating even deeper now. *(Rosa breathes deeply.)*

And when you're ready, you can reach out and take hold of your future self . . . to touch it . . . as you would touch the most delicate living presence . . . the most resilient amazing spirit . . . the most extraordinary gift of life . . . And as you touch it . . . feel it . . . and as you feel it, just really enjoy . . . *Your future is in your hands now* . . . And when you're ready, you can take that future self and slowly bring it into the center of your body–mind. Let your hands select which center. Let your hands guide that future self into its home in your center now. *(Rosa's hands begin to move to her heart.)*

That's it . . . bringing to heart your future . . . giving it a place . . . giving it a space . . . giving it a proper home in the deepest part of your being . . . *(Rosa takes some deep breaths.)* That's it, breathing it all the way inside . . . into the world of time and space . . . today and tomorrow . . . the world of the living . . . And just take a few moments to enjoy the completion of this amazing journey of self.

And then when you're ready to come back . . . to the world of earthlings . . . time and space . . . you may want to first make a simple commitment . . . in that place of honor . . . in that place of dignity . . . in that place of freedom . . . to continue this process for yourself and your hero's journey. *May you continue to care for this awakening presence . . . with your whole heart . . . with your whole mind . . . with your whole being.* And then when you're ready, let yourself slowly come back into the room and join the rest of us back here.

(Rosa opens her eyes, looking still deeply immersed in the experience.)

Good afternoon. *(Rosa laughs.)*

That was a really great experience to support you in. I wish you the best in continuing your hero's journey in the deepest, most fulfilling ways.

Rosa: *(Smiles.)* That was such a deep experience for me. Thank you. I can hardly find words for it.

SG: No need for words right now. Just enjoy what you have done for yourself and your future. Take some time to continue to stay connected to yourself, without words.

Rosa: OK, thanks.

SG: You're most welcome, Rosa. *(Smiling)* May the Force be with you. *(Laughter.)*

(To audience) Let's give Rosa a nice appreciation.

(Audience applause as Rosa leaves stage.)

The general sequence is: *Goal, energy ball, drop goal inside energy ball, four turns around the energy ball – first adding tenderness, then fierceness, then playfulness, then all at once. Then reach out, integrate the transformation into your center, make vows to the future, and come back.* Not so difficult. *(Laughter.)*

RD: So, you're just gently guiding the client to bring those three energies with each turn. The client puts the symbol of his or her goal in the middle, and just turns around three times, bringing those energies into the ball and the situation. So take some time and practice this process now.

(Participants find partners and begin to practice the exercise.)

Mindfulness and "Opening Beyond"

SG: We want to make a couple of points before continuing. You may be noticing that in the model of the hero's journey and the Generative Self, we're emphasizing how as you move to a generative level, you add another level of consciousness. One of the main ways this occurs is in the emergence of a *witnessing self* that allows you to detach from your *performance self*. The performance self is the one thinking thoughts, feeling feelings, expressing behaviors – all of the inner and outer "doing" by which a reality is created. The witnessing self is able to have what Buddhists call *mindfulness* and *metta*. *Mindfulness* is a non-reactive awareness of what's there; *metta* is the loving-kindness that touches and sponsors what's there.

For example, let's consider Robert here. *(Smiling, points to Robert.)* We can refer to him as the "Robert unit." *(Laughter.)* The Robert unit was a little spirit dropped into the world 54 years ago. Usually, whoever is doing the "dropping" senses who the spirit is, then searches for a family that will be unable to see or support that spirit's essence, making for a very interesting hero's journey. *(Laughter.)*

So, 54 years ago he was dropped into the world and he's been performing ever since, each moment using thoughts, images, behaviors, feelings, and so forth, to create a reality. To sponsor this performance self, we're looking to see how we can open a meta-position, a generative field of awareness that can hold, witness, bless, and help that spirit and the performance self to open up a beautiful, amazing life. *That's what moving to the generative level allows you to do.* So we're looking to develop this compassionate curiosity about how our life is unfolding, how to notice each moment of awakening, and how to gently support it into its most aligned, resonant, whole form. Remember, when we talk about detachment here, we're not talking about dissociation – it is a generative differentiation.

RD: Ken Wilber talks about this in terms of being able to "transcend yet include" whatever is there. This is very different from dissociation; it's a true meta-position.

SG: When you have these two levels of self, it means that you can think about your performance self either in terms of a first position – the "I" position – or in terms of third position – "he" or "she." Sometimes when you think about your performance self as he or she, it gives you new choices. Suppose, for example, you're in an experience of depression. You could say: *"I'm* depressed," using first person. That would identify you as the depression, and possibly make it worse. Or you could say, *"He* is depressed" or *"There's a presence inside of me that is filled with depression. And I'm really interested in being able to create a field of sponsorship and support for him."* This could differentiate you from the depression, opening up new possibilities of being with it. So again, moving to the generative level is literally opening a higher level of consciousness. Not to escape the lower level, but to be with it in a wider, deeper, and more creative way.

RD: This is a type of transcendent consciousness.

SG: To do that, we need this direct somatic sense that the field is alive, so your awareness is open beyond the problem. This sort of exercise is a simple technique, a metaphor for trying to train your attention to directly sense that everything in the world is living. And however big the challenge is, the space of the self is always bigger.

RD: Everything in the world produces some kind of energy through its relationships with everything else.

SG: And when you directly experience that, you are a part of the deeper creative force of the world. This is what we're looking to train in these exercises. To realize, *I am part of this amazing world of living consciousness.* And it's all so impermanent, so make use of it while you can. To have a human life is to be so lucky. The Buddhists like to say, when you get a human life, you've really hit the jackpot. The possibilities for awakening are relatively very great.

RD: You could have been a mosquito . . . again. *(Laughter.)*

SG: And at the end of your life as a mosquito, you might wonder, "What was that all about?" But a human life can be so much more. That's what we're exploring in the hero's journey – how to create a life that makes you happy. To do this, it's important to let your individual sense of self connect with this generative field of consciousness that is also part of your deeper self.

RD: This is what we're exploring in this section on the field mind. We've said that the generative principle of the somatic mind is *centering.* The generative principle of the cognitive mind is *sponsorship.* And we're saying now that the generative principle of the field mind is *open beyond* the content or the focal awareness.

To deepen awareness of this principle, we want to do another exercise. The generative principle of the field mind is to *expand* or *extend beyond.* In the next exercise you can experience that directly, and also experience the pragmatic value of thinking with a field mind when confronted with an impasse. The exercise is called "Seeing the Field." It is summarized in the following steps.

Exercise: Seeing the Field

1. Identify an experience where you have reached an impasse and select a physical location to be associated with it. Associate into that experience as fully as possible and step into the physical location you have chosen.

2. Step away from the physical location to an observer position. Center yourself and open to the "field." With your eyes closed, imagine you are looking through your center at the field or energy dynamics influencing the system. Allow a symbolic image to emerge.

3. Reflect upon your desired state and select a different physical location with which to associate it. Staying centered, step into that location and get a feeling for the desired state. Pay attention to the field or energy dynamics of this state. Allow a symbolic image to emerge for this state.

4. Step back into an observer position. Center yourself and open to the field. With your eyes closed, imagine you are looking through your center. Consider how the field or energy dynamics influencing the system would transform in order to reach the desired state. Allow a symbolic image to emerge for this state.

5. Taking the symbolic image that emerged in Step 4, step back into the impasse location and feel how it transforms.

RD: As we will see, there are several important principles in this exercise. The first is an extension of what NLP has always said, which is: *Don't put your attention on the content, put it on the form.* The solution will arise from the larger field of the relationships and their processes. So we're going to be attuned here to representing the field of relationships.

SG: We say in aikido, *Never give your eyes to the problem.* Put your first attention to the field. To get a simple perceptual example of this, experiment with your visual awareness as you look around your current environment. Instead of focusing on objects, let your eyes open to the peripheral. Let them be soft and open, and see if you can attune to the two corners of the room or space around you.

Let the larger peripheral field be your first attention. And from there, drop down and relax into your center, and see your environment from that perspective. It's a pretty big shift, isn't it? That's a major piece of what we're going to explore in this exercise.

RD: In particular, we're going to open to the larger generative field around a problem situation. How can you sense the field in which a problem is experienced, and how can you utilize that larger generative field to find a solution that is completely new? The basis for this is something similar to the previous exercise. It involves sensing the weave of energy within and beyond a problem state. In this larger field, you will also include the desired state.

SG: And then, as we did in the "Good Self/Bad Self" exercise, we'll be sensing the two complementary states in a larger unified field that holds "both, and much much more."

RD: You will be holding both present state and desired state within a space that extends beyond. This will give you a good example of what Albert Einstein meant when he said that *you can't solve a problem with the same thinking that is creating the problem*. So the question is, of course: How do you get to another level of thinking? How do you move to a more expanded level of consciousness? This exercise gives you some suggestions for how to do that with yourself and others.

We will be exploring a situation in which you come up against an impasse in your life; where you reach a place that you feel stuck; a place where you realize you can't go any further; a place on your hero's journey that you don't know how to get through. Very often these appear in the form of a double bind – where I'm wrong if I do, and I'm wrong if I don't.

SG: And by the way, these places of hitting a double bind on your journey are precise signals that you're standing on a threshold of generative change. When you're up against a double bind – I'm damned if I do, I'm damned if I don't – it tells you that nothing in your present or past awareness can help you get through this. At such threshold points, you must create a new response, beyond anything you've done before. Remember, this is our definition of a generative process. So you should train yourself to be happy when you recognize you're in a double bind. It means you're on the threshold of great change, if you can remember to activate a generative state! This exercise is an example of how to absorb the double bind in a way that creatively transcends it.

RD: One example of generative responses to double binds can be found in the Zen tradition of *koans*. These are purposeful double binds that the teacher gives the student to force a response that comes from beyond the box of the ego mind. So a Zen master might take a stick, hold it over the student's head and say, "If you say this stick is real, I'm going to hit you with it. And if you say it is not real, I'm going to hit you with it. Is this stick real?" *(Laughter.)*

SG: Sounds like the families that some of us grew up in. *(Laughter.)*

RD: So, what do you do if you are the student? How do you answer? If you stay in the either/or world of your ego mind, you're going to get hit. It's a double bind. The key is, of course, to let yourself respond with the ten thousand possibilities that are outside the either/or box. You might reach out and take the stick and hit the master with it. *(Laughter.)* Or you might find your own stick and start a sword fight. Or you could tickle the teacher and offer him a hot dog. *(Laughter.)*

SG: These are examples of the Marxist approach to double binds – and Groucho Marx was a very good spokesman for this approach. *(Laughter.)* It reminds me of the story of the two important Buddhist teachers who were going to have one of these major debates that Buddhist teachers have, where they quickly hurl questions and double bind-type techniques at each other, seeing how each responds without getting attached to the ego mind. They are seated across from each other on a stage. The first monk, a young guy known for his brilliance and scathing intellect, suddenly pulls an orange out from his robe, fiercely holds it out to the other monk, an old guy with a good centered presence, and says, "What's this?" It's a version of the *koan* Robert was just sharing. The young monk looks ready to pounce on any response the old monk comes up with. The old monk sits in silence for a while, breathing from his center, open to the field. He then leans over and chats briefly with his translator, who then gives his response, "What's the matter with you, don't they have oranges where you come from?" *(Much laughter.)*

Demonstration with Eric

RD: We would like you to have this generative level of conscious-ness. I'd like to ask somebody to volunteer who's interested in discovering a generative response to an impasse that they may be facing.

(Hands raise. Robert picks a man named Eric, who comes up on stage.)

Eric, we're going to begin by setting the context. What is the place where you feel stuck or at an impasse?

Eric: Well, it's that old story that Stephen mentioned earlier: sex, drugs and rock 'n' roll.

RD: Hmmm.

Eric: And I feel really stuck in my relationship with it. I feel this sort of desperation about it. I don't feel good when I do it. But it feels like if I don't do it, if I don't respond to what feels like a "call of the wild" . . . it's like . . . I feel I lose all my energy.

RD: So if I'm following you, Eric, you said you feel this sort of "call of the wild." In the States, we call it being a "party ani-mal." *(Laughter.)* But you feel this call . . . and there are some consequences.

Eric: I think basically it's like an addiction, you know? I enjoy it when I'm there, but then afterwards I pay the price. I'm not able to feel very present afterwards, and that's a big problem.

RD: I hear that and understand that. And you also said, if you don't do it, you feel like you're missing some kind of important life energy?

Eric: Well, it's like cutting myself off, like a constraint. I feel shut down and I don't feel free.

RD: Yes, I hear this double bind. If you do it, it's bad, because the consequences harm you. But if you don't do it, you're cutting off part of yourself, and that's also a problem for you.

Eric: Yes.

RD: OK. So are there particular moments or situations where this double bind is strongest for you?

Eric: *(Pauses)* Well, in intimate relationships . . .

RD: Can you think of one?

Eric: *(Nods)* Yes.

RD: Good. So far we've been talking about the content. What I'd like to do with you now is open a space in front of you *(pointing in front of Eric)* where you can place both the present state and the desired state. I'd like you to take a few moments to sense whether you feel if the present state – the struggle as you currently experience it – is more to your right or to the left in this space.

Eric: *(Pause)* The left.

RD: I'm going to ask you, when you're ready, to let yourself step into that space on the left side, and let yourself identify with what it's like when you're in that struggle. The whole struggle, both sides, OK? *(Eric nods.)* Both sides: *When I do it, I feel bad afterwards . . . but if I cut myself off, I feel shut down and not free.* And you mentioned this comes up with your intimate relationship. *(Eric nods.)* So when you're ready, step forward to the left side and connect with the whole of the problem state.

(Eric steps forward, begins to breathe deeply, looking conflicted and stressed.)

Yes, and really feel all the sensations that go with that struggle. What happens there?

Eric: It's like this . . . *(His hands show a twisting, pulling motion.)*

RD: So the sensations are like this feeling of a big pull.

Eric: Yes . . . feeling pulled between responsibility and desire.

RD: You notice a feeling of being pulled between responsibility and desire. Also notice if there are other presences, other people, in this field with you. Perhaps your intimate partner, or family members, or other people. Are there others present?

Eric: *(Nods, looks stressed)* Yes.

RD: And of course, you can also notice whether things from your past, from your history are part of this field. *(Eric nods, looking deeply absorbed in the conflict.)*

(To audience) And you see in his non-verbal patterns, it looks pretty difficult. You can see this is a field that completely possesses Eric, or anybody struggling with such an impasse. It's usually connected to many things – the past, the family, other people, and so forth. You just want to give the person an opportunity to identify with that whole field, then step back out.

(To Eric) What I'm going to ask you to do now, Eric, is to step out of that state, and take a step back to your original starting point, into a witnessing position. And as you do so, you can leave that whole field, that whole pattern, for now. *(Eric steps back out, takes a deep breath, reorients.)*

Hi, welcome back.

Eric: Hi.

RD: And Eric, as Stephen was saying, we're going to talk about Eric *over there (points to the "problem state" space)* – that's "him." And we can also notice that there is an "Eric" that is beyond the pattern. As we explored in the "Good Self/Bad Self" exercise, there is both responsibility and desire. *I see that you're responsible. I see that you are also pulled by desire. I see that you're both . . . . And I see that you are much, much more.*

That's the problem pattern, it's not the whole of Eric. *(Eric nods.)* So what I'd like to ask you to do here now is to really center . . . standing here, deeply within yourself . . . connected to a "you" that is beyond responsibility . . . and a "you" that is also beyond desire – this really unique energy of Eric. And really feel and sense your center as the place before and beneath thought . . . feeling grounded in your body and feet . . . a sense of your whole being here.

And as you do that, we're going to do some generative witnessing. As Stephen was saying, it's not dissociated. It includes the problem space, includes the solution space, but transcends them both. And from this space, Eric, I'd like to have you sense the whole field of that problem space, as one unitary field. We know that the content has to do with desire, feeling guilty, partying, intimate relations, and so on. What I want you to do is not put your attention on those things, but on the energetic field that holds all of that. So you are not looking from your head or your eyes, but looking from your center, to sense what's happening there. And rather than try to understand it literally, let yourself sense it more metaphorically, more symbolically. Maybe it has color, or some visual image, or some energy pattern, or a group of symbols. Let yourself sense with your field mind whatever is there.

(Pauses to let Eric sense the field.) And what do you notice?

Eric: I see the yin . . . and the yang . . . that symbol that represents both.

RD: Yes, you see the yin–yang symbol. And how about the conflict? How is that represented in the energy of this problem pattern?

Eric: It's like two very strong energies.

RD: So that's important to represent. Because we want to represent the problem here. And the problem, you were saying, is that you're not connected; there's something that's not in harmony. So sense the symbol of things not being in harmony . . . And as you feel that energy of the struggle, what is it like? You said you felt disconnected.

Eric: It is difficult for me to describe it . . . but I think that the starting point is that I'm just losing the perception of field because I'm involved in this judging and compulsive energy. It feels like with these persons, I am not centered to start with.

RD: That is important information, but I'd like you to notice how much of that description may be coming from the cognitive mind.

It makes sense, but it's more of an analysis of what's happening. *(To audience)* When you're coaching, it's very important to notice whether the description is coming from an experiential, symbolic field or from the cognitive mind.

(To Eric) So just let yourself take a deep breath, let go of your cognitive mind, and really come into your deeper mind. Let yourself tune into a different type of language, a language of pictures and images, symbols and metaphors.

Eric: What came to me was "trust" as the circumstance that can be the missing link.

RD: And that's also wonderful, but trust is a word. What I really want to have you receive is the symbol or image of the field of this problem. Maybe it's waves crashing on a shore, or thunder clouds, or a fire. Really drop into your body and feel the symbolic presence.

(Eric breathes more deeply and relaxes more.) That's right, that's good . . . And feel on this symbolic level. What is the symbol for this field?

Eric: A path under stars.

RD: Good, and notice in that image . . . a path under the stars . . . where is the problem? Notice where is the struggle?

Eric: I think the problem is that I feel a bit of fear, because I don't know where this path is going.

RD: How would you represent the energy of that fear? What is your symbol? Does it have a color? A movement?

Eric: Like a big wall of dust.

RD: A big wall of dust . . . That's good to notice. *(To audience)* Now Eric is beginning to enter more into the language of the field. It's dust. There's a path. When we use words like "trust," that's taking us right up into cognitive thinking. We really want to move to this level of metaphorical thinking. So there's this path, and there's a wall of dust.

(To Eric) And when you really tune into that problem of addiction, what other images come to you about this path, this dust? The images don't have to make any logical sense, just notice what's there.

Eric: I feel it's very difficult . . . This dust . . .

RD: And how do you see that in the image? What does it look like? What does this difficult energy look like?

Eric: Feeling paralyzed.

RD: Yes. Feeling paralyzed. And notice how feeling paralyzed looks in the image. Is it like glue? Notice the symbol of paralysis.

Eric: Well, it's like the wall is coming, and . . . I don't know what to do.

RD: Yeah. So there is a long path, and this wall is coming . . . this wall of dust.

Eric: I just feel the dust in my mouth.

RD: Yes, feeling dust in the mouth. *(To audience)* And by the way, you may notice that we're getting to a place which is not just dissociated or just associated. The thinking is not in the normal way of thinking. We're dropping into the field language of symbol, of metaphor, of image. So that's our field representation of the present state. And now we're going to move to the desired state.

(To Eric) So in just a moment, Eric, when you're ready, I'm going to ask you to let go of that field representation of the problem state for a moment. OK?

(Eric takes a breath and nods.)

And I'm going to ask you in a moment to go to the desired state over there *(points to right)*. And remember, you're letting go of the problem state. Let the problem state be over there *(points to left)*. And let yourself step into the desired state over there *(points to right)*.

(Eric steps into the space of desired state, and his non-verbal presence almost immediately shifts to a more centered, calm state.)

And really notice, as things are different, what are they like? The integration has happened, the problem is resolved, your self is integrated. Just notice what that's like. *(Eric breathes deeply, looks centered.)*

And let's start with your sensations. What do you feel in your body?

Eric: Hmmm . . . *(Smiles.)* I feel very quiet.

RD: Quiet . . .

Eric: I feel quiet . . . like my heart is . . . tranquil.

RD: Quiet, and your heart is tranquil.

Eric: Calming down . . . *(Makes sound with breath, a deep release happens.)*

RD: That's good. *(To audience)* And just notice, everybody, that we're not quite yet talking about the solution field. We're talking about bodily sensations, so this is the somatic state in the field. *(Eric breathes slowly and audibly again.)* The somatic state is different from the field. But we're starting with the somatic sensation . . .

Eric: Ahhh. I can move again.

RD: You can move.

Eric: *(Nods, smiles, and breathes.)* Instead of being paralyzed.

RD: Yes. So this is your desired state. And even as you notice the somatic part of the desired state, I want to see if you can open your awareness wider, to include but open beyond your somatic state, to the field as a whole. And as you let yourself do that, notice any images that emerge. What is the symbol that comes to represent this field? What images make it possible for the heart to quiet?

(To audience) I don't know if you could notice, but Eric was going back into his head. From the body tension, especially in the forehead, you can see the cognitive mind begin to reassert itself. So you want to keep coaching a person to open wider into the field mind.

(To Eric) And Eric, what is the symbol for your desired state?

Eric: It's like . . . it's like a fur. It's like a question mark.

RD: Like a fur, in the form of a question mark.

Eric: *(Deep breathing, looking very intense.)* It's a very intense energy. Wow.

RD: *(Nodding)* The energy of this desired state is very intense.

Eric: Yes . . . very deep . . . very nice.

RD: And what else is in the field of this desired state? What other symbols do you notice?

Eric: My vision is much clearer. I see the path and all the surroundings. It's a sunny desert.

RD: *(To audience)* Now Eric is speaking from a different level of language. It includes the body, but also the larger field.

(To Eric) And now we're going to go to the next step, which is to come back to the third position here *(points to starting place)*; the witnessing position for both states. When you're ready, step out of the desired state and come back to the meta-position.

(Eric steps out of desired state and into witnessing position.)

Good. And now from this meta-position, I'm going to ask you to hold both of these states, as if they're part of a deeper unified field. Hold both of the states and really reflect on them at the same time. One on side *(points and directs voice to the left side)* there's the problem state: the power struggle, on the path with a wall of dust overwhelming you. And on the other side, over there *(points and directs voice to the right side)*, there is the desired state: a sunny desert . . . a beautiful clarity . . . a deep calm and tranquility. And really hold your attention with both of them, equally and at the same time. *(Eric closes his eyes.)* That's right.

And as you do that, notice that there is field between these two: the path with a wall of dust . . . the sunny desert . . . and an energy connecting and unifying the two of them. And as you sense that, let another symbol come up. Let your deepest creative wisdom provide a symbol for that deeper field.

Eric: *(With eyes closed, looking deeply absorbed.)* Wow, it's this energy ball, like we were working with before.

RD: An energy ball.

Eric: Yes . . . and with the energy ball around the two states, it is like they are the same. It's very strange . . . very hard to describe . . . but it's like they're not that different.

RD: That's right. *(Eric breathes, looking like he's integrating something.)* And even as you do that, in the final step, I'd like to ask you to extend beyond even that. Extend even beyond that energy ball. Extend into a field of fields *(Eric looks deeply absorbed)* where there is an intelligence . . . a mind that is beyond the normal, ordinary mind . . . what Erickson might call "the unconscious mind" . . . what Bateson called "the larger mind" . . . A mind beyond mind. And from that place, you can experience another symbol. Just let another image come into your awareness from this superconscious mind . . . A generative symbol that comes to you as a gift from this larger mind. All you have to do is to stay open and extend beyond both the present and desired states. What's the symbol that comes to you?

Eric: I just realize . . . there are flowers . . . flowers.

RD: So the symbol that comes is there are flowers. Good, just let yourself receive the gift of those flowers . . . And as you do, I'd like to ask you to go back to the problem state . . . step back into the problem state . . . take your time . . . and bring this symbol, this gift of flowers and bring it into that state. Cross the threshold. Return back to this problem state with the resources from the larger mind. *(Eric steps into problem state. His breathing changes, becomes more quiet.)*

(To audience) You can see at this moment, he's more in his generative trance mind. There's not much cognitive thinking. Everything is smoothed out. The breathing is deep and calm. The physiology looks beautiful. I think you can see this is not the normal cognitive mind. There's a lot of generative somatic mind going on here. Standing near him, I can feel that there's a lot of heat coming from his body. The coloring in his skin is much darker, more blood and relaxation flowing through.

(To Eric) And just notice what happens here. What moves, what shifts or transforms, what intensifies, what disappears?

Eric: I feel a lot of calm energy here. It's a very good place. Yes, it's a good place . . .

RD: *(To audience)* Again, you see quite a big physical difference here than when Eric was first here.

(To Eric) And Eric, I'd like to have you now go and take the energy ball to the desired state. So if you walk to the desired state . . . taking your time. *(Eric walks slowly to the desired state on the right side.)* And bring to this sunny desert . . . the flowers and an amazing ball of energy that is beyond any particular state.

(To audience) You can see there's a lot going on. Not much verbal or cognitive effort, but you can see deep experiential absorption and processing.

(To Eric) And what is happening there?

Eric: *(Pauses, looking deep in processing.)* It's working . . . there's something swinging between two things . . . It's very amazing . . . I feel very good.

RD: Something is swinging between two states that feels very good.

Eric: Yes.

RD: What about that tension, that conflict that you felt over there – what's going on there?

Eric: I don't feel that tension.

RD: Great. As our final step, let's go back to the middle place, the meta-position in between the two . . . and bring the flowers to the energy ball that holds the two worlds.

Eric: Ah! Wow! *(Looks very happy, excited but centered.)*

RD: Yeah!

Eric: Ah! Ah! . . . Wow . . . Ahhhh! *(Looks like deep integration process, deep breathing and opening.)*

RD: *(Smiling)* That's what we call somatic syntax! *(Laughter.)* *(Eric continues to explore, eyes closed in integration process.)*

(To audience) This is an example of what we call third generation NLP. Were not just switching around some submodalities. We're seeing how it might be possible to do deep identity transformation. It's a third-order type of change. A rearranging of a human being, an awakening of the soul. You can see that the generative field mind is very different from the cognitive mind.

(To Eric) I'm curious if there is a symbol that comes to you for this place you're in now.

Eric: *(Looking beatific)* Well, it's just flowers everywhere! . . . and I can feel my bare feet really touching the ground.

SG: You've become an authentic flower child!

RD: *(To audience)* And you can see as Eric's breathing slowly begins to change, he's beginning to complete the process for himself. You could track a lot of Eric's work here through the breath. He's been processing lots with his breath, and you could see how it changed significantly at different points in the process.

Eric: *(Takes a deep breath and opens eyes back into the room, looking at Robert, smiling.)* Hey!

RD: *(Smiling back)* Hey! It's good to see you, flower child! Take good care of yourself on this journey.

(Eric hugs Robert, then Stephen, then leaves the stage to loud applause.)

Skills for Opening to the Field

RD: OK. Like most of our exercises, the basic formula for this process is very simple. A lot of stuff happens. It can be very intense and amazing, but the basic formula is very simple.

SG: In order to do this work well, it needs to stay simple. There's so much stuff going on that you need to stay grounded in a simple sequence. You don't need to micro-manage the details, which can often be non-linear, non-rational, and unexpected. On the contrary, you're looking to be guided by this language of the creative unconscious. But you're also being guided by the simple underlying structure of the work. Let everything flow through you, even as you gently steer with the experiential sequence you're using.

In this case, we're using the same basic model as with the "Good Self/Bad Self" exercise. There are four points of focus you're shifting between.

RD: There was the problem state.

SG: That's the first point of focus.

RD: The desired state.

SG: That's the second point of focus.

RD: The field between them.

SG: The third point of focus.

RD: And the bigger field extending beyond all of them.

SG: That's number four. One of the beautiful things you may have noticed with Robert as the coach, is that he imposed none of his own content. He was just guiding Eric between these four positions, asking Eric's creative unconscious, his generative field mind, to provide all the content along the way. That sequence was (1) step into the problem state, (2) step into the desired state, (3) step into the field that holds both, and (4) open into the "field of fields" beyond that. And everything else came from Eric.

RD: There are a couple of small nuances of the process worth mentioning. In stepping into the problem state, you want to get a description of the somatic sensations. Begin to bring the person from their cognitive intellect into their experiential knowing. This is crucial. At the same time, make sure the person is not limited to just their somatic perspective. The somatic state, and the personal self, is one important focal point of the field, but there are others as well. That's why I was asking Eric if there were other people, other memories, other associations connected with the space. You want to tune into the larger field, bypassing the cognitive intellect. Field intelligence requires a felt sense to guide you.

SG: You probably noticed that throughout the session, Robert was emphasizing, *Don't think the answer, let it come to you. Let yourself experientially sense it.*

RD: Once we touched the problem state, we went to the witnessing state, the field awareness. This meta-position is not about focusing on the specific content, but on the field as a whole. This was a very important part of the demonstration, because it took Eric a little while to shift from his ordinary cognitive mind into his somatic field mind. We've all been taught to try for conscious insight: "Oh, I see. This means that." But really what we want to do is to enter this deeper mind of experiential symbolic, energetic, field knowing.

SG: It's precisely being in the field mind that allows the process of holding opposites – holding the double mind – in a way that creatively transforms them. Attuning to the generative field mind is the way through the impasse. This is why we emphasize it as one of the crucial tools for the hero's journey. Carl Jung talked about the generative process of transforming opposites into a deeper unity as "the transcendent function," and emphasized it as the central process in the path of self-realization, which is intimately related to the goal of the hero's journey.

In this regard, you might say that the two parts Eric was struggling with – what he called "responsibility" and "a call to the wild" – are pretty deep archetypal patterns. That is, they don't just operate in Eric, but in each of us. And as such, they're probably connected to a field that holds many, many different experiences; not only in his own personal history, but in his family and ancestral history as well.

RD: Another way to talk about the archetypal struggle Eric was exploring is that "responsibility" is about others – how to take care of others; while desire is about self – how do you feed yourself?

SG: *(Smiling)* And which one is more important? This is part of your final test – 30 percent of your final grade is based on this question. *(Laughter.)*

RD: And of course we all know the answer to that question. The answer is . . . "Yes."

SG: This question is like the Zen master's stick. Which one do you say it is, responsibility or play?

RD: Which one do you need more in your life? The answer is "Yes."

SG: One final thing. Coaches, remember that one of your main responsibilities is to help the hero stay in a high quality state, regardless of what the content of their experience is. So remember the coaching principles of the somatic generative state (align and center), the cognitive generative state (accept and sponsor), and the field generative state (open beyond the content). If your partner is not in a high quality state, they won't have access to generativity. So monitor and gently coach things like breathing, erect posture, and relaxed muscles. These are your coaching responsibilities.

RD: If the client starts to go up into their head, just gently but clearly coach them. Breathe, drop into the center, relax, let go.

SG: Now it is time to find a partner and practice opening your awareness to this field level of consciousness.

Closing: The Pattern that Connects

SG: We hope you can begin to see from these exercises the outlines of the map for a hero's journey. We're emphasizing in this section how to shift to a generative field, where you can experience yourself beyond any position. This way, you can creatively hold all positions, so that you can be "relationship" itself.

RD: We're suggesting that to achieve your hero's journey, you need to pray. I don't mean that in a religious sense, but in the human sense of connecting with an intelligence beyond your local self.

SG: There are an infinite number of ways to practice this and realize this communion. However you get there, get there. Because you need to do healing and transformation. One of the main practical points we've been exploring is that when you're stuck, it's telling you that there's a clash, a violent resistance, between two different parts of the field. They could be inside of you – as with Eric, where it was responsibility fighting with desire – or interpersonal, as with two people holding very different positions. The question is, how do you transform conflict to cooperation? And the answer, we're suggesting is *you!* You are the generative field that can hold different parts of a field and integrate them. You are the deeper space that can "make love, not war." You are the self that can create harmony in the world. You are the field!

Once you've opened yourself as a generative field, you become curious about how to give place for each part of the field. You could do it in the space outside of your body, as Robert did with Eric. Or you could use your different body centers to hold and then integrate different energies or parts. For example, you could sense where in my body do I feel the energetic center of the part that wants to be responsible? (*Steve lets hand hover over his body, then touches it to his heart.*) And then you could ask, where do I feel the energetic presence of the call to be wild? (*Again, hand hovers over body, waiting to sense where this center is felt.*) Oh, I feel it in my belly, that's interesting. Then the next question is, how can I sense a feeling of connection flowing between these different centers? This represents the self that can unify opposites.

RD: So different parts may have different somatic centers. You might find it helpful to think in terms of the Hindu chakra system in this regard.

SG: That reminds me of the five Jewish boys who made good. The first one was Moses. And Moses said, "It's all here (*points at his head*). With the Ten Commandments, you can't go wrong." The second nice Jewish boy, Jesus, said, "No, it's all here *(points at his heart)*. This is the center." The third Jewish boy was Karl Marx, who said, "It's all here" *(fiercely pats the belly)*. Then Sigmund Freud came along and said *(looks down at pelvic area)*, "Go lower, young man!" *(Laughter.) (Looks down again and smiles.)* And the fifth nice Jewish boy is Robert's favorite, Albert Einstein, so I'll let Robert tell you what Uncle Al said.

RD: It's all relative! *(Laughter and applause.)*

SG: But seriously, we're emphasizing that it is your human spirit that is the pattern that connects. So it's good to know that in one somatic center you feel a particular part of yourself, and in another somatic center you feel another part. The even better thing to know is that neither of them is really you. *You are the spirit that connects and flows through all parts of your knowing.*

RD: Gregory Bateson talked about this as "the pattern that connects."

SG: So that's what we're looking to do on the great journey of the hero. Be the connection that heals. Be the connection that transforms. Be the connection that gives birth. So train yourself to feel excited when you feel really stuck, when you hit conflict, because it means you're standing on a threshold. You're standing in a place where two important parts of a whole are trying to integrate. These polarities, these dualities, are your friends. They are the means by which a Generative Self is born.

You see the polarities everywhere you turn. And while we're trained to pit them against each other or think of one as "good" and the other as "bad," we're saying that they're two peas in the same pod. For example, we ask you: Is it more important to care for yourself or to care for others?

RD: *Yes.*

SG: Is it more important to say "yes" or to say "no"? Is it more important to sense you're feminine or you're masculine? To be active or to rest? When we ask in this way, you can see how silly it is to think of the polarities as enemies or mutually exclusive, although this is how they are typically experienced in a symptom or problem. The good news is the relationship can shift from clashing to blending. You can make love, not war. You can be whole, not divided. The integration will not happen spontaneously; it takes human presence to do it. And what we're saying is that *you* are that presence.

RD: And for you to do it, you need a connection with a wisdom that is beyond your cognitive self. But that can only come through human presence. That's the channel of the divine.

SG: *(Playfully)* So praise the Lord! Praise the Lord!

RD: *(Also playfully)* Amen!

Day 4

Navigating the Journey

SG: I want to start this section with a poem by one of the great contemporary American poets, Mary Oliver. She has written a beautiful poem that I'd like to read to you called "Wild Geese" from her book *Dream Work* (1986). She lives in Cape Cod, Massachusetts, and every fall, the sky is filled with thousands of huge geese flying south for the winter. They're like me, they don't like cold winters. Then, in the spring, you see them all flying back home. And she uses this as a beautiful metaphor to talk about the return to one's self. You will hear in the poem references to the three minds of Generative Self – the mind in the head that often judges things in terms of good versus bad; the mind in what she calls "the soft animal" of the body; and the mind beyond us in the field.

Some people say that there's one line in every poem that is the most important line. For all the recovering Catholics in the room, it clearly is the first line. Here's what she says:

> You do not have to be good.
> You do not have to walk on your knees
> for a hundred miles through the desert repenting.
> You only have to let the soft animal of your body
>   love what it loves.
> Tell me about despair, yours, and I will tell you mine.
> Meanwhile the world goes on.
> Meanwhile the sun and the clear pebbles of the rain
> are moving across the landscapes,
> over the prairies and the deep trees,
> the mountains and the rivers.
> Meanwhile the wild geese, high in the clean blue air,
> are heading home again.
> Whoever you are, no matter how lonely,
> the world offers itself to your imagination,
> calls to you like the wild geese, harsh and exciting –

over and over announcing your place
in the family of things.

SG: In this poem, Mary Oliver offers this radical idea: the world
is alive. The world wants to help you in your journey. It's calling
you and supporting you. The capacity to sense that is a big part of
what we've been emphasizing these past days. How to quiet your
local mind and listen and feel that there's a deeper consciousness
that's trying to help us wake up, trying to help us become persons.
Will we let it?

RD: In honor of our Irish heritage, I'm going to offer an Irish blessing for my reading, which goes:

I wish you not a path devoid of clouds,
Nor a life on a bed of roses,
nor that you might never need regret,
nor that you should never feel pain.
No, that is not my wish for you.
My wish for you is:
That you might be brave in times of trial,
when others lay crosses upon your shoulders.
When mountains must be climbed,
and chasms are to be crossed.
When hope can scarce shine through.
That your gift God gave you
Might grow along with you
and let you give the gift of joy
to all who care for you.
That you may always have a friend
who is worth that name.
Whom you can trust, and who helps
you in times of sadness.
Who will defy the storms
of daily life at your side.
One more wish I have for you
that in every hour of joy and pain
you may feel God close to you.
This is my wish for you,
and all who care for you.
This is my hope for you,
Now and forever.   Anon.

RD: This blessing touches on the value of having guardians – friends who are worthy of the name, of feeling close to that calling from the larger field. So you're not just focused on material comfort or safety, but attuning to how your gifts and your goodness grow through all the challenges of life. We're suggesting that this is what the deepest satisfaction of the hero's journey comes from. It's not that "If I just did everything right, then I wouldn't have pain anymore, or I wouldn't have sadness, or I wouldn't have difficulties." All those things will be there in life. Those are what we call the trials on the hero's journey. But the good news is that something deeper is also there. May you find it each day.

SG: *(Smiling)* And the days just get worse as you get older! *(Laughter.)* When I work with clients and they make these wonderful changes and say, "This is great, I feel so wonderful!" I try to break the news gently: "Enjoy it while you can, it won't last." *(Laughter.)*

RD: The drugs will wear off. *(Laughter.)*

SG: The drugs will wear off, and now that you've created this bigger solution space, your next problem is going to be even bigger. Isn't that great to know? *(Laughter.)*

RD: Life is out to get you – it will not let you be a couch potato! It's going to keep giving you challenges.

SG: What can change is your relationship with these challenges. You can learn to not take them so personally. You can learn that however big the problem is, the space of self is always bigger.

RD: This comes through a generative relationship with yourself.

SG: And to something beyond yourself, beyond your problems. This is the big shift we're looking to make. Problems come, problems go.

RD: These are the trials and ordeals on the hero's journey.

SG: But your life is not a problem. You are not a problem. But, technically speaking, in English we say: "Shit happens." *(Laughter.)* But we also say: "Shift happens." So we're looking to develop a shift to your shit. *(Laughter.)*

RD: Frequently, I will have a client who comes in and works on a challenging situation. When they return the following week, I'll ask, "How is everything going?" And they reply, "Well, the situation is still the same, but it's not a problem anymore." How do we shift ourselves so that the problem is no longer a problem? How do we find the calling in the trial, the opportunity in the problem?

SG: We're bringing this up in this last section as we begin to sense what it might be to bring some of these learnings back into your everyday life. It's really great to be able to take time to step back from your usual life and explore these deep connections and transformational changes. But a crucial part of the hero's journey is the return back home. It can sometimes be a bit of a shock to discover that the world out there is not as nice and accepting as the world we've created in this program. There are many presences in the world that really don't want you to wake up. Isn't that great to know? *(Laughter.)*

RD: And they're going to be the ones that test your commitment to your calling. They're going to be the ones that hold up a mirror to your shadows.

SG: So we want to anticipate that, to have a clarity that this is going to happen, but also have a clarity about what each of us can do when we encounter those demons, those presences that really don't support us.

RD: So, we've been following this path of the hero's journey . . .

SG: . . . and really looking at it as a metaphor for the awakening of the spirit into the human world. We've been exploring how you are something more than your thoughts; something more than what other people think about you. You're this amazing human presence who has come here to bring your gift into the world.

The Importance of Practice

RD: And in bringing that gift – to also heal the wounds of yourself and the world. To explore this, we want to start with a process that has to do with what we would call "practices." In the hero's journey, we emphasize *practices* more than *techniques*. Practices are what allow you to have an ongoing transformation of identity. This is different from techniques. In emphasizing techniques, the focus is often more narrow. You focus on a single situation and think, "Gee, which technique will I use to fix this?" You use some technique, and if it makes a change, you say, "Great!" If it doesn't, you say, "Oh darn, the technique didn't work."

But this deep transformational path of the hero's journey is not a one-shot deal. To hear your calling, to live that calling, to turn demons into guardians, you need practices – repetitive activities that you do over and over. Just like in mastering anything – sports, music, relationships, business. You don't use a single technique to achieve lasting success. You use a set of practices every day to create an amazing journey of mastery. This is how we see the hero's journey. So some of our basic coaching questions are: *What are your practices? What are the things that you do every day, not for your job, not for your family, but for you to become a better person?*

SG: We look at the amazing changes you can create with these exercises, whether in a seminar or in a coaching or therapy session, not as final results – they are the beginning of some incredible possibilities. The seed has burst into the world. You can now feel what is possible. But to make the possible actual, to grow that seed into its full maturity, takes tremendous devotion to practices. If you don't have good practices, the promising changes will wither away quickly.

RD: The experiences you have in the work you do are reference experiences upon which to build the path, to live the journey.

SG: So when you do coaching or therapy, this conversation about practices is very, very important. Freud used to say there are two pillars of the good life – one is what Robert has alluded to as "work" and the other is "love" – by which Freud generally meant "family." So according to Freud, it's all about how you connect with your work and with your family. We're saying that's not enough. You need a third pillar, which is your relationship to yourself. To build this third pillar, you need daily practices. Time and attention that is just for you with you. Because when you're with your family, or your loved ones, it's not just about you. You have responsibilities to attend to them as well. Obviously at work, it's not just about you – you have responsibilities. So in your relationship with work and family, you are accountable to others. But with your practices, it is just about your relationship with yourself. So to live the hero's journey, you must have a commitment to practices.

RD: And if you don't commit to those practices, the attention to self will usually be forced through symptom development.

SG: Robert has mentioned his dad and his cigarette smoking, and how he said about his smoking: "This is the one thing I do for myself." That was his centering practice.

RD: Exactly.

SG: But we would say it's a pseudo-centering practice. It brings you back to yourself, but you have to give up your center to get there.

RD: If you don't commit to connect with yourself in centered ways, you will end up connecting with yourself in uncentered ways. It comes out in all these symptomatic expressions, uncentered desires – smoking, internet pornography, and so on.

SG: Overeating.

RD: Addictions are essentially uncentered practices people do for themselves.

SG: This can be seen very easily by asking somebody with an addiction: "Take a moment and recall the first time that you engaged in that addiction; for example, the first time you smoked a joint." And as the person reconnects, you'll usually see this sense of "Ahhh." A sense of release of ego control and surrendering to the field. If there weren't this initial positive experience, the addict would not be drawn back to it. You'd probably say, "Oh, I felt terrible doing that. I've got to find a different addiction." (*Laughter.*) "That addiction technique doesn't work. But there are plenty more to try!" (*Laughter.*)

RD: But we're saying that the addiction connects you to something deep within yourself, beneath your ego control. We're saying this is a basic need for all of us, and if we don't feed it with our presence, it will be done without our presence, as in an addiction. Sometimes I will say to a client, "Isn't it a sad thing that this is what gives you the most pleasure in your life? You must not have explored very much."

SG: If your most intimate relationship is with a cigarette, maybe you should at least consider a few other possibilities. *(Laughter.)*

RD: So what we're saying is that to feed the connection with your center in a positive way, you need practices. Practices that align you with your center, your calling, and your resources. You need them in order to successfully live your hero's journey.

SG: And by the way, what is the number one excuse for not doing a practice?

Different audience members: I don't have time!

SG: Isn't that amazing? It's not only you that uses this cheap excuse – you can see that it's *everybody*! And since you can see that everybody uses this excuse, you can see it's not even your idea. It's an equal-opportunity "alien" or "demon" that possesses every possible human being. These alien thoughts are the hypnotic internal dialogue that "alienates" you from your center and your resources. Be on the lookout for them!

Sometimes I suggest to clients that they imagine a group of ghouls camped out a short distance from their body. They're just watching for when you leave your center, because that's when they invade and start eating your soul. *(Laughter.)* This usually happens whenever you curse or reject some part of you, since that requires that you dissociate from your center. As soon as that happens, they say, "OK boys, she's gone. Let's move in." And the next thing you experience is this gnawing feeling that something is eating you inside. *(Steve imitates a ghoul eating human flesh.)* And that's the feeling of aliens eating barbecued soul. *(Laughter.)*

RD: And your energy for your calling starts drifting away, diminishing. And the TV starts looking better and better. The whining and complaining seem more compelling.

SG: So we have this saying, "A centering practice each day keeps the aliens away!" *(Laughter.)* To make sure you do them, you need to look at the hypnotic techniques you use not to do them. And "not having time" is at the top of the list. "But I don't have time now. When I get more time, then I'll do it." We guarantee: you will *never* have more time.

RD: People often ask me: "Oh, how do you find the time to write books?" I say: "You never find it. You won't find it. You have to create it." Remember the top manager I talked about who rode his bicycle as a problem-solving practice? Many people hear that and say, "Oh, that's nice. I wish I had time to ride my bicycle!" For him, he was saying: "That is an absolutely essential practice for me to be able to be on my journey to be a good manager. I have to make the time to ride my bicycle."

SG: Otherwise you cannot master what Robert was calling "the inner game."

RD: Remember the top manager who said, "As a leader, it is imperative that I maintain my energy"? He made the time to sing out the negative energy, and he also did physical activities. Those were things he did just for himself, to manage and to feed his own energy. So we're saying that to realize your journey, you need to find your practices. We're going to offer some suggestions about how you can do that.

Self-Sponsorship through Expanding Awareness

SG: The first exercise we want to guide you through is known as a self-trance method. You can also think of it as a self-connection or self-sponsorship practice. When people would ask Milton Erickson about self-hypnosis, he would say, "Oh yes, Betty likes to demonstrate that." Betty was his wife. This was the 1970s, and he had an intercom connecting his office to his home next door. He would press the intercom and say, "Betty, they want to know about self-hypnosis!" And she would say: "All right, I will be out in a while." And she would come out and share a version of what we are going to share with you.

At the core of this practice is self-acceptance as a creative strategy. We've been emphasizing that to walk the hero's journey requires that you don't oppose or clash with energy. Instead, you practice how to blend with it and creatively engage it. The word "acceptance" is one of those tricky words that can mean so many things. We hope you sense at this point that we don't mean it as passively submitting to what's there – "OK, whatever" – but a more vibrant practice of receiving it in a centered, generative field, then becoming curious about how it can open further in a positive way.

RD: As my Irish blessing was implying, you're not only on your hero's journey in times of joy. It's also in the times of pain. And you've got to take both the joy and the pain, and transform those into energies that take you forward.

SG: You're practicing this relational sequence of: (1) center within yourself, (2) align with your intention, (3) open to the field, (4) receive whatever is in the field through your center, (5) add your own resources, (6) align it with your intention, and (7) release it back into the world with whatever changes it has just developed. Then notice what's there next, and do it again. So you're really training yourself as this exquisitely tuned channel; a centered intentional field that absorbs and transforms in positive ways.

RD: You're an energy transformer. Like the top manager I mentioned, whatever comes, take it in and turn it toward the fulfillment of the calling. Turn it toward the mission.

SG: A good analogy for this is Robert's wife Deborah, who interprets for him in France. And she's such an amazing interpreter. She is also a dancer, and she just stands there with this beautiful centered presence and takes in what Robert is saying, holds it for a moment, and then expresses it . . . better than Robert! (*Laughter.*) She somehow takes away all his impurities, in a way that the nuns couldn't! (*Laughter.*)

RD: It's true. I say something, and when I hear her speak it in French, I go, "Yes, *that's* what I really meant to say!" (*Laughter.*) She somehow manages to distill down the essence and intention of the idea and trim away all the unnecessary content.

SG: This is the process we're talking about developing in yourself. How to attune your nervous system, your body–mind, to deeply receive and give through this creative loop with a generative field.

RD: Receiving, transforming, filtering, and then giving.

SG: So, usually what we call "thinking" blocks all of them. It blocks receiving, so you're not getting any new information from the moment. It blocks processing, and it blocks giving. And you really won't be able to do anything creative or transformative if you've shut the door to receiving, and blocked the passageway to giving. So this is a little practice to open the door, and allow yourself once again to be a transformative presence in the world. The basic steps are summarized as follows.

Exercise: Self-Sponsorship for Health and Healing – Utilizing Ongoing Awareness

1. Develop a comfortable, receptive position.

2. Set intention.

3. Induction: repeat cycle of statements, filling in new content each time:

   - **Now I am aware that I see** _____

   - **Now I am aware that I hear** _____

   - **Now I am aware that I feel** _____

4. Next cycle of statements:

   - **Now I am aware that I see _____, and I give permission for it to take me deeper into myself (breathe and relax)** . . .

   - **Now I am aware that I hear _____, and I give permission for it to take me deeper into myself (breathe and relax)** . . .

   - **Now I am aware that I feel _____, and I give permission for it to take me deeper into myself (breathe and relax)** . . .

5. Once entranced: note, accept, and allow each experiential form to contribute to the solution:

    • **Now I am aware that _____ is happening, and I can allow it to open toward a generative solution** . . .

6. When ready, allow integration and movement beyond the problem:

    • **And now I can allow all to integrate into a generative solution** . . .

7. Sense yourself in this new response in the future.

8. Gratitude and vows.

9. When ready, reorient comfortably.

SG: To begin, take a few moments to get into a comfortable position. This is a pretty simple process. It starts with getting yourself settled in and settled down. And shifting from orienting to other people to giving yourself all of your loving awareness.

RD: Bring your first attention to your center . . . to your body.

SG: Begin to allow yourself to shift into that witnessing mode.

RD: Bring your awareness into your breath.

SG: Align through your spine . . . nothing to do in the body, except relaxation . . . nothing to cling to or to hold on to in the mind.

RD: Feel your body all the way from your feet . . . up through your legs and spine.

SG: Once you've settled in and settled down . . . sense the setting of an intention . . . and for today's work . . . we invite you to sense your calling. What have you been sensing as your calling at this point in your life?

RD: Let your breath remind you over and over and over again of your deepest calling.

SG: Don't hold on to that calling in your mind . . . see if you can hold it in your center . . . without any muscular tension . . . you don't have to cling to it . . . weightless body, weightless mind.

RD: Bring it into the breath. Breathe that calling.

SG: And once you have that sense of an intention, developing a generative trance is a process of opening and receiving and utilizing whatever is there in each moment of consciousness.

RD: Transforming whatever is there into something that propels you more and more toward your calling.

SG: And the simple form that we would like to guide you with is just using three statements over and over and over. The first statement is, *"Now I am aware that I see . . ."*

RD: And notice what images, what visions are present in your mind's eye or your visual field, and just let them be there.

SG: And then continue by saying, *"I draw them down through my spine . . . into my center . . . out from my center . . . . to enter into the field . . . and relax."*

RD: The second statement is: *"Now I am aware that I hear . . ."*

SG: External voices, internal dialogue . . .

RD: . . . inner questions . . . critical voices . . . whatever is there.

SG: For example, now I'm aware that I hear my daughter's voice. Then continue, "I draw it down into my center . . . let my center open into the world . . . to allow me to achieve my goal . . . and then . . . relax . . . let go . . . let it all go."

RD: Use your breath to allow you to bring it down and let it go.

SG: The third statement is, *"Now I'm aware that I feel . . ."*

RD: For instance, "Now I'm aware that I feel tension in my shoulders."

SG: And I draw this energy through my spine . . .

RD: . . . into my center . . .

SG: . . . opening from my center . . .

RD: . . . out into the world . . .

SG: . . . allowing my goals to be realized.

RD: Let it go and relax.

SG: Nothing to do.

RD: Then repeat the first statement, *"Now I'm aware that I see . . ."*

SG: And notice whatever visual images are there.

RD: Draw them down.

SG: Open your center . . .

RD: . . . out into the field . . .

SG: . . . energy reaching toward the goal.

RD: Let it go.

SG: Nothing to do . . .

RD: . . . but relax.

SG: *"Now I'm aware that I hear . . ."*

RD: Draw it down into the center.

SG: Opening through your center.

RD: Let it out . . . into the field.

SG: A beautiful energy entering the world.

RD: *"Now I'm aware that I feel . . ."*

SG: Let in the awareness . . . become the energy.

RD: Let it go . . . and relax.

SG: Now I'm aware that I see . . .

RD: What? Images of space . . . memories?

SG: Drawing them all down through the spine . . . through the center . . .

RD: . . . out into the field.

SG: Like a star opening into space . . . radiant energy . . . light.

RD: Let it go . . . nothing to do.

SG: Enjoy the path . . . and relax.

RD: Now I'm aware that I see . . .

SG: So many different things come into your mind . . . letting them be rivers that flow through your being.

RD: Down through the center . . .

SG: . . . opening into the world . . . a beautiful circle . . . trance . . . forming.

RD: Letting go . . .

SG: . . . receiving . . . opening . . . releasing. So you can begin to feel that sense. Everything that comes into your consciousness, receive it . . . breathe it through . . . let it orient you even more deeply to your path.

RD: Now I am aware that I hear . . .

SG: What do you hear here? Music? Voices?

RD: Breathe it down.

SG: Energy flowing.

RD: Holding it in the center.

SG: A cosmic channel.

RD: Letting it go onto the path.

SG: All this is a circle within . . . beginning the flow once again.

RD: Deeply relax.

SG: Letting it flow through every organ. Letting it flow through the blood of your soul .

RD: Now I'm aware that I feel . . .

SG: Let it flow . . . into the earth . . .

RD: . . . now.

SG: Seeds . . .

RD: Symbols . . .

SG: Opening . . .

RD: Opening . . .

SG: Flowers . . .

RD: Let go . . .

SG: In your body . . .

RD: Relax . . .

SG: Your organs can heal. Self-healing is happening.

RD: Self-connection.

SG: So as you follow, simply let attunement . . . awareness of each moment . . . what you see . . .

RD: . . . what you hear . . .

SG: . . . what you feel . . . Let all of it flow to your center.

RD: Transform it through your presence.

SG: And then like a shining star . . . on a beautiful dark night . . . let your center radiate into the world . . . there's your calling . . . there's your calling.

RD: And relax.

SG: So you can begin to sense in this process that your most creative self is beneath the world of control. It rests deeply in your center . . . radiating support.

RD: Generativity and transformation are a natural part of your existence.

SG: So take a few moments just to sense the channel. And remember the words of Martha Graham: "Keep your channel open." That is your gift to yourself.

RD: That is your business and your work: "Keep your channel open."

SG: So maybe you'd like to make a simple vow.

RD: A commitment.

SG: A promise . . . about your relationship to this place . . . And may you always be the first to touch it . . . May you always be the deepest connection with it . . . For there, you will find love and freedom . . . Love and freedom. The freedom to slowly begin to return to the room . . . feeling that connection . . . bringing back that gift.

RD: And as you re-enter this present environment . . . as you connect to this outside world, what do you see, as you open your eyes? What do you hear? What do you feel?

SG: Welcome back! Welcome back, ye heroes of the great journey.

RD: And when you're ready, take a couple of minutes, find somebody and share what that experience was like for you.

The 5Rhythms® of the Journey: Flowing, Staccato, Chaos, Lyrical, and Stillness

RD: Gabrielle Roth's 5Rhythms® form the foundation of a body-based movement practice that teaches us to ground in our bodies, open our hearts, still our mind, and feel our connection with the larger field of which we are a part. The rhythms are both a map and a practice, the fruit of Gabrielle Roth's many years of observation of how energy moves in people and in life. As Roth says in *Sweat Your Prayers* (1997): "Energy moves in waves. Waves move in patterns. Patterns move in rhythms. A human being is all of those: energy, waves, patterns, rhythms."

She identifies five rhythms – flowing, staccato, chaos, lyrical, and stillness – that form a *wave*, a type of "meta-model" for transformation.[1] These rhythms are types of "archetypal energies" through

---

[1] Like all true works of genius, the 5Rhythms® are universal and can seem deceptively simple. While the rhythms are based on a series of maps, the learning happens first and primarily in the body. The intelligence of the somatic mind will nurture the cognitive mind, but this is a learning process that begins (and remains) in the feet, rather than trying to go from the head down. If you're moved by this practice, Gabrielle Roth and her group The Mirrors have created CDs for dancing the rhythms. The music itself will guide you through the 5Rhythms®: bones (tracks 2–6), initiation (tracks 1–5), trance (tracks 4–8), tribe (tracks 1–5), and endless wave (vols. 1–2) – Gabrielle's voice guides you through a wave.

In many parts of the world, you can find workshops and courses led by teachers who have gone through extensive training with Gabrielle. She has also written three inspiring and practical books: *Sweat Your Prayers: Movement as Spiritual Practice* (Los Angeles, CA: J. P. Tarcher, 1997), *Maps to Ecstasy: A Healing Journey for the Untamed Spirit* (Novato, CA: New World Library, 1998), and *Connections: The 5 Threads of Intuitive Wisdom* (Los Angeles, CA: J. P. Tarcher, 2004), that will deepen your relationship with your practice. Consult her website, www.gabrielleroth.com, for information about classes, teachers, music, and books. You can also visit www.movingcenter.com for more classes and workshops.

which our individual centers/sources become progressively more defined, open to, and connected to the field. In Roth's words:

In flowing you discover yourself. In staccato you define yourself. Chaos helps you dissolve yourself, so you don't end up fixed and rigid in the self you've discovered and defined. Lyrical inspires you to devote yourself to digging deep into the unique expression of your energy. And stillness allows you to disappear into the big energy that holds us all so you can start the whole process over again.

Gabrielle Roth's 5Rhythms® form a wave.

RD: We begin the wave in the rhythm of *flowing*. We have already explored some of the characteristics of flowing in the "Active Centering" exercise. It begins by being grounded in the feet. From this rooting to the earth you begin to move *(Robert demonstrates)* in continuous easy movement, Nothing is forced. And, as we practiced in "Active Centering," the movement is in circles. Roth says flowing is the rhythm of the feminine.

We have also already seen what happens if you become ungrounded or uncentered while flowing. You experience its shadow. You become stuck in inertia or begin to "blow with the wind."

SG: *(Stephen playfully gets lost in the looseness of flow)* Oh, yes, I can go with that. *(Laughter.)*

RD: And this is one of the reasons why you need *staccato*. Staccato *(Robert demonstrates with strong, discrete movements)* sets limits. You could say it is the rhythm of masculinity. It is the yang to the yin of flowing. The centered form of staccato is focus, concentration, commitment, setting clear boundaries, and so on. The uncentered form is rigidity, aggression, and violence.

Chaos is the rhythm that will keep you from getting too rigid. Chaos is the energy of release, of letting go, especially in the head and the neck *(Robert demonstrates)*. You're releasing the frames, letting go of the fixed positions. The uncentered, shadow side of chaos is confusion, disorder, and feeling overwhelmed. But the positive function of chaos is to let go.

Once you let go, you're free to express the new, to express the subtle. And that's where you get what Roth calls *lyrical* – where you're light, creative, and playful. If you're not grounded, you will also get the shadow of lyrical, which would be superficiality, shallowness, or downright schlockiness.

After the lightness and freedom, comes the rhythm of *stillness*. Stillness is not the absence of energy; it is the full presence of energy that allows us to connect both to ourselves and beyond ourselves. Gabrielle Roth says it's the rhythm through which you open yourself into the meta-field. The shadow side of stillness is lethargy, dissociation, and becoming disembodied and lost in the field. Centered stillness is that form of disappearing where you're still fully present – you are a center connected with a field.

SG: So what we're saying is that as you travel your path of a hero's journey, you are going to need the energies and the gifts of all five of these different rhythms. You start from a centered stillness, then begin the flow of exploration, then move to organizing things into small chunks and emphasizing differences. You then need to let that go and release into something bigger: a freedom that allows you to express the subtle energies in a creative way. After this journey, you return to the stillness of center, to reconnect with yourself and the larger field, and realize the gifts of wholeness that have been developed.

RD: In fact, we can relate the 5Rhythms® to the phases of the hero's journey. Flowing (discovering oneself) may be linked to finding one's calling. Staccato (defining oneself) provides the strength and determination to commit to the calling and cross the threshold. Chaos (dissolving oneself) allows one to enter into the inner state necessary to transform demons and shadows. Lyrical (expressing oneself) can be related to the full connection with one's unique resources and the completion of the task. Stillness (connecting beyond oneself) is a powerful resource for "returning home" and preparing for the next journey.

SG: These five rhythms give you a way of sensing your state when you're trying to achieve something or when you're struggling with a problem. You may find, if you're coaching somebody or looking into your own state, that as you engage with something, you may be missing one of these. Or be in an uncentered form of one of them, which would tend to make you stuck in it. For example, you may find that when you start thinking about your future, you lose your capacity for flow.

RD: Each of these rhythms can have many forms of expression, dance and "somatic syntax" being the most obvious. They also, however, have corresponding visual and auditory expressions (as in art and music) and may appear as driving factors at the basis of various techniques.

You can sense these energies in any conversation. Certainly you'll hear them in the voice tone. So you can hear a flowing voice *(Robert demonstrates)* . . . or a staccato rhythm *(demonstrates with sharp voice)* . . . a chaotic voice *(starts stuttering)*, a lyrical voice *(speaks melodically)* . . . or a very still voice.

SG: Eckhart Tolle, the guy who wrote *The Power of Now*, is a good example of that still voice.

RD: A very . . . . . . very . . . . . . slow . . . . . . still . . . . . . voice. *(Laughter.)*

SG: Yes, he speaks soooooo slowly. I'd hate to have to eat dinner with him. It would take him 20 minutes to ask you to pass the butter. *(Laughter.)* Actually, if you like books on tape, you probably shouldn't get his. It takes three years to listen to him reading his book on tape. Because most of it is the stillness of longggggg pauses between words. Now . . . . . . I . . . . . . want . . . . . . You could go out and get a sandwich between words. So Eckhart could probably use a little more flow. *(Laughter.)*

RD: Or lyrical. He needs a little more Irish in him. *(Laughter.)* Actually, when I go into a company, I'll sense which of these rhythms is in the field. Is it flowing? Is it rigid (the shadow of staccato)? Or perhaps staccato is completely missing and there are no clear limits or boundaries. Frequently it is chaos, many different conflicting energies. Is it lyrical – light, playful, creative, expressive? Is there a place for stillness? One of the big, big missing things in companies is there's no place for stillness. It's go, go, go, go, go! Do, do, do, do, do!

SG: And that creates a lot of do-do. *(Laughter.)*

RD: And when stillness is not sponsored or allowed, it will typically show up in the form of symptoms that stop you, that force you to rest.

We'd like to do a brief exercise to help you explore these rhythms. I think it is important to realize that Gabrielle Roth developed this as a movement practice, not as a theoretical model. It's something to be experienced in the body. I've been dancing these rhythms now for more than four years, and I find it to be a very powerful, transformational practice. For those of you who know NLP, I would suggest that these are the meta-programs of the somatic mind.

In the exercise, we'll guide you through dancing the 5Rhythms® with a partner. One of you will be Person A, the other Person B. We'll start by connecting with centering and energetic mirroring, as we have done in previous exercises. Each of you will bring an intention – it could be a goal, or perhaps something to heal, or maybe a demon you need to transform. You don't have to share it, just bring it into your field with your partner.

Once you are in rapport energetically, Stephen and I will guide you through each rhythm. To demonstrate, as Person A, I'm going to begin to bring the rhythm of flow in and Stephen (as Person B) will mirror me. *(Robert begins to move as "flow," Stephen matching him.)* And as Person A flows, you are keeping a sense of connection to your center and also to your partner. *(Robert and Stephen continue to "flow" with each other.)* Let yourself explore flow. Let it bring you to your edge, while staying connected to your center.

And then at some point, we'll be switching leads, so that now Stephen leads and I'm following. *(The flow dance shifts as Stephen leads and Robert attunes.)* And there's going to be a moment where neither of us will lead. We'll be sensing where and how the field is guiding us. *(Laughter as Robert and Stephen open the dance of flow.)*

(Jokingly) I know it's good for me, is it good for you, too? *(Laughter.)*

And then into that field we'll both attune to our intention, and see how we can dance flow with our intention. So we begin to explore what it's like to explore an intention from each of the different rhythms.

Then we'll move to the staccato. Again, A will lead and B will follow. *(Robert begins to dance staccato, Stephen is following.)* Then B will lead, and A will follow. *(Stephen begins to lead.)* Then neither leads, and you sense the field guiding you both. You're looking to sense a place where you're neither leading nor following, but you are both guided by something between and beyond us. And then you'll bring in your intention, and see what happens as you explore your intention with a staccato rhythm.

As with flowing, we're exploring: Who am I when I dance this rhythm? Who is my partner? What is our deeper relational field? What happens when I explore my intention with this rhythm?

Then we'll shift to chaos. *(Laughter as Robert and Stephen dance chaotically.)* When you go into chaos, it'll be more spontaneous, more free form. You're really letting go. *(Energy increases, Robert and Stephen and audience all laughing.)*

SG: I became John Travolta for a second. *(Laughter.)*

RD: Your proximity to each other can shift. You don't have to be constantly touching.

Then you'll shift to lyrical following the same sequence. *(Laughter as Robert and Stephen move in lyrical dance.)*

SG: *(Laughing)* Here comes the Easter bunny dance. I hope this isn't being filmed! *(Laughter.)* Cameras off! *(Laughter.)*

RD: Then you go into stillness. And that's when you connect more deeply within yourself, returning to yourself. *(Robert and Stephen slow down into stillness, breathe deeper, touching their belly centers.)* And again, notice your relationship to your intention through stillness.

So you can see that the exercise allows you to use the rhythms to find a connection first with yourself, then someone else, then to a field beyond your separate selves. In that field, you then bring your intention and see how all the connections and rhythms allow you to explore the intention in a generative way.

When you're dancing, it's your quality of rhythm, not how big or little the movements are, that makes the difference. You can be very staccato with very small movements. And people of all ages can dance the 5Rhythms®, from very young to very old.

SG: Or somebody in a wheelchair.

RD: I was with a quadriplegic person doing the 5Rhythms® recently. She participated fully, finding whatever parts of her body she could move applying each rhythm. Each person finds the possible movements that allow him or her to sense the rhythms while staying connected to his or her center and then opening to field. So it's about quality, not quantity.

SG: We hope you sense that beyond the idiosyncrasies of the exercise, there's the powerful idea that connection to each of the 5Rhythms® is essential to live the hero's journey. To realize your calling, you'll need centered forms of flowing, staccato, chaos, lyrical, and stillness. If you don't, you'll get stuck in your creative journey. Naming these rhythms can allow you to deepen your relationship with each of them, thereby allowing the realization of your highest calling.

Exercise: Exploring the 5Rhythms®

RD: So now it's your turn to explore them. You need to find a space around you. So, with your partner, make sure you have enough space. Spread out, find enough space, and then face your partner. Take a few moments to decide who is Person A and who is Person B.

We hope you allow yourself to have a very powerful experience with this simple exercise. Not only in terms of developing rapport and connection, but also exploring how the rhythms can help you transform challenges and realize your goals and intentions.

SG: And just be aware that the easy way would be to just be silly during the exercise. As hopefully we demonstrated, it's great to laugh and have fun during the work. But at the same time, keep attuned to the deeper space of your hero's journey and how these rhythms can positively help you with it.

RD: One simple way to do this is by intentionally creating a sacred space at the outset. Of course, this involves first taking some time for centering. So to start, face your partner, your hands by your sides. And let yourself close your eyes for a few moments and settle into your center. And as you begin to sense your center, you might find it helpful to take your hands and touch that place in your body where you most feel your center. Be sure to feel your feet. Bring your mind into your feet.

SG: Time to let go of your performance mind . . . the part of you that is trying to please others all the time. Take this time for self-care . . . self-witnessing . . . self-discovery.

RD: Really make sure that you feel centered, grounded, and connected with yourself. And then take a few moments to attune to your intention. What is the goal you want to achieve? Or the problem you want to resolve? Or the wound you want to heal? Feel whatever the call is . . . even as you stay connected to your center.

And when you have that goal, then open your eyes . . . and connect with your partner. Keep that sense of your awareness on your own center . . . and expand your awareness out to include your partner. Once you're ready, move your hands from your body and face them toward your partner. Don't touch your partner's hands . . . but mirror the energy.

SG: Come right to the point where you can feel the magnetic field between the hands. Almost physically connecting, but not quite.

RD: And you're mirroring, so that it's not that one of you is more dominant, or less. Explore that sense of connection, giving and receiving in a way that allows you to nurture safety, trust, and rapport.

And when you're ready, Person A, let yourself begin to gently allow your hands and your body to slowly move in a flowing motion. Let it start slowly. Stay connected to center and your partner, and sense how flow can begin to move through the connection. And B, you're mirroring A. It doesn't need to be perfect, just let yourself feel and follow the connection. Keep your eyes soft and peripherally wide open, so you can let your somatic mind be the lead system.

And person A, just really allow that sense of flow to come in . . . in your shoulders . . . in your knees. Explore the range within which you feel comfortable, while also attuning to your intention. What goal or intention do you want to bring into the field? And as you bring it in, let yourself flow around it . . . Flow with it . . . Flow through it, let it flow through you.

SG: Stay connected to both the intention and your partner. And notice how the two complement each other.

RD: It could also be a wound or demon that you bring into the dance. Just flow with it, as you stay connected to your center and to your partner.

And now Person B, you begin to lead . . . And A, you follow. Feel that sense of a connection between you. Feel the energy of flow always be with you.

SG: Stay tuned to that resonant sense of the intention that you're holding. And you can notice how that resonant image allows your body to relax more deeply into flow . . . and how your movement into flow allows the image to be more fluid, opening into new dimensions . . . a creative flow developing on many levels.

RD: And now, let the rhythm of flow guide you both. Neither of you lead, neither of you follow. Feel that rhythm of the flow and let it move you both.

SG: And let the rhythm of flow allow your intention to open and flow in new pathways of expression.

RD: Feel that generative space between you. And let the energy build in that space more and more now.

And A, let yourself begin to sense a rhythm of staccato beginning to come into you. Feel the beat. Feel the intensity. Follow it, let it begin to be your rhythm. And again, stay centered. Keep your center, and keep the intention in your center.

SG: Beginning to sense the intention in a different way, as you engage it with staccato energy.

RD: Staccato is about defining yourself. Let yourself express movements that are repetitive, so your partner can follow . . . a beautiful somatic syntax of staccato . . . And now B, you be the lead and A, you follow. Define yourself. *(Rhythmic clapping noises can be heard, vocal grunts and shouts as well.)* Remember that intention. Keep yourself centered. *(The noises increase and form a pattern.)* . . . Good.

And now let the field guide you into chaos . . . Feel deeper into your center . . . Person A, let go deeply into the center of chaos . . . Letting go of all order, all form . . . And now B, connect with that . . . Feel and follow the centered rhythm of letting go . . . of chaos . . . And A, you follow . . . And now both A and B, neither of you lead . . . Find the integrated field of chaos guiding you both. *(Rhythmic noises continue, become slightly faster.)*

SG: And whatever energy is in the field, guiding you, remember your intention . . . Stay centered . . . Let go . . . Let the energy guide the exploration of the intention. *(Clapping continues.)*

RD: And now that you've surrendered to letting go, Person A, find and feel the lightness of lyricism begin to flow through you . . . Person B, follow the lyrical dance of A. Feel the lightness, the playful expression of lyricism.

SG: Always sensing the intention in the dance . . . How the playful dance allows the intention to be experienced and expressed in so many delightful ways.

RD: Stay centered . . . feel light . . . Person A, express the intention in a way that is uniquely you . . . And Person B, now you begin to lead in the dance of playful, gentle lyricism. Person A, you follow. And then both of you release into the field that is guiding you. Let this energy of lightness guide you both.

SG: Let the field become a sweet nest . . . that lyrically hatches the eggs of so many unique expressions.

RD: And let the field of lyrical lightness . . . of magic . . . of creativity, play . . . Let it flow to . . . through . . . and beyond the intention that you're holding . . . Let lyrical energy infuse and allow the intention to be experienced through the forms of lyricism. And notice that as that lyrical expression unfolds, it naturally begins to draw you to stillness . . . to centered stillness. Find stillness in each small movement . . . each finger . . . each shoulder movement . . . in the hips . . . in the space beyond. Make the movements of stillness that open you to the larger mind . . . And B, mirror those movements.

SG: The poet T. S. Eliot wrote: "At the still point of the turning world there the dance is . . . And do not call it fixity . . . for that is to place it in time."

RD: And B, now you go to your place of stillness, and A follow B. *(Deep silence.)* In his great work *The Four Quartets*, T. S. Eliot also wrote:

> *I said to my soul, be still, and wait without hope*
> *For hope would be hope for the wrong thing; wait without love*
> *For love would be love of the wrong thing; there is yet faith*
> *But the faith and the love and the hope are all in the waiting.*
> *Wait without thought, for you are not ready for thought:*
> *So the darkness shall be the light, and the stillness the dancing.*
> ("East Coker")

RD: So let stillness be within you and between you. Feel that sense of connection within and beyond. Hold both of your journeys between you. Feel the presence of your partner. That unique energy that is your partner. And feel your own special energy.

SG: As you support the deep vision of your life path, something within you is now beginning to dance into the world . . . to give birth . . . give breath . . . give movement . . . give love.

RD: And then allow your hands to begin one more time to face each other so that you slowly feel the presence of the energy of your partner. Feel your center in the full presence of yourself. And sense how in the field between you that you are held in a larger field around you.

And then when you're ready, you can allow your hands to come back to your own center. Coming fully back to yourself. Close your eyes, if it helps coming fully into yourself.

And then when you're ready, open your eyes to your partner and offer some gesture of gratitude non-verbally to say thank you for this dance.

SG: Thank you for this dance. And then take a couple of minutes to share with your partner what that was like.

Finding Guardians

RD: We have a final exercise – one that has to do with gathering your guardians to support you as you move back out into the world to navigate the trials and tribulations of your journey.

SG: We want to emphasize that on the one hand, this journey is yours and yours alone. But an equally important truth is that, "We get by with a little help from of our friends." Was it George Bush who said that?

RD: No, that was Groucho Marx. *(Laughter.)*

SG: Seriously, we can't do this journey without guardians. Carl Jung used to say that one of the most important tasks for each person was to develop what he called a "community of saints." He didn't mean this religiously. He meant that we need to develop in our psyche a circle of sponsors who love and support us on our journey.

RD: Beings who see you and bless you on your way. Beings who can mentor you, teach you, coach you, and awaken you. So this exercise explores how to do that in an inner way; how to realize that we have the support of many guardians, even when they're not there physically.

SG: If you want to identify who is in a person's community of saints, ask the question, *Who has really seen you or given you blessing in your life?* Because none of us would be here were it not for such people. Not people who tried to do something to you, but who reached in and touched and awakened your spirit. So we ask you all, *Who has really seen you?* Milton Erickson was such a person for me. He gave me a blessing. I was this confused kid of 19 when I met him, and he really touched me with this message of, *You have something very special to contribute!* And it lit a fire in my soul. And despite various efforts to extinguish it, that fire won't go out! *(Laughter.)* Now, Erickson saw and blessed many people, but I'm *really* glad he saw me. So he is one of the beings in my community of saints.

RD: These sponsors and guardians don't have to be living people. They could be historical figures, spiritual beings, or even natural phenomena. I worked with a woman who grew up in an extremely dysfunctional family. As a child, there weren't any human beings she could trust. But when she would go into the forest, something would happen. It was as if the forest saw her, and she suddenly felt at home. She could talk with the forest, and it offered tremendous wisdom and understanding. So the forest was her guardian and sponsor.

SG: You may find that your community of saints includes writers or artists. When I was in high school, I was so depressed that I considered suicide. Somehow I got introduced to poetry, and some of those poets awoke something deep and amazing within me. The poet's voice would reach in and touch me, each word saying with love and wisdom, "We have been here before. It's okay, there's a way through and beyond this." And it opened a deeper aesthetic field beyond pain and suffering, beyond my personal situation.

For many people, artists and writers can awaken your center and transpose your experience into a generative realm, lifting you out of "the dust of everyday living." So there are a lot of possibilities of who can be legitimately in your community of saints.

RD: One aspect of the community of saints has do with what we might call *lineages*. For every part of our journey, we stand in a lineage of those who have gone before us.

SG: In Japanese, the word for "teacher" is *sensei*. The *kanji*, or Japanese character, for *sensei* includes a river with two people standing next to it, one in front of the other. *Sensei* means "one who is on the same path as you but who started a little bit before you." So our sponsors and guardians are ones on the same path who have started a little bit before us, and they can send back resources and guidance. We may attune and receive from these positive presences.

RD: So we have our family lineages – our parents, grandparents, and so on, from whom we carry both gifts and wounds. We also have our spiritual and vocational lineages – the healers, artists, warriors, lovers who have lived their journey before ours. We can find our guardians in these and other lineages.

SG: So, you're asking the question: What is the path that you are on? Or as Jung asked: "What is the myth you are living?" What is the journey you are making? What is the legacy of your soul? And which lineages are you walking in? By attuning to the generative beings who are in that lineage, you can find the community of saints to guide you on your path.

RD: I read a very interesting story on the internet some months ago. Some guy in Germany was in a very distraught, angry state. It got so bad that he got a gun and decided to go to the local shopping mall and just start shooting and killing people. He was literally on his way to do this, when a cute, adorable, little puppy came up to him. The guy was in no mood to play, but the puppy was! The puppy relentlessly approached the guy with such innocence and sweetness, that finally something was touched and released in this guy. It was as if the puppy connected him to a field beyond his own darkness. The result was that the man went back home and put his gun away. The puppy was a guardian from beyond that probably saved a number of lives and at least one man's soul!

SG: So you never know who will show up to help you. What we're saying is that there are many positive presences in the world that want to support you on your journey. As you open into the field to discover them, they'll find you.

Exercise: Gathering Your Guardians

RD: The following is an overview of the exercise we will be going through to find your guardians.

1. What is the "demon" (challenge) you are currently facing? What is a situation in which you feel more of a victim than a hero?

2. What is your "threshold"? What is the unknown territory, outside of your comfort zone, that either (a) the challenge is forcing you into or (b) you must enter in order to deal with the challenge?

3. Given the demon you are facing and the threshold you must cross, what is the "call to action" – what are you being called to do or become? (It is often useful to answer this question in the form of a symbol or metaphor, e.g. "I am being called to become an eagle/warrior/magician, etc.")

4. What resources do you have and which do you need to develop more fully in order to face the challenge, cross your threshold, and accomplish your calling?

5. Who are (will be) your "guardians" for those resources?

When you have identified your guardians, imagine where they would be located physically around you in order to best support you. One by one, put yourself into the shoes of each of the guardians, and look at yourself through their eyes (second position). What message or advice does each guardian have for you? Return to your own perspective (first position) and receive the messages.

RD: We're going to take you through the first part of the exercise as an introspective reflection, then demonstrate the second part interactively and have you practice it with a partner. The first part involves establishing some reference points for where you are currently on your journey, and some of the challenges you are facing. During the course of this journey we've been on you've probably sensed some of the demons who are likely to visit you, some of the shadows that are still living within you. You'll continue to face them at different points ahead, hopefully now with greater resources and confidence.

So please take a few moments now to center, so you can sense which demons you are likely to meet again. Those situations, those feelings, where you feel more like a victim than a hero.

SG: Another way of asking this is, *As you think about the coming week or month, what is most likely to knock you out of your center?*

RD: What are the situations, the people, the parts of yourself that are most likely to give you negative sponsorship messages? *You're not capable. You're not good enough. You don't exist. You are not welcome here.* Take a few moments and identify those demons, those shadows, those trials, those ordeals, those tests. Also think about your thresholds. Where are those places of uncertainty, the places of risk, the points of no return? What is it that you need to do that is going to take you out of your comfort zone? Which risks do you need to take? Where are the places that you need courage?

Stephen and I sometimes talk about how important it is to really look forward to those times in the future when you will fail miserably. Isn't that good to know that this will happen? *(Laughter.)* By allowing those possibilities you can comfortably begin to appreciate all the ways you can positively respond at such times. As we say in NLP: there is no failure, only feedback. There are no mistakes, only outcomes. How you respond to each outcome is what determines whether it ultimately is a failure or success. So if you open to your hero's journey, you are opening to great risk and challenge. Identify what some of those challenges may be for you.

SG: And as you do, you may notice that you almost automatically begin to reactively brace against them. You go into what we have been calling "fight, flight, or freeze," those non-generative responses that will ensure the problem will not be transformed. So when you come up against your demons, remember that old Buddhist suggestion, "Don't just do something, sit there." Don't feed the demon with anger or fear. Don't give your center to the problem. Take it as a signal: *Let go and center. Let go and center. Let go and center. Feel the vertical axis of connection within you. Let go of the attachment to the demon. Let your center be your first relationship.*

RD: Siddhartha said: "I can think, and I can wait." There are times to think. There are other times to "wait without thought." When confronting the demon, let go of thinking and reacting, and find your center first. Then resonate with the questions: *What resources can help you? What are the resources you need to face this difficult future?* Certainly every hero's journey requires courage and fierceness.

SG: But also softness and kindness.

RD: And let's not forget playfulness, humor, and creativity. Just sit with the question of what resources you need. Maybe it's not a capability, maybe it's a belief; a belief in yourself.

SG: Maybe it's not a belief in yourself, but a connection with something bigger than yourself – something that you can draw from.

RD: A sense of trust. Really find, right now, deeply, truly, what are the resources that you're going to need if you are truly going to share your gift and heal your wounds. What are the inner resources? What is inside you to help you with your inner game?

SG: Really rejoicing in this awareness that *however big the problem is, the space of your self is much bigger*. Deeper . . . wider . . . stretching before and beyond the problem. Much bigger. So what resources, which connections, what beliefs do you need to be able to extend into your expanded self?

RD: And then the key question for this exploration: *Who are your guardians for those resources? Which sponsors and mentors – people in your life, historical people, archetypal beings, spiritual beings – will help you to remember, access, and utilize your resources?*

SG: Who are some of the people who have gone before you on this path? Don't try to find the answer cognitively. Just hold the question and see what and whom comes to you. Let yourself be pleasantly surprised at who appears in your field.

RD: What is the lineage to which you belong?

SG: Just enjoy the awareness of different guardians beginning to appear in the field around you.

RD: There may be spiritual guardians . . . spiritual teachers . . . angels . . . symbols . . . archetypes. Maybe guardians from nature: mountains, oceans, rivers, forests, or flowers.

SG: Somebody who believes in you . . . Somebody who believes in your capacities . . . Somebody that can let *you* know, *"This is possible. What you are longing for on your journey is possible* . . . And we are here to give you support . . . and guidance. *Your path is possible.* You can do this . . . *You can do this . . . Yes, indeed, you can do this!"*

RD: Somebody who inspires in you courage, confidence, creativity, connection, determination.

SG: And just notice what it is like to release from your own individual mind and surrender to the community of saints . . . *There* . . . within you and all around you . . . the field of the community of saints . . . Let that be your deeper mind.

RD: And as you do, really get a sense of several key guardians. And then when you're ready, return back to the room.

So we just did the first part of the process which involves identifying some key guardians. We want to now demonstrate the second part, where you're going to explore how to use these guardians when you're encountering a demon or challenge. We need a volunteer, someone who is facing one of these trials, one of these ordeals.

(Alice volunteers and comes on stage.)

Demonstration with Alice

RD: So the first step is to find out what challenges or ordeals you are facing. Alice, can you tell me what you'd like to work with today?

Alice: I have been experiencing conflicts in my life that have afflicted me personally, up to the point where I have been between life and death. I ended up with tumors on my liver. I don't really understand it, but I believe they were symptoms to force me to admit my life conflicts.

RD: Do you have liver tumors right now?

Alice: No. I had two operations, one a year ago and one six months ago. I had three tumors total. They cut off half of my liver to remove them.

RD: Yes, I see that you are definitely on a hero's journey. You have clearly confronted demons already, and have further trials to come. In terms of our exercise, the "demon" seems pretty evident. It's the tumors themselves, is that right?

Alice: Yes.

RD: So we could say the tumor is a demon to be faced on your hero's journey. You said you don't really understand it, but you want to. We've been exploring here the idea that the demon is a reflection of our shadow self.

Alice: Yes.

RD: You were saying something about your conflicts. Let's tune to that for a few moments. When you think about the tumors, just notice what happens inside. What gets mirrored back from your unconscious? Is it fear? Anger? Notice what's there.

(Alice closes her eyes, breathes deeper, seems to emotionally connect with something.)

(Gently) That's right. That's right. What do you feel there? Notice what's in your somatic mind.

Alice: *(Emotionally)* I'm alone.

RD: Yes . . . and what else do you notice?

Alice: There's a coldness. It's painful.

RD: A coldness. And what are the messages that seem to cause you pain?

Alice: *(With tears)* They say that my life has no value.

RD: Those messages are telling you that your life has no value. Usually, those messages can't be powerful unless they resonate with something that *you* believe about yourself. So I wonder if there is a part of you that thinks, "You are right, I have no value." The demon is usually able to hurt you if it can hook with your shadow. So I'm curious, what inside of you resonates with the message, *You have no value.*

Alice: I don't exist.

RD: I don't exist. Yes.

Alice: I'm being manipulated.

RD: What about being manipulated? Can you say more?

Alice: When I want to cry out, I receive the message back: "Shut up!"

RD: What feeling does that bring in you? When you want to cry out – and you get "Shut up!" – what do you feel in your body?

Alice: Pain.

RD: Where do you feel that pain?

Alice: In my soul.

RD: So, a pain that you feel in your soul. That's good to know. And as it feeds on your soul, perhaps it also takes on the physical manifestation of feeding on your body. Now here's an important part of our hero's journey exploration. Let's imagine this demon is pushing you across a threshold, into a new territory for yourself. That as a result of this demon, you're forced to move into new places for yourself. What is that threshold for you? What is the edge of your comfort zone that you're being pushed to?

Alice: You mean, where I want to be?

RD: Not quite. That's more your desired state. We're talking about the edge of your comfort zone. These tumors and the conflicts are moving you to a threshold, to a place outside of your comfort zone. They're calling you to do something new. It's very challenging what you're being asked to do as a result of these symptoms. What is the new thing you have to do that is not easy for you?

Alice: My challenge?

RD: Yes.

Alice: *(Pauses, becomes emotional)* To speak out what I really feel. What I think, feel, and want to do!

RD: Yes. That's what it is. And clearly that's difficult for you. That's a place of challenge. You have the demons and shadows, the tumors, the pain, the "shut up" . . . And also the fact you need to be able to speak out what you feel. So what is all of this calling you to do or to become? The loneliness, the tumors that make you speak out. They're calling you to grow and do something new. They're saying, "You can no longer stay as you were. You can no longer stay small." What is it calling you to?

Alice: *(Still emotional, more settled)* Happiness and love.

RD: Yes, happiness and love. That's good to know. And I wonder if you can let a symbol come to you, a symbol that represents who you would be if you had happiness and love. What would be the symbol for the kind of person that you're being called to be? Would you be like a star? Would it be something else? Just pay attention to the symbol that comes from within.

Alice: The infinity sign.

RD: Infinity sign. What does that infinity sign mean to you? Let a symbol come. What is it that you'll become? What does this infinity sign represent? If you speak out, if you heal these tumors, what is it that you'll be?

Alice: A secure person.

RD: What does this look like? What is your symbol for this secure person? As a secure person, who are you? What is that symbol? What is that metaphor? Just notice the first image that comes to you.

Alice: The ocean.

RD: The ocean.

Alice: Hmmm . . . *(Looks absorbed.)* Yes. *(Takes a deep breath.)*

RD: There is a call within you to be the ocean. *(To audience)* You can notice that as soon as she moves from the abstract words to the metaphorical image, she relaxes. The somatic mind begins to think for her. That's really important, especially given her physical symptoms. She needs to let her body think and exist, creating its own realities. Otherwise, the demons will do it for her.

(To Alice) So, to be this ocean, to heal these tumors, to heal with this pain, and these voices that say "Shut up!", what are the key resources that you need?

Alice: Strength and confidence.

RD: Confidence in yourself?

(Alice nods her head.)

Anything else?

Alice: Self-esteem. *(Begins to tear up.)*

RD: Yes. Self-esteem. Mmmm, I see that touches you very deeply. *(Alice nods.)* That's very important. Self-love, self-esteem. That's great.

So now we come to the key part of this exploration, which is to gather your guardians. To do this, I'm going to ask you to think of a very specific situation in your future where you're going to need strength, self-confidence, and self-esteem. Is it with others? Is it in the hospital? Is it with family? Where would it be? Give me a specific time and a place when you need those resources. What are the moments that you most doubt, that you lose your strength, that you lose your confidence?

Alice: *(Emotionally absorbed)* With my spouse.

RD: With your spouse.

Alice: And my family.

RD: Are there specific times? Would you, for example, be trying to talk with your spouse or your family about some issue? It's important that you tune into one such time, or one such situation. Can you do that?

Alice: Yes.

RD: And as you do that, I'm going to ask you to become curious about who will be your guardians – for strength, confidence in yourself, and self-esteem. Which presences, which people, which beings can help you to remember, when you're with your family and spouse, these important resources of strength, confidence, and self-esteem? Who or what, for instance, would be your guardian for strength?

Alice: My guardian angel.

RD: Your guardian angel.

Alice: Yes. I feel her standing behind me.

RD: There is a guardian angel. What does she look like?

Alice: A huge angel with large wings.

RD: Huge angel with large wings . . . Great . . . And who is your guardian for self-esteem? Who is it in your life that lets you know you exist, you are valuable, that you deserve to be heard?

Alice: It's a mantra.

RD: A mantra. What will be your symbol for this mantra? Where is it going to be around you, as a support to you?

Alice: I hear it . . . as a support.

RD: Where do you hear it? It's really important that you sense the specific details. Who is speaking it? Make a picture of it. Your body needs concrete images, not abstract. It's the specific languages coming from you that will allow you to inhabit and heal your body. It's important to feel it and bring it into your body.

Alice: I am repeating the mantra.

RD: Notice who you are that is repeating it? What does that look like? See what she looks like, the you that is repeating the mantra.

Alice: I see a kind of light.

RD: A kind of light. Is it a star? Is it a sun? Is it a flame?

Alice: (*Looks very absorbed*) Hmmm . . . There is light. A ball of light.

RD: A ball of light. What color?

Alice: It's white.

RD: A ball of white light. And where do you sense the presence of that ball of white light in the field around you?

Alice: To my right. (*Alice points.*)

RD: To your right. OK. Now I'm curious; so far the guardians are an angel and a ball of light. That's good. But I notice there are no human guardians so far. You'll need some human presences, I think. So who is a mentor for you in the human world?

Alice: *(Pauses)* It's hard to find, because I've always been physically and mentally alone.

RD: I understand. That is why I'm suggesting you find a human guardian, to remind you that you belong to the human community as well as to the non-human communities. Notice who can be your human guardians. Take your time. Who would that be?

(Tears well up in Alice's eyes.)

Who is this guardian?

Alice: *(In tears)* My daughter.

RD: Yes. Yes.

(Alice continues crying.)

Yes. And where do you feel her presence in the field right now. You said the angel is behind you. Where do you feel the presence of your daughter. Is she in front of you? She won't be inside of you; she's physical, she doesn't fit in. Is she behind you, in front of you? Where do you feel her, with your body? She has a body, you have a body. Where is she?

Alice: She's in front of me.

RD: She's in front of you. *(To audience)* It is important that we develop these guardians and images in relation to the physical body. Alice needs to think and feel and talk within her body in the external world. One of her survival strategies has been to leave her body and dissociate out in the bodiless inner worlds. She feels the pain and loneliness in her physical body, and so leaves it for another world. We've been emphasizing that to be generative – to be able to create, or heal, or transform – you have to be centered within your body, and then extend through it and beyond it, while remaining centered. So what we're exploring here is which guardians can help her stay in the body, to connect with everything that's there, and walk in the world with that centered, resourceful connection. Without that, spiritual connection becomes spiritual avoidance. That's escape, not a resource.

Alice: *(Looking very absorbed)* Hmmm . . .

RD: *(To Alice)* So someone needs to help you stay here in the world. Like your daughter, saying something like, "Stay here, mom."

Alice: Hmmm . . .

RD: People cannot see you when you go away. If you want them to see you, you have to stay visible and sometimes that means you have to hurt . . . *(Alice nods.)* So as a final step, we're going to receive the messages of these guardians. So when you interact with your husband, for example, these guardians will be with you. We've touched upon so far the angel, the ball of white light, and your daughter.

Alice: Yes.

RD: So I want you to imagine yourself about to meet your husband.

Alice: OK.

RD: I'm going to ask you now to step outside of yourself and behind yourself, into the position of the guardian angel. Just let yourself physically move to the location of the guardian behind you, so you are watching yourself from the guardian angel's perspective. Feel free to move your body into whichever position and posture that allows you to enter the place of that guardian angel.

(Alice steps back, breathes deeply.)

In NLP, we call this second position – putting yourself in the perspective of another individual or entity. Let yourself step into the field of the guardian angel and perceive yourself through the perspective of the guardian angel. Become the guardian angel. And as you do, notice the messages you're giving to Alice over there. *(Robert points to where Alice has been standing.)* You're her guardian. What message do you have for Alice as she prepares to see her husband and her family. You are now the guardian of Alice's self-confidence. What is your message to her? Guardian angel, what is it that you want to say?

(Alice extends both hands with palms facing forward, like a blessing gesture.)

So it's less words and more this kind of touch. What is the message of the touch? What is it that you want to communicate to Alice with that touch?

Alice: *You can do it.*

RD: *You can do it.* That's important . . . Now take a step forward and step into Alice again. *(Alice steps forward.)* And as you do, feel the touch of the guardian angel from behind you. She's saying, *You can do it. You can do it. You can do it* . . . And as you feel those messages, notice where in your body you receive those messages.

Alice: *(Laughs.)* My legs.

RD: In your legs. *(Alice laughs again, looks excited.)* That's good to know, you've got legs! I'd love to see those legs come alive for you.

Alice: *(Excited and happy)* I feel like I can run!

RD: There's this old song, "These boots are made for walking." *(Alice, who is wearing boots, laughs with excitement, stamps her feet a few times.)*

Wow, that's great. It's great to see a little staccato in your energy finally. Life is not all about stillness, is it? You need a little staccato. Especially with your spouse, I think.

Alice: Yes, you're right.

RD: OK, now we have the next guardian. There's this mantra, this ball of light. Let yourself step out of yourself and to your right-hand side, when you're ready, and enter into the field of the white light. *(Alice steps in front of herself and to her right and turns around.)* Be the ball of white light. And as the ball of light, what is your message to Alice? As her guardian, as a ball of light, what is your message to her body?

Alice: *You exist.*

RD: Yes. *You exist, you have a voice in this world* . . . Good. Now come back over and step into yourself again. *(Alice returns to her initial position.)* Feel your guardian angel saying, *You can do it. You go, girl!* Feel that in your legs. *(Alice laughs.)* And now in your belly, that ball of light, saying, *You exist. You're here. I see you. It's good to see you.* *(Pause while Alice deeply experiences the process.)*

Finally, we have your daughter. I want you to step into her and face yourself. She's there, she's in front of you there. Let yourself become her. What's her name?

Alice: Janet.

RD: Become Janet. Go into Janet's energy. Her body. Her energy. *(Alice steps forward and turns around.)* Janet, your mom needs you as a guardian. What is your message to your mom? What do you say?

Alice: Janet tells me . . .

RD: No, not Janet tells you, you are Janet. *(To audience)* This part is very important to coach, because Alice has a tendency to leave herself. And when she leaves her body and her center, other stuff can take over.

(To Alice) You're Janet. Not an abstract idea of her. If you're Janet, you speak as Janet, to your mom.

Alice: *Mom, I love you.*

RD: Yes . . . Yes . . . *Mom, I love you!* . . . That's right . . . and now take a breath and move back into your own perspective over here. *(Alice moves back into "self" position.)* And now you have your guardian angel behind you, who is touching you and communicating: "You can do it!" You've got the ball of white light to your right, that is saying: "You exist." And then, there is your daughter Janet in front of you, and she is wrapping her arms around you and saying: "I love you, Mom." Where do you receive that message in your body?

(Alice moves her hands around her whole body.)

Great. And sensing all those messages, now step into that difficult situation with your husband and your family. Hear the messages that usually are there: *Shut up! You don't exist! You'll be alone again!* But as you do, feel the presence of your guardians. See them. Hear them. Not as an abstract concept, but really, deeply in your body. You don't have to leave your body to find them. They're in your body. The messages of the guardians are now in your body. Feel them in your liver. In Chinese medicine, the liver is often associated with fire. Emotional fire, anger. So your liver needs to be alive. It's OK to feel. It's OK to express pain. Expressed pain heals. Unexpressed pain grows . . . What happens now as you sense all of that?

Alice: Many different feelings. Pain . . .

RD: Good. Be with that. And bring your guardians into your belly, your heart, into your legs, into your shoulders. All around you, all inside of you. Hear the guardians' messages. *I love you. You exist. You can do it.* These are the messages to guide you, to guard you, to allow you to be with your spouse and your family in a powerful way. You're a hero, not a victim. Face the demons. Meet and transform them. Stand your ground or move out of the way of negative energy. *(Alice relaxes, looks radiant, spreads her hands around her body like a blessing.)* Yes, see and feel your second skin opening up all around you.

(Alice looks deeply in transformational process for another minute or so. She then takes a deep breath, touches her heart, then opens her eyes and smiles. She looks like a new woman.)

Alice: Thank you so much!

RD: *(Hugs Alice.)* You're welcome. In the 5Rhythms® Gabrielle Roth likes to say, "Follow your feet." That guardian angel will let you know where to go. Thank you, Alice.

Alice: Thank you.

(Loud applause as Alice leaves the stage.)

RD: So that was a demonstration of how to find and use the guardians that you'll need to do your hero's journey. I hope you could see some of the different core elements of the journey that we've been emphasizing: the hero, the call, the demon or challenge, the resources, and the guardians. A key part of the hero's journey is to find the resources and guardians needed to transform the demons and cross the threshold, in order to complete the journey. We've been showing how to do that within yourself, and also how to help others to do it.

So, find a partner and take some time to help each other find your guardians and the messages they have for you at this stage of your journey.

Conclusion: The Return

SG: I want to begin our last section by sharing a poem by the great soul poet of Chile, Pablo Neruda. As you'll hear, it's really about the hero's journey. In fact, I think it's one of the great poems of all time regarding the hero's journey. In the poem, called "Poetry," Neruda is talking about an experience he had when he was 17 years old. As will be obvious, it's his receiving the call to the journey. Here's what he has to say:

And it was at that age . . . Poetry arrived
in search of me. I don't know, I don't know where
it came from, from winter or a river.
I don't know how or when,
no, they were not voices, they were not
words, nor silence,
but from a street I was summoned,
from the branches of night,
abruptly from the others,
among violent fires
or returning alone,
there I was without a face
and it touched me.

I did not know what to say, my mouth
had no way
with names
my eyes were blind,

and something started in my soul,
fever or forgotten wings,
and I made my own way,
deciphering
that fire
and I wrote the first faint line,
faint, without substance, pure
nonsense
pure wisdom
of someone who knows nothing,
and suddenly I saw
the heavens
unfastened
and open,
planets,
palpitating plantations
shadow perforated,
riddled
with arrows, fire and flowers,
the winding night, the universe.

And I, infinitesimal being,
drunk with the great starry
void
likeness, image of
mystery,
I felt myself a pure part
of the abyss
I wheeled with the stars,
My heart broke free on the open sky.

SG: Now, that's a hero's journey! *(Applause.)*

RD: That's a tough one to follow. But this one also stands on its own as a great poem. It's by Hafiz, the great Sufi poet of long ago. It's called "For No Reason." As you will hear, it's about the important part of generative consciousness and the rhythms of lyrical; namely that there are realities beyond the ego-intellect. Here's what Hafiz says:

And
For no reason

I start skipping like a child.

And
For no reason
I turn into a leaf
That is carried so high
I kiss the Sun's mouth
And dissolve.

And
For no reason
A thousand birds
Choose my head for their conference table,
They start passing their
Cups of wine
And their wild songbooks all around.

And
For every reason in existence
I begin to eternally,
To eternally laugh and love!
For every reason in existence
I begin to eternally,
To eternally laugh and love!

When I turn into a leaf
And start dancing,
And I run to kiss our beautiful Friend
And dissolve in the Truth
That I Am.

(Applause.)

RD: Now that these dances and poems have hopefully opened you up to a deeper presence within yourselves, we want you all to take a few moments for a closing process. In this process, to prepare you for your return to ordinary reality, we will be asking you to sense and gather your community of saints.

So just take a few moments to close your eyes . . . take a few deep breaths to return to center . . . Remember the two-part process of drop into center, open into field . . . Drop into center, open into field . . . and as you do that, let your awareness begin to tune to who will be your guardians for the road ahead.

SG: As you begin to sense at many levels, the beginning of the orientation back into the ordinary world. *I begin to return from the timeless infinity of ritual space . . . where many beautiful things have been discovered . . . where I have touched some of the great mysteries of being . . . where I have felt love . . . once again . . . Now begins the return . . . the movement to bring the gift back into the ordinary world.*

RD: The good news is: you will not do that alone. There are lineages of many that have come before, that will walk with you and behind you. Maybe there'll be a thousand songbirds choosing your head for their conference table.

SG: Jesus said: "Be in this world, but not of this world." A beautiful way of beginning to sense that your deep self . . . the deepest reality . . . is light itself.

RD: And in that field of light and love . . . let yourself begin to feel the presence of those guardians. Where are they around you? Who is over your left shoulder? Who is over your right shoulder? Who stands behind you?

SG: Who is above you?

RD: Who stands in front of you, calling you forward?

SG: Perhaps whispering . . . reminding you: *You are here for a deeper purpose. You are not here to be lost in illness. You are not here to be trapped in sadness. You are not here to be grounded by bitterness. You are here to live your gift into the world.*

RD: And as you live that gift, be open and aware of the guardians that will appear; guardians that you can't even imagine now. Maybe in some moment a week or two weeks from now, you'll find yourself struggling and dealing with something that's happening yet again. And maybe you'll suddenly feel Stephen's presence over your left shoulder, saying: "Isn't that nice to know?" And I will be over your right shoulder . . . and will add: "And it's not a problem."

SG: And truly sense . . . the beings within you and around you . . . that are there to help you keep coming *back* . . . to your center . . . keep coming *back* . . . to the timeless, weightless place of pure light.

RD: And at the same time you keep coming back to the specific reality . . . in the present moment . . . within and around the presence of your physical body.

SG: So that those beings can remind you once again: *You are here for more than mere suffering. You are here for a deeper purpose. Let your life live from that deeper purpose.*

RD: And grow along with your gifts.

SG: Knowing that time and time again, you will forget. So may you use all of these different signs . . . may you use your unhappiness and your happiness to remember . . . *There is a deeper place than this, all around me now . . . there is a deeper wave than this, listen to me now.*

RD: The Greeks say, "I lose myself a hundred times, no, a thousand times each day." The key is to remember to return.

SG: You are here to be happy . . . You are here to be healthy . . . You are here to be helpful . . . You are here to be healed. So keep remembering that you have been given this amazing gift of life . . . to live that hero's journey . . . and that you walk with the support of guardians . . . an amazing community of saints.

RD: So take a few moments now and listen in silence for the message or messages of the guardians that walk with you.

SG: What do they say? Listen . . .

RD: What are their messages?

SG: Listen with your heart.

RD: Listen with your soul.

SG: Receive the blessings . . . of the spirit . . . of each of these kind beings . . . There's a wonderful Irish writer . . . his name is John

O'Donoghue . . . who just passed from this world several weeks ago . . . and he wrote a wonderful book called *Anam Cara* . . . And *anam cara* is Gaelic meaning "a friend of the soul" . . . so may you sense each guardian . . . as a friend of the soul . . . and in receiving their mirroring . . . discover the great joy in realizing you too are *anam cara.*

RD: You are a friend of the soul. You are a guardian for your own life. You are *anam cara* for the souls of your children.

SG: May you be *anam cara* for your family . . . your co-workers . . . for your community . . . May you be *anam cara* . . . a friend of the soul . . . a hero on a great journey.

We were mentioning Milton Erickson, and how we were poor college students when we were studying with him . . . we didn't pay him any money. Milton Erickson was a friend of the soul.

RD: And the question is: How do you pay back friends of the soul? You don't give them money. You don't give them television sets. You don't even necessarily buy them dinner. What you do?

SG: *(Smiling)* The way that you can repay?

RD and SG: *(simultaneously) Pass it on!*

SG: Pass it on to your community. Pass it on to your family. And please pass it on to the demons that you encounter. *(Laughter.)*

RD: After a successful journey, the hero typically is filled with many experiences, not the least of which is gratitude. What are you grateful for? Let yourself sense a few of the most important things you are grateful for with respect to the hero's journey that you have been on. And then let the feeling of gratitude come, let it wash all over you, let it fill you as we approach the return home.

I think it was Eckhart Tolle who said: "If the only prayer that you ever said in your whole life was 'Thank you,' that would be enough." So all we have left to say is this prayer from us to you . . .

RD and SG: *Thank you!*

(Thunderous applause.)

The International Association for Generative Change (IAGC)

As a next stage in our own hero's journey, we have recently established the International Association for Generative Change (IAGC) – http://www.generative-change.com.

Like those explored in this book, generative processes are those that promote innovation, evolution and growth. To 'generate' means to create something new. Thus, the core focus of generative change is *creativity*: How do you create a successful and meaningful work life? How do you create great personal relationships? How do you develop a great relationship with yourself – your body, your past, your future, your wounds and your gifts? These are the basic challenges in leading an extraordinary life, and the processes of generative change offer a way to succeed at them.

Generative change means creating something beyond what has yet existed, either in one's personal or one's professional life. It is not merely a cosmetic change, but a deep contextual shift that allows new levels of mastery. Generative change techniques assume that we construct our reality through personal and perceptual filters, and that this creative process can be mindfully engaged for positive outcomes. To do this, a person's state of consciousness is the *difference that makes the difference*. Generative change processes teach you how to build the generative states, for yourself and others, needed to transform ('imagineer') dreams into reality. These processes then focus on how to maintain these states in dealing with whatever challenges and obstacles arise on one's journey, so that new and meaningful results can occur.

We have been studying the dynamics of generative change in individuals and organizations for the past four decades. This exploration has led us to the development of programs on generative change, including The Hero's Journey, Generative Coaching, Generative Leadership, Generative Psychotherapy and Generative Collaboration, as well as others. These programs form the basis for the IAGC.

The purpose of the IAGC is to bring generative change to multiple professions throughout the world. The IAGC offers training, certification and other resources that promote generative change in personal, professional and organizational contexts.

The vision of the IAGC is a world where coaches, psychotherapists, leaders and entrepreneurs are living and sharing principles of generative change and creating a world to which people want to belong – a world where people have the tools and models to be able to creatively transform obstacles and to use seeming conflict as the basis for creative innovation.

The mission of the IAGC is to provide the training, standards and infrastructure necessary to create and support a global community of professionals dedicated to practicing the principles and methods of generative change.

The ambition of the IAGC is to be an international hub for generative change with representatives in many different countries, serving thousands of people from all over the planet. Within five years the IAGC will have a substantial team of trainers who will bring generative change work into an increasing number of different professions with a sense of passionate authenticity.

Thus, the role of the IAGC is to be a type of attractor – a magnet for like-minded people to be able to come together and build something that is unique, solid and influential by providing concrete ways to collaborate, create communities, and share values and modalities that make a positive difference in people's lives.

If you are interested, please visit: http://www.generative-change.com.

Bibliography

Bateson, G. (1972) *Steps to an Ecology of Mind: Collected Essays in Anthropology, Psychiatry, Evolution, and Epistemology* (Chicago, IL: University Of Chicago Press).

Campbell, J. (1948) *The Hero with a Thousand Faces* (Princeton, NJ: Princeton University Press).

Gallwey, W. T. (1986) *The Inner Game of Tennis* (London: Pan Books).

Gershon, M. (2000) *Second Brain: A Groundbreaking New Understanding of Nervous Disorders of the Stomach and Intestine* (New York: HarperCollins).

Gilligan, S. (1997) *The Courage to Love* (New York: W. W. Norton & Co.).

Gilligan, S. (2004) "The five premises of the Generative Self" (Workshop handout: Stephen Gilligan).

Jung, C. (1971) (Edited by J. Campbell) *The Portable Jung* (New York: Penguin Group).

Lakoff, G. (1981) *Metaphors We Live By* (Chicago, IL: University of Chicago Press).

Mille, A. de (1991) *Martha: The Life and Work of Martha Graham* (New York: Random House).

O'Donohue, J. (1997) *Anam Cara: Spiritual Wisdom from the Celtic World* (London: Bantam Press).

Oliver, M. (1986) *Dream Work* (New York: Atlantic Monthly Press).

Pearsall, P. (1998) The *Heart's Code: Tapping the Wisdom and Power of Our Heart Energy* (New York: Broadway Books).

Pearson, C. (1989) *The Hero Within: Six Archetypes We Live By* (San Francisco, CA: Harper & Row).

Roth, G. (1997) *Sweat Your Prayers: Movement as Spiritual Practice* (Los Angeles, CA: J. P. Tarcher).

Somé, M. (1995) *Of Water and the Spirit: Ritual, Magic and Initiation in the Life of an African Shaman* (New York: Penguin).

Tolle, E. (2001) *The Power of Now: A Guide to Spiritual Enlightenment* (Marina Del Rey, CA: Mobius).

Whyte, D. (1996) *House of Belonging* (WA: Many Rivers Press).

Wilber, K. (2001) *A Brief History of Everything* (Boston: Shambhala).

Williamson, M. (1992) *A Return to Love: Reflections on the Principles of "A Course in Miracles"* (London: HarperCollins).

CPSIA information can be obtained
at www.ICGtesting.com
Printed in the USA
BVHW032125061022
648883BV00003B/25